SPAM NATION

THE INSIDE STORY OF ORGANIZED CYBERCRIME—FROM GLOBAL EPIDEMIC TO YOUR FRONT DOOR

BRIAN KREBS

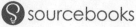

Published by Sourcebooks, Inc.
P.O. Box 4410, Naperville, Illinois 60567-4410
(630) 961-3900
Fax: (630) 961-2168
www.sourcebooks.com

Library of Congress Cataloging-in-Publication Data
Krebs, Brian.
    ⁺ the inside story of organized cybercrime—from global epidemic to your front door / Brian Krebs.
        pages cm
    1. Computer crimes—United States. 2. Internet fraud—United States. 3. Spam (Electronic mail) 4. Phishing. 5. Organized crime—United States. I. Title.
    HV6773.2.K74 2014
    364.16'80973—dc23
                                        2014023007

Printed and bound in the United States of America.

VP 10 9 8 7 6 5 4 3 2 1

CONTENTS

WHO'S WHO IN THE CYBERWORLD

PAVEL VRUBLEVSKY, a.k.a "RedEye"— Cofounder of ChronoPay, a high-risk card processor and payment service provider that was closely tied to the rogue antivirus industry. Cofounder of Rx-Promotion pharmacy affiliate program.

YURI KABAYENKOV, a.k.a. "Hellman"— Co-owner of Rx-Promotion along with Pavel Vrublevsky.

IGOR GUSEV, a.k.a "Desp"—Cofounder of ChronoPay, and co-owner of the pharmacy spam partnerships SpamIt and GlavMed.

DMITRY STUPIN—Co-owner, along with Igor Gusev, of the pharmacy partnerships SpamIt and GlavMed.

IGOR VISHNEVSKY—A spammer who helped develop the "Cutwail" spam botnet, and a onetime business partner of Dmitri "Gugle" Nechvolod, a major spammer.

DMITRY NECHVOLOD, a.k.a. "Gugle"— One of SpamIt and Rx-Promotion's most successful spammers, Gugle rented out his "Cutwail" spam botnet for use by many other junk emailers.

GENNADY LOGINOV—A Belarusian man and leader of a militant organized crime group known as "The Village." Partner with Alexander Rubatsky and involved in the kidnapping and ransom of Evgeny "Pet" Petrovsky—a rival businessman.

ALEXANDER RUBATSKY—A Belarusian hacker closely tied to the child porno-graphy industry who later founded the Russian Business Network (RBN) in St. Petersburg, Russia.

EVGENY PETROVSKY, a.k.a. "Pet"— Belarusian owner of companies Sunbill and BillCards, credit card processing networks that were deeply involved in processing payments for child pornography sites.

NIKOLAI McCOLO, a.k.a "Kolya"—The young entrepreneur behind McColo Corp., which until its demise in 2008 was among the most popular Web hosting providers in the cybercrime underground.

LEONID KUVAYEV—A convicted spam-mer who ran the RxPartners pharmacy spam affiliate program. Kuvayev is currently serving a ten-year prison sentence in Russia for child molestation and child pornography.

IGOR AND **DMITRY ARTIMOVICH**, a.k.a. "Engel"—Brothers who allegedly operated the "Festi" spam botnet and were close allies of Vrublevsky. The brothers were convicted in 2013 of using Festi to attack the website of Assist, a ChronoPay competitor, although they deny this.

COSMA—Spammer for both GlavMed-SpamIt and Rx-Promotion and principal author of the massive Rustock botnet.

SEVERA—Spammer for both GlavMed-SpamIt and Rx-Promotion and the apparent author of the Waledac and Storm botnets.

PREFACE

S ince the original hardcover publication of *Spam Nation*, I've spoken at multiple speaking engagements and book signings about the issues of cybercrime and cybersecurity. One question I'm often asked is, "Why did you choose to include the word 'spam' in the title of your book? Nobody likes junk email, so why would they even crack the cover?" Also, readers seem to be curious why—if so many of the cybercrooks that I write about are based in Russia and the former Soviet states—does the book have a picture of the United States on its cover?

I chose that title for several reasons. First, like it or not, spam is the primary vehicle for most cybercrime. Most people associate spam with junk email, which is something they don't feel they need to care about, but the term also encompasses malicious email, including missives that bundle malicious software and disguise it as a legitimate-looking attachment, as well as phishing attacks designed to steal your banking credentials and other account information.

Second, I wanted to express that—at least traditionally—Americans have been the reason for and the target of most spam and cybercrime. Spam would not exist were it not profitable for those that send it, and incredibly millions of American consumers are responding to and buying from spam—thus perpetuating the cycle of fraud and abuse that affects us all.

Finally, as described in detail in Chapter 2, the early cybercrime pioneers who built most of the spam industry were able to do so because they operated undeterred for years out of U.S.-based hosting providers that seemed completely oblivious to or willfully ignorant of the reputation of the partners with whom they'd chosen to do business. But recently, it's become impossible for any of us to ignore these spammers' and hackers' actions because they are now hitting us where it hurts most: our wallets.

Stephanie Bowen, my gracious and tenacious editor at Sourcebooks, had lobbied for the initial hardcover publication of *Spam Nation* to include a discussion about the epidemic of credit card breaches over the past year at retailers around the globe, but principally here in the United States. At the time, I didn't think the topic exactly fit with the flow of the narrative, but she ended up sneaking a mention of the December 2013 breach at Target Corporation into Chapter 1 anyhow.

Upon further reflection, I now see that she was right: these card breaches do have much to say about the state of modern organized cybercrime (a major focus of this book). It's worth noting that the Target breach began with a spam email sent to a heating and air conditioning (HVAC) vendor that worked with Target and had remote access to portions of Target's network. That spam message contained malicious software disguised as a document related to the company's business. Once inside the HVAC company's computers, the attackers were able to abuse that access to break into Target's network. The rest is history.

According to sources interviewed by this author, the malware was sent to the HVAC vendor by a collection of hacked PCs known as the "Cutwail" botnet, the very spam crime machine built by two characters profiled extensively in this book. As I wrote in the final chapter of *Spam Nation*, cybercrooks at the helm of massive spam engines these days are spending more of their resources churning out malicious spam designed to target consumers' account information as opposed to commercial pitches for dodgy products like knockoff pharmaceuticals.

I was able to break the Target breach story because the thieves who stole forty million credit and debit card numbers from the retail chain turned around and sold them on open-air bazaars online. I determined that Target was the source of the stolen cards by discovering these and utilizing the same knowledge gaps in the financial industry that the crooks are exploiting to steal data— but I was doing so to help these companies get to the bottom of these cyberattacks.

What are those knowledge gaps? Prior to the Target breach discovery, I'd spent a great deal of time building sources at smaller banks, which it would seem would want to invest in cybersecurity to protect their and their customers' assets. This might be surprising to many readers, but anti-fraud experts at many of these institutions actually tend not to have adequate money or resources to fight fraud, and they generally do not have the best visibility into what goes on in the underground cybercrime markets either. Instead, these banks—and there are thousands of them—are quite eager to share information if they think it will get them better intelligence about fraud trends that could end up costing them big money (such as early notice on a big retail breach).

The large, Wall Street banks pay cyber intelligence firms to dig up and share information about how their brands are being abused in the shadowy online forums and markets, and as such they possess a much more holistic view of fraud patterns. This is helped both by virtue of their size—the sheer number of accounts they have—and also because these colossal institutions have their fingers in so many financial pies that when a big fraud event occurs—like a Target breach—they tend to see spikes in fraud across many different business lines. So they have more resources to recognize fraud, if it's big enough, as soon as it occurs.

What's bizarre is that Visa and MasterCard and the other card brands will tell the banks about specific cards they've issued to customers that the card brands have determined were compromised in retail breaches, but they won't tell the banks which hacked merchant was responsible. The bigger banks can generally figure it out on their own which merchant got hacked—again, if the breach is big enough. On the other hand, the smaller banks are running around trying to figure out who's responsible so they can block transactions at that breached merchant going forward and limit their financial losses due to fraud on those cards.

Remarkably, it is this very disconnect in the financial system that organized cybercrooks exploit: the longer the banks spin their wheels trying to figure out who got hacked, the longer the crooks who hacked the merchant can continue selling the stolen cards and making money. Meanwhile, the card brands keep racking up fees from banks and merchants for the charges whether they're legitimate or not. Thus, if you want to know who just got hacked, the best place to find that intelligence is in the underground stores—not from security firms or the card associations.

It's become clear (to me, at least) that the entire credit card system in the United States is currently set up so that any one party to a transaction can reliably transfer the blame for an incident, dispute, or fraud to another party. The main reason the United States has not yet fully transitioned to a more secure standard for handling credit cards—such as chip-and-PIN—has a lot to do with the finger pointing and blame game that's been going on for years between the banks and the retail industry. The banks have said, "If the retailers only started installing chip-and-PIN card readers, we'd start issuing those types of cards." The retailers respond: "Why should we spend the money upgrading all our payment terminals to handle chip-and-PIN when hardly any banks are issuing those types of cards?" And so it has gone for years, with the cybercrooks hitting one major retail chain after another, laughing all the way to the cash machine.

The same crime machines responsible for pumping spam also are typically used to launch blunt "denial of service" attacks to knock people, companies, and organizations offline. Denial of service attacks have grown to epic proportions in recent months. My site, KrebsOnSecurity.com, has been under near constant attack for almost a year now. The same miscreants who've been attacking my site used their crime machine to knock millions of users off of Sony and Microsoft's online gaming networks on December 25, 2014.

That said, let me stress this is *not* because the misguided youngsters at the helm of these assaults are in any way sophisticated hackers. To the contrary: most of them probably couldn't hack their way out of a paper bag. But the sad truth is that it's now shockingly easy to launch massive attacks capable of knocking Fortune 500 firms offline for sustained periods of time.

The majority of these attacks are launched from point-and-click online criminal services (most of them even accept PayPal). Some of those services draw attack power from hacked computers they've taken over, but the majority of them seem to take advantage of the fact that there are currently more than thirty million misconfigured or seriously outdated systems on the Internet— mostly old DSL routers being used by people like you and me (and even provided to us by our cable and Internet providers)—that can be remotely and trivially abused to launch these crippling attacks. Some of these systems are here in the United States, but the vast majority of them are at ISPs in developing countries around the world.

I'd like to see a more global, systematic effort to drastically reduce the number of these outdated, largely unfixable, and unprotected systems. Much like we fund efforts to eradicate polio and malaria and other preventable diseases that kill millions of people each year, there really is little excuse not to fund a hard target effort to get these systems replaced and keep our data, our companies, and our identities safe (not to mention save billions of dollars in the long run). It would be expensive, for sure, but maybe there should be a sort of virtual "homeowners association" for the Internet that the United States and its wealthy allies pay into each year to help address some of these cybercrime problems and tidy up the neighborhood a bit. Though even a moderately successful eradication effort won't reduce the number of abuseable systems from thirty million to zero overnight, it's possible to get pretty close, and it's worth doing.

Incidentally, Sony suffered another kind of malicious cyber assault in late 2014; its Sony Pictures Entertainment division was the victim of a massive hacking attack in which the intruders stole gigantic volumes of employee and proprietary Sony data, and then threatened to release the information unless Sony executives paid a ransom demand. Sony declined, and the hackers leaked the data online for the whole world to see. They also unleased malicious software into the company's internal networks designed to destroy much of the company's internal computer systems.

The U.S. government has said publicly that it believes North Korean hackers were responsible for the malicious attack on Sony, but many in the security community remain unconvinced of this version of events. Nevertheless, the attack was the perfect end to a year marked by increasingly destructive attacks aimed at stealing data and extorting victims from corporations and from companies alike.

This rapidly increasing cyber threat—known as "ransom-ware"—encrypts all of the files, pictures, videos, and documents on your computer, unless and until you pay some arbitrary amount of money to get them back. Perhaps unsurprisingly, ransomware is most often spread through malicious spam, but it is also spread when Internet users fail to vaccinate their computers with the latest software security updates.

The Internet of today is a truly transformative communications and learning tool that radically enriches the lives of billions each day. Yet, never before in the history of the Internet has this medium been more fraught with snares and ne'er-do-wells looking to fleece the unwary. You may not understand the value of your computer, your Internet connection, your inbox, or your digital files, but I guarantee you the bad guys do, and they've become quite adept at extracting full value from these digital assets.

Every one of us online has an important role to play in making the Internet a safer, more productive place. But make no mistake: those who endeavor to remain blissfully unaware of their role in becoming part of the solution will almost invariably end up becoming part of the problem. That's why it's so crucial to read this book; it will help you understand your role in all of this and what you can do to stop it—and protect yourself.

For tips on how to protect yourself and your loved ones from the latest online attacks and scams, check the information in the final chapter of this book as well. And stay safe.

—*Brian Krebs*

Chapter 1

PARASITE

T he navy blue BMW 760 nosed up to the crosswalk at a traffic light in downtown Moscow. A black Porsche Cayenne pulled alongside. It was 2:00 p.m., Sunday, September 2, 2007, and the normally congested streets adjacent to the storied Sukharevskaya Square were devoid of traffic, apart from the tourists and locals strolling the broad sidewalks on either side of the boulevard. The afternoon sun that bathed the streets in warmth throughout the day was beginning to cast long shadows on the street from the historic buildings nearby.

The driver of the BMW, a notorious local scam artist who went by the hacker nickname "Jaks," had just become a father that day, and Jaks and his passenger had toasted the occasion with prodigious amounts of vodka. It was the perfect time and place to settle a simmering rivalry with the Porsche driver over whose ride was faster. Now each driver revved his engine in an unspoken agreement to race the short, straight distance to the big city square directly ahead.

As the signal flashed green, the squeal of rubber peeling off on concrete echoed hundreds of meters down in the main square. Bystanders turned to watch as the high-performance machines lurched from the intersection, each keeping pace with the other and accelerating at breakneck speed.

Roaring past the midpoint of the race at more than 200 kilometers per hour, Jaks suddenly lost control, clipping the Porsche and careening into a huge metal lamppost. In an instant, the competition was over, with neither car the winner. The BMW was sliced in two, the Porsche a smoldering, crumpled wreck close by. The drivers of both cars crawled and limped away from the scene, but the BMW's passenger—a promising twenty-three-year-old Internet entrepreneur named Nikolai McColo—was killed instantly, his almost headless body pinned under the luxury car.

"Kolya," as McColo was known to friends, was a minor celebrity in the cybercriminal underground, the youngest employee of a family-owned Internet hosting business that bore his last name—McColo Corp. At a time when law-enforcement agencies worldwide were just waking up to the financial and organizational threats from organized cybercrime, McColo Corp. had earned a reputation as a ground zero for it: a place where cybercrooks could reliably set up shop with little worry that their online investments and schemes would be discovered or jeopardized by foreign law-enforcement investigators.

At the time of Kolya's death, his family's hosting provider was home base for the largest businesses on the planet engaged in pumping out junk email or "spam" via robot networks. Called "botnets" for short, these networks are collections of personal computers that have been hacked and seeded with malicious software—or "malware"—that lets the attackers control the systems from afar. Usually, the owners of these computers have no idea their machines have been taken hostage.

Nearly all of the botnets controlled from McColo were built to blast out the unsolicited junk spam advertisements that flood our inboxes and spam filters every day. But the servers at McColo weren't generating and pumping spam themselves; that would attract too much attention from Internet vigilantes and Western law-enforcement agencies. Instead, they were merely used by the botmaster businesses to manipulate millions of PCs scattered around the globe into becoming spam-spewing zombies.

By the time paramedics had cleared the area of Kolya's accident, gruesome images of the carnage were already being uploaded to secretive Russian Internet forums frequented by McColo's friends and business clients. Among the first to broadcast the news of Kolya's death were denizens of Crutop.nu, a Russian-language hacker forum that counted among its eight thousand members some of the world's biggest spammers. The same Crutop.nu members who spread pictures and news of the incident were some of McColo's most successful web hosting customers, and many felt obligated (or were publicly shamed by forum administrators) to shell out funds to help Kolya's family pay for his funeral expenses. This was a major event in the cybercrime underworld.

Days later, the motley crew of Moscow-based spammers would gather to pay their last respects at his service. The ceremony was held at the same church where Kolya had been baptized less than twenty-three years earlier. Among those in attendance were Igor

"Desp" Gusev and Dmitry "SaintD" Stupin, coadministrators of SpamIt and GlavMed, until recently the world's largest sponsors of spam[1]—and two figures that will play key roles in this book.

Also at the service was Dmitry "Gugle" Nechvolod, then twenty-five years old and a hacker who was closely connected to the Cutwail botnet. Cutwail is a massive crime machine that has infected tens of millions of home computers around the globe and secretly seized control over them for sending spam. Nechvolod had already earned millions of dollars using the botnet to send junk email for GlavMed and SpamIt to millions of people around the world. To this day, Cutwail remains one of the largest and most active spam botnets—although it is almost undoubtedly run by many different individuals now (more on this in "Chapter 7: Meet the Spammers").

So why is it important to note these three men's presence at such a momentous event for cybercrime? Because their work (as well as Kolya's and hundreds of others') impacts every one of us every day in a strange but significant way: spam email.

Indeed, spam email has become the primary impetus for the development of malicious software—programs that strike computers like yours and mine every day—and through them, target our identities, our security, our finances, families, and friends. These botnets are virtual parasites that require care and constant feeding to stay one step ahead of antivirus tools and security firms that work to dismantle the networks. To keep their bot colonies

---

1.   It should be noted that Gusev has publicly denied sending spam and running SpamIt, though not to me directly in my interviews with him.

thriving, spammers (or botmasters—the term is interchangeable) must work constantly to spread and mutate the digital disorders that support them. Because antivirus programs routinely clean up infected PCs used to send spam, botnet operators need to continuously attack and seize control over additional computers and create new ways to infiltrate previously infected ones.

This technological arms race requires the development, production, and distribution of ever-stealthier malware that can evade constantly changing antivirus and anti-spam defenses. Therefore, the hackers at the throttle of these massive botnets also use spam as a form of self-preservation. The same botnets that spew plain old spam typically are used to distribute junk email containing new versions of the malware that helps spread the contagion. In addition, spammers often reinvest their earnings from spamming people into building better, stronger, and sneakier malicious software that can bypass antivirus and anti-spam software and firewalls. The spam ecosystem is a constantly evolving technological and sociological crime machine that feeds on itself.

Thus far, the criminals responsible for unleashing this daily glut of digital disease are doing a stupendous job of overwhelming the security industry. Antivirus companies now report that they are struggling to classify and combat *an average of 82,000 new malicious software variants attacking computers every day*, and a large percentage of these strains are designed to turn infected computers into spam zombies that can be made to do the attacker's bidding remotely. Security giant McAfee said it detected more than twenty-five million new pieces of malware in the fourth quarter of 2014.

But that also comes at a price to the spammers. In the case

of Cutwail, the maintenance needed to sustain it required 24-7 teams of software developers and technical support staff. That's because the software that powers botnets like Cutwail is typically rented out for use by other spammers, who frequently demand code tweaks or add-ons to help the bot programs work properly within their own criminal infrastructure.

Moscow resident Igor Vishnevsky, in his early thirties, was one of several hackers who worked closely with Nechvolod on Cutwail. (Vishnevsky would eventually strike out on his own, developing a rival version of Cutwail that he too used to spam and rent to other spammers. He agreed to act as our virtual "Virgil" and walk us through this strange and unfamiliar spammer underworld, and he appears throughout this book.) "We had an office for Gugle [Nechvolod, pronounced "Google"] with coders and support. Sometimes I visited it, but I didn't work from there," Vishnevsky recalled in an instant message conversation. He said Gugle's office employed at least five full-time coders and as many support staff who rotated shifts around the clock and on weekends to better meet the demands of clients.

Hosting firms like McColo attracted clientele like Cutwail's producers because they stayed online in the face of significant pressure from domestic and foreign law-enforcement agencies to unplug unsavory or illicit sites they hosted. According to Vishnevsky, McColo's servers were legendary for their consistent speeds and for being "bulletproof," or immune from shutdown requests lodged by other Internet service providers (ISPs) or foreign law-enforcement officials.

Shortly after Kolya's death, McColo was quick to assure the

cybercrime community that, while the organization's most recognizable member had passed away, the hosting provider would continue business as usual. Kolya's partner, Alexey, spread the message on a number of top cybercrime-friendly forums, seeking to reassure the firm's client base that the incident would result in no disruption of service.

The cybercrime community needed little convincing to stay. The service was mainly hosted in the United States, and was cheap, reliable, and fast. For the year following Nikolai's death, Nechvolod and most of the top spam botmasters would keep their botnet control servers parked at McColo.

That is, until the evening of November 11, 2008, when an exposé in the *Washington Post* about the high concentration of malicious activity at the hosting provider prompted the two suppliers of McColo's connection to the larger Internet to simultaneously pull the plug on the firm. In an instant, spam volumes plummeted by as much as 75 percent worldwide, as millions of spam bots were disconnected from their control servers and scattered to the four winds like sheep without a shepherd.

The McColo takedown hit botmasters like Nechvolod and Vishnevsky directly in their pocketbooks. Spammers who were renting the botnets flooded Crutop.nu and other underground fraud forums with complaints that they had lost substantial investments, demanding to know what was going to be done about it.

"On McColo, we hosted servers in the USA that had good speed," Vishnevsky recalled. "When McColo went down, we had to rent much slower servers in China and other countries that suck," in their ability to withstand abuse complaints, he said.

In a sign that few thought McColo's operations would ever go away—even after Kolya's death—many spammers actually kept another major and expensive component of their operations— huge email address lists—directly on the company's servers.

"Everyone lost their lists there," Vishnevsky said, noting that he and Nechvolod lost a particularly large and valuable list of more than two billion email addresses after the takedown.

Kolya's death and the dissolution of McColo were watershed events because they signified the beginning of the end of an era in which spammers and cybercrime lords were allowed to operate under the radar with relative impunity. At the time, more than 90 percent of all email sent worldwide was unsolicited junk, the bulk of it advertising fly-by-night Internet pharmacy sites. In the ensuing four years, a series of similar takedowns of rogue ISPs, hosting providers, and large spam botnets would make a major dent in worldwide junk-email volumes and coincide with the arrest or imprisonment of several top spammers.

However, McColo's demise also marked the dawn of a new age of spamming through the genesis of a protracted and costly turf war we'll explore in this book. Dubbed the "Pharma Wars" by bystanders in the cybercrime and cybersecurity worlds, it exploded into a vicious feud between two of the largest sponsors of pharmaceutical spam—with unsuspecting users like you and me trapped in the middle.

On one side of the battle were the aforementioned Dmitry Stupin and Igor Gusev and their sister pharmacy operations GlavMed and SpamIt. On the other was Rx-Promotion, a competing rogue Internet pharmacy started by Gusev's former business partner, thirty-five-year-old Muscovite Pavel Vrublevsky. Officially, Vrublevsky was the top executive at a company called ChronoPay, one of Russia's largest online payment-processing firms and a company that he and Gusev cofounded.

In secret, he had deep ties to the cybercrime underworld, helping online miscreants of all stripes obtain credit card processing for their shady endeavors, and taking a hefty cut of the action. Vrublevsky also is the cofounder and administrator of the popular spammer forum Crutop.nu and another pivotal figure in the cyber wars that have made us into a spam nation—or in reality, a world of spam—today.

By 2010, I had spent more than a year investigating and reporting on allegations of corrupt business practices by Vrublevsky and his reputed ties to spammers working for the Rx-Promotion rogue pharmacy program, first as an investigative reporter for the *Washington Post* and then for my own cybersecurity news website, KrebsOnSecurity.com. But as I dug deeper and deeper, I wanted to know more about the spam email and cybersecurity problem: who was driving it and how to solve it. It was clear others did, too.

Prior to the war of attrition between spam kingpins that this book will explore, there was shockingly little public and reliable information available to answer the most basic questions facing the spam problem, such as:

- Who is buying the stuff advertised in junk email, like Viagra, prescription drugs, and even Gucci purses? And what drives people to purchase and ingest pills pushed by these intrusive and unknown marketers?

- Are these drugs real or ineffective—and possibly lethal—fakes?
- Who is profiting from sending spam? How are the profits being divvied up, and where is the money going?
- Why is the pharmaceutical industry—one of the richest and most influential businesses in the world—seemingly powerless to stop the wholesale theft and hijacking of its products, trademarks, and customers?
- For that matter, why is it so easy to pay for these blatantly spam-advertised knockoffs with a credit card?
- Do customers have their credit card accounts hacked or resold after buying from spammers? What if they don't even buy from them? Are they still in danger?
- And what can consumers, policymakers, and law enforcement use to get control of the cybercrime epidemic?

These are some of the questions people asked when I told them I was writing a book about spam. At the beginning, I could offer only my best guesses for answers. Even as I sought advice from purported spam experts, I discovered that some of the world's top authorities on spam didn't have a firm grip on the answers either. Many offered canned responses that seemed to be based on a handful of well-worn case studies, some of which were sponsored by major pharmaceutical or security companies, or both.

Leaked pharmacy spam databases that I was able to obtain from Rx-Promotion and GlavMed-SpamIt during the Pharma Wars changed all of that by providing a deep insider look at almost every significant aspect of the world's largest spam organizations.

Perhaps ironically, the spammers themselves provided this glimpse into their shady doings that affect each of us every day.

Hackers loyal to Gusev and Vrublevsky leaked this information to certain law-enforcement officials and to me in an attempt to sabotage each other. Instead, their databases offered unprecedented insight into the day-to-day operations and profits of these secretive, international drug cartels, which comprise a loose affiliation of spammers, virus writers, shadowy suppliers, and shippers. The information in these databases also forms the basis of my reporting for many portions of this book.

More importantly—and alarmingly—this cache of documents also contained the demographic, health, and financial information of millions of customers—mostly consumers in the United States—who had purchased prescription medications from the spam networks upon receiving a solicitation by junk email or after searching for prescription drugs online.

The databases offered an unvarnished look at the hidden but burgeoning demand for cheap prescription drugs, a demand that appears driven in large part by Americans seeking more affordable and discreetly available medications.

Given the increasing menace of spam email and related cyber-security assaults that directly affect consumers and companies (like the major news story I broke to the media in December 2013 about the Target credit-card database breach—a cyberattack that compromised millions of Americans' financial information and forced an even greater number of us to get new credit cards), you may be wondering why governments, law-enforcement officials, and corporations aren't taking a stronger and more significant stance to stop the tidal wave of spam and cybercrime impacting us all.

Part of the reason for the Internet community's stunted response to the malware and spam epidemic to date is that many policymakers and cybercrime experts tend to dismiss spam as a nuisance problem that can be solved or at least mitigated to a manageable degree by the proper mix of technology and law enforcement. For many of us, spam has become almost the punch line of a joke, thanks to its close association with male penile-enhancement pills and erectile dysfunction medications such as Viagra and Cialis. We assume that if we don't open the emails or don't purchase anything from them, we aren't affected.

Unfortunately, that attitude underscores a popular yet fundamental miscalculation about the threat that spam poses to every one of us: namely, the sheer destructive power of the botnets and the misguided computer programmers who keep them going. Indeed, the botnets built and managed by members of SpamIt, Rx-Promotion, and other spam affiliate programs were not only used for distributing spam. Web criminals routinely rent access to these crime machines to mask their true location online, because botnets allow miscreants to bounce their Internet traffic through a myriad of infected systems that are largely untraceable.

Crooks running these botnets also regularly use them to harvest usernames and passwords from host PCs, stealing everything from people's online banking credentials to digital keys that can unlock valuable corporate secrets at companies large and small. Indeed, the miscreants at the helm of some of the world's most active botnets already control thousands of zombie systems inside

Fortune 500 companies that allow attackers to spam people using these corporations' more powerful servers, and to siphon sensitive and proprietary data from internal company systems.

Botnets pose other serious threats. Frequently they are rented out as powerful hired muscle in high-stakes Internet extortion schemes known as distributed denial of service or "DDoS" attacks. In such assaults, crooks demand tens of thousands of dollars in protection money from businesses. If business owners refuse to pay up, the botnet masters will order their armies of infected PCs to pelt the targeted company's website with so much junk Internet traffic that it can no longer accommodate legitimate visitors. The extorted business either pays up or stays offline until the attackers relent (or, if the targeted business can afford it, hires a legitimate anti-DDoS company to help deflect the attacks).

Politically or ideologically motivated DDoS attacks are capable of unplugging entire nations and silencing critics or protesters of certain issues. In 2008, a politically motivated, sustained DDoS attack against the ultra-wired former Soviet nation of Estonia knocked most government sites offline for several days, interrupted electronic banking for several hours, briefly incapacitated that country's largest cellular network, and disrupted the national network that Estonians rely on in the event of medical emergencies.

Such firepower has gained the attention and concern of the U.S. government and its military operations as well. Cyberattacks have been identified as a potent and current threat to today's network-centric war-fighting machine. In a seminal speech at the White House in May 2009, President Obama declared the cyber threat to be one of the most serious economic and national security challenges facing America today.

Despite government concerns, the public policy response to all of the organizational and technological machinery that powers the spam epidemic has been lukewarm at best and, in some places, virtually nonexistent. Here is a threat that is capable of disrupting entire countries' infrastructure, diluting vital communication networks, poisoning people with its spread of counterfeit consumer products, and fueling the development of an entire illegal underground economy, yet governments around the world have done little to protect their citizens from these invasive cyber armies.

Many lawmakers in the United States and elsewhere are using the cybercrime epidemic to lobby for changes to the laws that govern how police and federal authorities can gather data on their citizens. But more stringent penalties against cybercrime have done little to deter attackers or the activities of fortune-seeking pill spammers and modern e-thieves. Most of the recently proposed and approved Internet security laws in the United States have focused on vague initiatives to beef up the security of the nation's critical information infrastructure—the computers and interconnected systems that run everything from manufacturing plants to water treatment facilities and the power grid.

Recent legislative efforts in the United States aimed at combating cybercrime have also met with stiff resistance from privacy advocates and the public at large. When the U.S. Congress tried to pass a law that would have forced ISPs to cease providing connectivity to websites that were deemed to have trampled on trademarks by peddling pirated or counterfeit goods, lawmakers were confronted with nothing short of a popular revolt from constituents opposed to the idea. Most of that resistance was organized and executed in artfully planned online demonstrations.

Meanwhile, a handful of key arrests and disruptive actions against spam botnets and top players in the cybercrime underground appear to have done more to destabilize the industry than any of the half-baked legislative proposals put forth so far. As numerous examples in this book illustrate, governments around the world can perhaps achieve the most impact on cybercrime not by passing new laws or increasing penalties for various cybercriminal offenses, but by better enforcing existing laws and by creatively applying pressure on and incentivizing global corporations to address this problem in ways that suit their own interests and extend the reach of domestic law-enforcement agencies.

This is not to say that the answer to combating spam and botnets rests only with the governments of the world. On the contrary; as we will see later in this book, some of the most effective actions against these dual scourges have come from efforts by corporations to protect their own financial interests, customers, trademarks, and public image—and from consumers themselves.

Ultimately, spam and all of its attendant ills will diminish very little without a more concerted, cooperative push from some of the richest and most powerful interests in the world, including the pharmaceutical industry; the credit card and banking sectors; lawmakers and law enforcers around the globe; and people like you and me, most of whom are the unsuspecting targets and victims of these spammers and hackers every day. It's time to do something about this global epidemic, to protect our identities, our bank accounts, our families, and our lives before it's too late.

Chapter 2

BULLETPROOF

To understand the threat that email spam poses for all of us, it's crucial first to peer into the dark corners of the cyberworld and understand what's lurking there. Kidnapping. Bribery. Extortion. Blackmail. Corruption. These were among the business skills commonly employed by the men who built the earliest cybercrime havens—the virtual pirate coves of the Internet.

These web hosting businesses—mostly based in Russia and the former Soviet states—were often referred to as "bulletproof networks" or "bulletproof hosting providers" because they had secured enough political and operational protection through a variety of methods (some legal, some illegal) to make them virtually untouchable by the law. Indeed, they had so much clout that they could often stay online in the face of withering pressure from foreign governments and law-enforcement agencies to disconnect them and their customers, who were invariably trafficking unsavory or illicit goods and services on the web.

One of the leaders, McColo Corp., was a master at this. Nikolai, the young entrepreneur whose violent death by car accident we witnessed at the outset of Chapter 1, certainly didn't invent the business of attracting and hosting cybercrime-based enterprises online. Rather, like innovators in other fields, he stood on the shoulders of cybercriminal giants before him, refining a time-honored business model by focusing on efficiency: cutting out middlemen, slashing prices, and investing in more dependable, faster networks.

Most of all, McColo distinguished itself by earning a reputation as a bulletproof hosting provider that offered top-notch technical and customer support. These were qualities that early pioneers in the business tended to overlook, probably because they had so little competition.

But to understand how McColo came to dominate the cyber-crime underground, it helps to know how and why its predecessors failed. As it happens, the bulletproof hosting providers that laid the groundwork for young Nikolai's business also are closely intertwined with the early careers of the two cybercrime kingpins whose lengthy feud forms the basic story arc of this book. And one network above all paved the way for the rise of McColo, the Pharma Wars, and many of the junk email and cybercrime practices that threaten us and our online security today.

By the middle of 2007, the Russian Business Network (RBN)—a shadowy web hosting conglomerate based in St. Petersburg, Russia—had cemented its reputation among security experts as the epicenter of cybercriminal activity on the Internet. In case after case, when computer crime investigators followed the trail of money and evidence from sites selling child pornography or pirated software, web properties at RBN were somehow always involved. When cyber sleuths sought to shutter sites that were pumping out colonies of computer viruses and "phishing" scams that use email to impersonate banks and lure people into entering account passwords at fake bank sites, more often than not, the offending site was a customer of RBN.

RBN epitomized the early bulletproof hosting providers, virtual safe houses where web hosting customers could display and offer practically any online content—no matter how illegal or offensive—as long as they kept paying exorbitant hosting fees that were prone to increase without notice. A basic web server at RBN commanded prices between six hundred and eight hundred U.S. dollars per month, more than ten times what most legitimate hosting providers charged for regular customers at the time.

These fees didn't just line the pockets of the bulletproof providers; they were essential to those providers' survival. For example, a share of the income from those lofty fees trickled down from RBN's ringleaders to local authorities and corrupt politicians in the region, some of whom were all too ready to look the other way when law-enforcement officials from other nations came inquiring about sites promoting illegal activity that were hosted on RBN's networks.

David Bizeul, a French security researcher who compiled a massively in-depth analysis of RBN during its heyday in mid-2007, said RBN had a dedicated team responsible for fielding abuse complaints, but that this team only served to make RBN appear more like a legitimate Internet service provider (ISP) than anything else.

"RBN has an available abuse team—used to give it a respectable image—and this abuse team will ask you to provide a Russian judicial indictment in order to process" an abuse or takedown request, Bizeul wrote in 2007. "Of course, this indictment is very difficult to obtain. Isn't it a paradise for fraudsters?"

The exact origins of the Russian Business Network are shrouded in mystery. Perhaps for that reason, many experts in the computer security industry have for years ascribed most malicious Internet activity to the ringleaders behind RBN, whether or not that activity had any obvious connections to the infamous hosting network.

Still, if RBN has become a kind of digital boogeyman for many, that reputation was hard-earned. According to press reports and sources familiar with the company, RBN was born out of cybercriminals' need for more stable and reliable web hosting for a variety of their illegal businesses—most especially extreme pornography and child porn. Indeed, RBN's roots trace back to the child porn industry and to organized crime groups based in Minsk, Belarus.

At the dawn of the new millennium, a bright, twenty-two-year-old Belarusian named Alexander Rubatsky was being groomed to follow in the footsteps of his father—a well-respected lieutenant colonel in the Belarusian police force. But Rubatsky was far more interested in and skilled at computers, and eventually dropped out of the police academy.

Victor Chamkovsky, a Belarusian filmmaker and investigative journalist who documented Rubatsky's early career, said Rubatsky's talents made him an attractive acquisition by local organized crime groups who saw big money in processing payments for Internet businesses, particularly pornography. According to Chamkovsky, in 1995 Rubatsky started hanging out with Gennady Loginov, a young tough whose brother was the leader of a militant organized-crime group in Minsk known as "The Village." Rubatsky's job was not to strong-arm people, but to simply find databases to plunder and acquire credit card accounts that could be drained or sold for cash.

In Spring 2001, Rubatsky began looking for a real job and was hired as a computer specialist with CyberPlat, at the time Russia's largest processor of online payments. As part of his position, he was given the funds and authority to hire more than a dozen other programmers. His assignment: to assemble a team that could build the next generation of CyberPlat's payment platform.

As noted by the Belarusian newspaper *BelGazeta*, CyberPlat also paid Rubatsky to rigorously test its systems for security vulnerabilities that might expose it to data breaches. But the company would later allege that he abused that access by downloading a copy of the company's client database. Rubatsky told prosecutors that he grabbed the data merely so that he could demonstrate the security weaknesses his team had found. But his employer wasn't buying that explanation. The local police raided the cabin where Rubatsky and his hackers worked, and carted off enough evidence to put him on trial for theft. The Belarusian courts ultimately sided with CyberPlat, sentencing Rubatsky to six months in jail. (That sentence was later suspended.)

But Rubatsky would exact his revenge. Before his trial ended, CyberPlat's customer list was leaked to law-enforcement officials. Cybercrime investigators from the United States and other nations had long suspected that most of the payments to sites selling child pornography were being processed through merchant accounts tied to CyberPlat and its Moscow-based partner Bank Platina, and now the authorities had a smoking gun.

By mid-2002, CyberPlat found itself ensnared in an international scandal when it was reported by the Russian news publication *Kommersant* that among CyberPlat's customers were dozens of websites selling access to child-porn images and videos. CyberPlat fired 40 percent of its staff—including top managers—in the wake of the scandal.

Meanwhile, Rubatsky was left to continue pursuing the extremely lucrative market of processing child-porn payments for shady sites that offered it. At the same time, Rubatsky's strongman Loginov was determined to beef up operational and physical security for the enterprise. Never again would local police forces be able to so easily raid the hacker hut.[2]

Prefiguring his later work as a pioneer in the bulletproof hosting business, Rubatsky sought to secure local and physical protection so that he could continue to operate his business without interruption or interference. If the local police decided to conduct another raid, at least Rubatsky would see them coming and have a chance to hide or destroy incriminating evidence of his business.

According to a documentary by Chamkovsky called *Operation Consortium*, and as documented in other Russian news sources, Loginov and his associates rigged the cottage with a variety of

---

2.   I was unable to track down Rubatsky, but according to the Belarusian Telegraph Agency (the state-owned national news agency), Rubatsky is currently a fugitive who is wanted by Interpol, the international criminal police organization.

security devices, including closed-circuit cameras and alarm systems. Loginov's team also acquired firearms, police radios, and uniforms. They even received combat training under the tutelage of a former officer from the Russian KGB—the secret police and intelligence agency of the Soviet Union.

Loginov's gang was reportedly subjected to a crash course in KGB field service, including a battery of physical and psychological endurance tests, as well as specialized instruction in a variety of medical and technical skills. "Initially, they even had to take [written] tests," said Igor Parmon, a deputy in the Belarusian Ministry of Internal Affairs, in Chamkovsky's documentary. "They were even punished for missing classes."

A 2004 story in the *Belarusian Business News* describes how Loginov's group reacted when they learned that a local businessman named Evgeny "Pet" Petrovsky was building his own credit-card processing business catering to the child porn industry—a company called Sunbill (later renamed BillCards). The organized crime gang decided to put their newfound combat training to work by eliminating—or at least intimidating—the competition. Petrovsky's alleged role in setting up card processing for child porn sites was also documented in 2004 by the Computer Crime Research Center, a nonprofit organization based in Odessa, Ukraine, that gathers data on transnational cybercrime.

Petrovsky was stopped in his car by a man posing as a local policeman, and when he stepped out of the car as directed, he was kidnapped by masked men. Once they reached their safe house in the outskirts of Minsk, the abductors contacted Petrovsky's associates and demanded a million U.S. dollars for his safe return. But no money would be forthcoming. When local authorities began to close in on their location, the assailants fled with Petrovsky to Moscow. By November 2002, Russian and Belarusian authorities had located the Loginov gang's hideout and arrested the kidnappers. They found Petrovsky alive and relatively unharmed.[3]

According to Chamkovsky, Rubatsky was intensely focused on hacking and plundering online stores of financial data, and was not aware of his comrades' paramilitary activities. But when Rubatsky got word that Loginov's group had been rounded up by law enforcement for kidnapping and extortion, he fled Belarus for St. Petersburg, Russia.

From a rented office space in downtown St. Petersburg, Rubatsky reportedly worked with contacts at Moscow's Alfa Bank to set up an entirely new payment system called "Alfa-Pay." The system was designed to process payments for child pornography and to shield the business from disruption or prying eyes. As described in a 2006 story in the Belarusian newspaper *Evening Minsk*, the business relied on a network of holding companies that served as intermediaries for employees back in Belarus who handled everything from photographing teenage and preteen models to the distribution of the content and the payment of commissions to resellers of the photographic content.

"With Rubatsky's help, a huge holding was developed, which encompassed everything from photo-shooting and pornography distribution to the administrative work of a holding company,

---

3.   Loginov and several associates were later prosecuted and found guilty of kidnapping and other crimes. According to a report in the *Ecommerce Journal*, Petrovsky is thought to be in hiding somewhere in Ukraine.

[including] regular payments, billing, and commissions," Chamkovsky wrote. "Rubatsky's know-how on…sites dedicated to child pornography was in creating [a] cookie-cutter system that could be easily cloned."

All of this may have seemed like an issue isolated to Russia and Eastern Europe, where these shadowy cybercriminal companies are allowed to exist. But the truth is that the vast majority of the business's customers were actually Americans who were willing to pay more than forty dollars per month for subscription access to the child porn sites, known in the underground as "strawberry" and "lolita" sites (the latter being a literary reference to the novel of the same name by Russian author Vladimir Nabokov). According to press reports on the operation, Rubatsky's network of child porn sites attracted more than 100,000 visitors per day and generated revenues of nearly $5 million per month.

But before long Alfa-Pay found itself at odds once again with Petrovsky's BillCards payment-processing business. By this time, Petrovsky had allied himself with Igor "Desp" Gusev, who was rumored to have been the administrator of a secret online forum called Darkmasters.com, which catered to webmasters (website owners) engaged in selling extremely hard-core porn, including child pornography.[4]

Rubatsky's Alfa-Pay and Petrovsky's BillCards were soon

---

4. In an email interview, Igor Gusev acknowledged that someone using his unusual nickname "Desp" was listed as an administrator on the homepage of Darkmasters.com, but denied that he himself was ever an administrator of Darkmasters. Instead, Gusev said he had merely agreed to lend his imprimatur on the site in exchange for money from the true administrator—another adult webmaster who used the nickname "Master." Vrublevsky, on the other hand, insists this is "proof" that Gusev was closely aligned with the Russian Business Network.

vying to destroy one another, said Pavel Vrublevsky, cofounder and owner of ChronoPay, the Russian company mentioned in Chapter 1 that got its start in 2003 processing payments for adult webmasters. (In 2003, Gusev would join Vrublevsky as a fifty-fifty cofounder in ChronoPay, which would later eclipse CyberPlat as Russia's largest processor of online payments.)

"Alfa-Pay got in a huge fight with BillCards, and they both started launching computer attacks against one another, trying to start criminal cases against each other, and sending all kinds of incriminating information to mass media and all that crap," Vrublevsky recalled in a 2010 interview that would eerily prefigure the turf battle then already underway between himself and Gusev over cornering the market for knockoff pharmaceuticals online. "As a result, both businesses fell apart, and it was a big scandal."

That's when Rubatsky decided it was time to go into another lucrative but less dangerous line of work: web hosting. According to Vrublevsky, the Belarusian set up a meeting with the men running Eltel, a local ISP whose networks connected much of St. Petersburg to the rest of the public Internet.

Vrublevsky maintains that Eltel's management had bought political protection for their business from agents of the Russian Federal Security Service (FSB), the successor to the Soviet Union's KGB. This type of cover, known as *krusha* or "roof" in Russian, was considered necessary for any business capable of generating healthy profits—because such income made the business vulnerable to criminal and governmental interference and even violence.

According to Vadim Volkov, author of *Violent Entrepreneurs: The Use of Force in the Making of Russian Capitalism*, FSB officers are frequently embedded as employees of Russian companies, ostensibly as a means to help them fight extortionists who might try to steal the company's profits.

Volkov writes that Russian law allows FSB agents, while remaining in service, to be "assigned to work at enterprises and organizations at the consent of their directors... This provision allowed thousands of acting security officers to hold positions in private companies and banks as 'legal consultants,' as the position was modestly called. Using their ties with the state organizations and information resources of the FSB, they performed what has become known as 'roof' functions—protecting against extortion and cheating by criminal groups and facilitating relations with the state bureaucracy. Expert estimates suggest that up to 20 percent of FSB officers are engaged in informal 'roof' businesses."

"The Eltel guys were famous for being really crazy and hosting child pornography and crap like this, because they had a good relationship with the local cops," Vrublevsky said in a telephone interview. "But the ISPs upstream from Eltel were constantly blacklisting their sites, so [to get around that issue] Rubatsky came up with the idea of having a direct link to big [Internet backbone providers] like Telia and Tiscali."[5] With a direct link, bulletproof hosting providers would no longer be at the mercy of smaller, intermediary ISPs that could be bullied into pulling the plug on RBN at the slightest sign of interest from law enforcement.

To circumvent this obstacle, "this Rubatsky guy ended up

---

5. Now part of TeliaSonera, Telia was the dominant Swedish telecommunications company with operations throughout Europe and Asia. Tiscali is an Italian telecommunications company that provides domestic service but at one time offered services throughout Europe and Hong Kong.

spending a shitload of money so [Eltel] could have their own channel of Internet coming from abroad," Vrublevsky recalled. "And they called it the 'Russian Business Network,' or RBN for short."

According to Vrublevsky, Rubatsky appointed as head of the RBN project a smart, young technician named Eugene I. Sergeenko, a twenty-year-old hacker better known in the underground by his handle, "Flyman."

Flyman would soon become synonymous with both RBN and the global spam epidemic, as RBN emerged as the global epicenter of malicious cyberactivity, including everything from phishing schemes to the penis-enlargement spam that bombards each of us every day.

◆　◆　◆

By 2007, RBN had evolved into a cybercriminal force to be feared. The rogue hosting provider had become a massive magnet for online criminal schemes of all kinds. Researchers in academia and at private Internet security firms had been sounding the alarm about RBN for more than a year, churning out countless reports about huge volumes of phishing scams, male enhancement spam, and sites hosting malicious software emanating from the troubled ISP and contaminating millions of Internet-connected systems around the world. But most of these reports were fairly technical analyses that examined just one or two aspects of the multifarious badness emerging from RBN—such as a new malware innovation, a botnet command center, or another orchard of malicious websites that had sprung up in RBN's backyard.

It occurred to me that nobody had centralized all of the disparate research on RBN or sought to pull it all together into a single report revealing all of the malicious activity there. At the time, these various reports had gradually worn down the support infrastructure that kept RBN's network online, so it seemed to me that a major exposé in a widely read publication might topple the entire enterprise once and for all.

I'd recently carved out a cybercrime beat as a reporter at the *Washington Post* and was eager to centralize the intelligence on RBN in a report that I hoped might bring broader attention to the size of the threat. I firmly believed that the cybercrime community had made a major strategic blunder in concentrating so much badness in one place. If somehow RBN was ostracized and shunned by the rest of the Internet community, many cybercriminal businesses would be unplugged from the web.

Cybersecurity experts I spoke with about the idea said such an action could increase the costs of these criminal operations and make it more difficult for them to find a stable home. One possible end result would be much less spam for everyday users and fewer sites pushing malicious software or peddling child porn. To me, the positive implications were huge. Not only could this decrease or possibly eradicate junk email and all of the viruses, malware, and other security problems that come with it, but it could also possibly decimate an illegal and shocking industry that harmed children for the perverse pleasure of a small minority of adults.

In June 2007, I began badgering dozens of sources for quantifiable data about malicious activity that persisted at RBN. Over the next four months, the reporting aspect of the story came together almost on its own, as facts pouring in from different sources about the location of websites both malicious and atrocious began to paint a truly frightening picture of this rogue Internet hosting firm and what it was doing to clog our networks with destructive spam email.

Nearly identical damnations of RBN came in the form of incriminating data from some of the most noted security firms in the industry, including Cisco, Dell SecureWorks, FireEye, HostExploit, Marshall/M86, the SANS Internet Storm Center, Shadowserver, Sunbelt Software (now GFI), Symantec, Team Cymru, Trend Micro, and Verisign, to name just a few.

Ken Dunham, then director of rapid response for Verisign's iDefense cyber intelligence unit, said his team examined all of the web properties hosted at RBN and couldn't find a single redeemable quality there. "We went through and correlated all of their information, and we couldn't find one good thing at RBN," Dunham said. "We've seen virtual safe houses for criminal groups in the past, but virtually everything within this hosting provider has always been illicit or malicious." In short, there was no redeeming reason for this criminal ISP to remain online.

Perhaps because of the mystery and aura of Russian organized crime that surrounded RBN, convincing sources to speak openly and plainly about what they knew of the ISP's operations was far more challenging. One source, an academic who fed investigators at the Federal Bureau of Investigation daily dossiers on the sale of child pornography and other criminal activity at RBN, said he was worried for his physical safety if he spoke out publicly on what he knew.

"The Russian Mafia is behind RBN, and they have big guns and small morals," the academician explained. "I'd love to be an 'expert' for you, but I really don't want to get my family whacked."

That was one of dozens of candid quotes I could never attribute, and I desperately needed experts to state on the record what they knew about RBN in order to expose this malicious network that was affecting the lives of millions of unsuspecting people. After much cajoling, I eventually convinced enough experts to speak the truth. On October 13, 2007, the *Washington Post* ran the story "Shadowy Russian Firm Seen as Conduit for Cybercrime," in the front section of the paper and featured the piece prominently on their website.

Not long after that story, the *Post* also ran a pair of supporting pieces on its Security Fix blog, detailing the malicious activity at RBN and explicitly calling out which ISPs were providing RBN connections to the rest of the Internet. The jig was up. Now that their names were out in the open, these providers would need to justify taking money from RBN—an indefensible position given RBN's horrid reputation as safe haven for any material, no matter how illegal or offensive.

Over the next few weeks, tens of thousands of Internet addresses previously assigned to the Russian Business Network were gradually abandoned. The cybercrime enterprises that had once occupied these "cyber lots" vanished, scattering to new bullet-proof hosting providers in Italy, China, Korea, and elsewhere. The result was that for a short time, while the spam bots continued blasting out junk advertisements and links to malware-laced sites, the sites advertised in those emails sat unresponsive. Although on the surface this was a hollow victory, for many in the security community it was a welcome shot across the bow alerting the cybercrime underground that the online security industry was finally fighting back.

Not everyone was thrilled about this development. Whereas before RBN had been a concentration of known bad hosters that ISPs could easily block or filter with a handful of firewall instructions, such blocking became much harder once the sites at RBN were dispersed to dozens of networks. Now, ISPs had to spread their security nets farther to ensure that malicious websites, botnets, and spammers couldn't get through. But ISPs, government officials, and corporations were finally starting to pay attention to this cybercrime underworld spreading beneath their feet.

That was the tip of the iceberg. In August 2008—almost a year after RBN was scattered to the four winds—I wrote a series about cybercrime activity concentrated a bit closer to home at a shadowy ISP called Atrivo. Like young Nikolai's McColo, it was a Northern California-based hosting provider that had also ignored requests from law enforcement agencies and from the security community to unplug abusive websites that had become synonymous with botnet-hosting and huge numbers of sites set up to foist malicious software. I relied on the same evidence collected by some of the security firms that had gathered data on RBN, and in particular a report from HostExploit, an organization of international respected Internet professionals dedicated to researching, exposing, and raising awareness about cybercrime.

That series, and growing attention from other media outlets and security experts, led to Atrivo being gradually excluded from the Internet, as its partners in the ISP industry who provided connections to the larger Internet for it and its cybercriminal users were publicly shamed into severing ties with the company one by one over a period of approximately two weeks.

One of the significant fallouts of Atrivo's shutdown was the hastened demise of the Storm worm, an infamous botnet that had infiltrated and compromised millions of Americans' PCs and "was once responsible for sending more than 20 percent of all spam," I explained on the *Washington Post*'s Security Fix blog on October 17, 2008. Atrivo had hosted a number of the master servers for the Storm worm; the worm discharged its final blast of spam three days before Atrivo was forced off the Internet by its final remaining Internet provider.

A week after Atrivo went dark, I heard from a trusted source who had contacts with many unsavory individuals in the cyber-crime underworld. My source said he had a message to pass on from an unnamed cybercrook who'd been mildly inconvenienced and grudgingly impressed by the organized ostracism of Atrivo I had started.

"Tell Krebs 'Nice job on Atrivo,'" the mysterious miscreant told my source. "But if he's thinking about doing McColo next, he's pushing his luck."

I wasn't sure what to make of this communication, which seemed like an amused observation backstopped by a veiled threat. But by the time my source relayed that message, it was too late to turn back. I was already knee-deep in an investigation of McColo, the ISP company led by Nikolai "Kolya" McColo. It was a logical progression, mainly because many of the miscreants and botmasters who had parked their botnet and crimeware operations at Atrivo also had portions of their infrastructure hosted at McColo. And now that Atrivo was wiped off the Internet, McColo had become an even more critical bulletproof provider for the underground cybercrime community.

On the afternoon of November 11, I sent several months' worth of data detailing McColo's offenses to the company's two ISP partners that connected it to the larger Internet: Global Crossing and Hurricane Electric, both of which had headquarters in the United States. The information was arranged in a map that showed how the servers used to control all of the top five most active spam botnets—Internet-connected programs responsible for sending most of the world's junk email—were parked at just a handful of servers in McColo's Northern California hosting facility. I had a hunch that, once presented with the record of malicious activity there, McColo's Internet partners would sever business ties with the hosting provider and effectively cripple it.

Hours later, I heard from a source who monitored global spam activity daily, and who knew I was working on a piece about McColo.

"Krebs, what did you *do*?" the source asked with a praising laugh. "I'm hardly seeing any more spam, and it looks like McColo has been unplugged from the Internet!"

I don't recall saying thank you or good-bye—I only remember swearing loudly and slamming the receiver down to quickly dial several other sources on my mobile phone. All of them confirmed the same findings: McColo was gone, and none of its Internet address space was reachable from anywhere on the World Wide Web. Mission accomplished—for the time being.

A call to Benny Ng, Hurricane Electric's director of marketing, revealed the reason. The ISP had severed ties with McColo that afternoon.

"We looked into it a bit, saw the size and scope of the problem you were reporting, and said 'Holy cow!'" Ng said. "Within the hour we had terminated all of our connections to them."

Within a few minutes of confirming the takedown, I wrote and published a blog post about the McColo outage—which quickly became one of the biggest cybercrime stories, in terms of immediate global impact, up until that date—and then began working on a longer story about the incident that was intended for publication on the *Washington Post*'s site and possibly in the dead-tree edition (as the print version was affectionately known among us dot-com reporters) the following day.

I worked from my home office that evening and well into the morning, toiling over the follow-up piece until eventually falling asleep in my pajamas at the computer keyboard as I finished the story around dawn.

The piece was edited and published on washingtonpost.com later that morning, and for a brief time the story was featured "above the fold" as one of the most popular on the site that day. That is, until a lawyer for washingtonpost.com found it and went positively ballistic. Apparently, nobody had asked the lawyers for their input, and now the attorneys were clamoring for the story to be unpublished from the website until facts could be triple checked and certain language about alleged illegal activities at McColo could be toned down.

Editors at the *Washington Post* and other major publications typically request that a pending story be "lawyered" when it contains statements of fact or allegations that could lead to legal trouble down the road, particularly from the parties named in the story who might wish to pursue libel charges. One washingtonpost .com lawyer was extremely uncomfortable with any language that even hinted at illegal activity on the part of McColo's owners, who had repeatedly ignored requests for comment. (To give a sense of how shady the dealings at McColo were, the sole points of contact listed on its website were anonymous instant messenger accounts.) After all, there was no evidence that anyone associated with McColo had been charged with any crime, so why were we alleging it?

(An important note: The story that ran that morning was full of links to supporting evidence of illegal goings-on at McColo, as gathered by countless security experts in the industry. Unfortunately, the washingtonpost.com lawyer who objected to it being published initially viewed the piece on her mobile phone, which had stripped out all of the hyperlinks that readers could use to view voluminous third-party reports and evidence of said criminal activity. To the attorney, the story appeared to be hurling all kinds of baseless and potentially libelous accusations at McColo, whose business at this point seemed all but ruined.)

The attorney demanded that the McColo story be pulled from the washingtonpost.com website, and after a brief period of defiance, the website news desk acquiesced without asking me whether the story was accurate or what supporting evidence I had to back up my reporting. The piece was simply yanked off the site, with no explanation to the tens of thousands of readers who found dead links and were eventually redirected back to my original blog post about the takedown. My inbox quickly filled with emails from mystified readers wondering where the story had gone.

For nearly five excruciating hours, the follow-up to one of the most important cybercrime stories to date remained in editorial and legal limbo, as the lawyers hashed over the piece line by line, changing or deleting potentially objectionable bits and pieces.

The piece was eventually republished later that evening, albeit in a shorter and much redacted form. But from that day forward, any story of mine that contained even a whiff of information about alleged online criminal activity had to be forwarded to at least one senior editor at washingtonpost.com and often run through a gamut of lawyers. Since I considered my beat to be cybercrime, this usually happened several times a week.

After the McColo fiasco, investigative stories that took weeks and sometimes months to produce could sit just as long in the inboxes of higher-ups whose approval I had to get before the stories could be published. In some cases, subsequent stories were placed on indefinite hold by washingtonpost.com editors, the lawyers, or both.

One of those pieces was an investigative story I'd spent six months reporting and writing, about a pattern of cybercrime activity that traced back to Vrublevsky's ChronoPay. At the time, the fastest growing and most lucrative cybercrime scheme worldwide was the spread of fake antivirus software. Also known as "scareware," fake AV uses misleading pop-up alerts and other ruses to frighten unsuspecting Internet users into purchasing worthless security software. Adding insult to injury, the bogus security programs often are bundled with malware that turns host machines into spam zombies.

Security experts who had been closely tracking the scareware scourge told me they'd found that ChronoPay was nearly always responsible for processing the credit card payments for scareware scams, and that the company's founder—Russian Pavel Vrublevsky—appeared to be heavily and personally involved in engineering and profiting from these schemes.

I knew very little about Vrublevsky until late 2008, when a Russian source (who will remain anonymous) urged me to look up ChronoPay's incorporation records in the Netherlands, where ChronoPay was founded. Those records showed that ChronoPay was created in 2003 as a fifty-fifty partnership between Vrublevsky and Igor Gusev. The same sources that led me to the incorporation data said that in 2005, the two men parted ways. Gusev would go off in 2006 to found the GlavMed-SpamIt rogue online pharmacy partnership. Not to be outdone, a year later Vrublevsky would cofound Rx-Promotion, a competing rogue Internet pharmacy.

I had no clue about Vrublevsky's ties to Rx-Promotion at the time, or even who Igor Gusev was. What I did know was that ChronoPay had very recently been associated with the Conficker worm, a computer contagion that remains one of the most virulent and heavily scrutinized strains of malware ever unleashed. An early version of the worm instructed millions of infected computers to download a rogue antivirus program from Trafficconverter.biz, an online business that made tens of millions of dollars by paying scammers to foist fake antivirus software on PC users. And ChronoPay was the company responsible for processing payments for TrafficConverter.

In March 2009, I turned in the first version of an exposé on ChronoPay's pivotal and lucrative role in the spread of fake antivirus software. The piece also presented evidence indicating that Vrublevsky was the founder, owner, and creator of Crutop.nu, the shadowy online forum that catered to the spammers and scammers who had attended McColo's funeral.

The story cited published research from several esteemed security experts about ChronoPay's history. Nevertheless, it was held in editorial limbo for months, punted from one washingtonpost.com senior editor to another. The editors were convinced ChronoPay would sue the *Washington Post*, which was understandable. In our phone interview, Vrublevsky had promised his company would do just that if we ran the story.

The same dithering delayed another big scoop related to the ChronoPay piece. When McColo went dark, much of the illegal activity that had made its home there quickly shifted to another Northern California hosting provider, Triple Fiber Networks, or 3FN as it was known in the underground. The same spam botnet controllers that had called McColo their home for years had begun using 3FN after McColo's demise. A review of postings at the online forum Spamdot—a closely guarded virtual den of thieves where most of the most successful Russian spammers gathered at the time—showed that 3FN's owners actively picked up McColo's stranded customers when the company's operations were shuttered in November 2008.

At the time, 3FN also was the Internet's largest host of sites that pushed fake antivirus software. The 3FN website was eerily similar to McColo's. Again, the only way to contact the company's owners was through ICQ ("I seek you"), an instant messaging protocol that for years was the de facto communications medium for many Russian hackers.

I pressed for these stories to come to light. Having exposed the malicious activity that eventually knocked RBN, Atrivo, and McColo offline, I believed that the *Post* had an obligation to its readers—and to the wider world—to keep the spotlight trained on those Internet providers that offered safe haven to a huge swath of the cybercrime community. Bad press on these companies from major media would force more law-enforcement agencies into taking action against them and thus reducing the threat they posed both to Americans and people all over the globe. But my editors were hardly anxious for a repeat of the McColo story, even though it hadn't resulted in any lawsuits or issues for the *Post*.

When I mentioned in an editorial meeting in early 2009 that 3FN had emerged as the central focus of a U.S. law-enforcement investigation into cybercrime, it was strongly suggested that we get confirmation of that fact from at least two sources, or wait for an on-the-record law-enforcement comment about the investigation or for proof of legal proceedings to be filed against the hosting provider before moving forward with any story alleging badness at 3FN. The case documents had been sealed by a federal judge, and my law-enforcement source was the only one I knew who had even heard of 3FN. The story was held.

Then, on June 2, 2009, more than fifteen thousand websites hosted at 3FN were yanked offline after the U.S. Federal Trade Commission (FTC) convinced a Northern California district court judge to have the company's upstream Internet providers stop routing traffic for the provider. The FTC alleged that 3FN operated "as a 'rogue' or 'black hat' Internet service provider that recruited, knowingly hosted, and actively participated in the distribution of illegal, malicious, and harmful content," including botnet control servers, child pornography, and rogue antivirus products.

The FTC's action provided the backstopping I needed to finally gather sufficient support to move ahead with my investigation into Vrublevsky, ChronoPay, and their role in fostering the fake antivirus market that was plaguing millions of consumers and threatening their identities, finances, and security. Crutop.nu also was hosted at 3FN and was even named in the FTC's action. The FTC called Crutop a place "where criminals share techniques and strategies with one another" and a Russian language website "that features a variety of discussion forums that focus on making money from spam." A review of multiple discussion threads at the Russian adult webmaster forum indicated that Crutop's more than eight thousand active members had been 3FN's single largest customer base.

Tellingly, directly after 3FN was taken down—but before washingtonpost.com ran the story on ChronoPay's ties to the rogue antivirus industry—Crutop.nu's homepage was changed to a lengthy screed about the FTC's action against 3FN. This would be my first introduction to Vrublevsky's epic rants. The message read, in part:

And in conclusion we would like to add, that while paragraph 1 of our rules has never been taken seriously before and was written as a joke, but related to recent events we would like to know how it was possible that five (5!) reputable experts-agents (including NASA experts and Mr. Brian Krebs) from the USA (where every tenth person speaks Russian, source: Wikipedia), could not figure out that on Crutop.nu in the SPAM sub-forum, discussions have nothing to do with mail spam or other cybercrimes?

The story on Vrublevsky and ChronoPay's key role in 3FN finally ran more than four months after I turned it in. No lawsuit from him or ChronoPay followed. But the editors at the *Washington Post* said they were still deeply concerned about my focus on Internet bad guys. The *Post* higher-ups were nervous about my reporting on a crime-heavy subject in which the standard forms of documentary evidence don't typically exist. Also, they took the position that my focus on cybercrime—as opposed to a broader beat such as consumer technology or technology policy—was too narrow, and that I was getting too close to my sources to remain objective.

I shared their concerns—to a degree. No journalist wants to depend on a handful of sources to the exclusion of others; doing so risks publishing stories that lack perspective and balance. But I knew the solution here was that I merely needed more and better sources—particularly those actively engaged in the cybercrime community. I also was convinced that the 3FN story was too important not to pursue, and that setting the story aside would be a waste of a good opportunity to expose—and potentially stop—a great deal of cybercrime activity.

At a meeting in mid-2009, the washingtonpost.com editors

explained that, although my Security Fix blog attracted a loyal and admirably large following given the niche subject, the angle of my reporting didn't quite fit into the *Post*'s emerging strategy of being the go-to source for news "for and about Washington, DC."

That turn of phrase encapsulated the new strategy that was the centerpiece of a protracted and painful effort to merge the separate operations of the *Washington Post* newspaper with the newsroom of washingtonpost.com, mainly for cost reasons.

The *Post* leadership had concluded that one way to save money was to shift the paper and site's news coverage so that it more closely focused on local events in the nation's capital and on explaining to readers how the events in Washington, DC, affect the rest of the world. The company also opted to close some of its major U.S. news bureaus and to rely more on wire services like the Associated Press and Reuters for breaking stories.

The editors were hoping I could spend most of my time writing about technology policy, specifically technology regulation and policy, or the future of technology innovation as it relates to policy. But I had no desire to shift the focus of my reporting away from cybercrime. I'd covered the tech policy beat for several years early in my career at the *Post*, and had found it tedious and stultifying.

Moving back to tech policy would also mean abandoning my previous four years cultivating clueful and connected sources in both the security industry and the cybercrime community. I was in the midst of a yearlong series about increasingly costly and sophisticated cyberattacks being perpetrated every month against countless small to mid-sized organizations across the country. After all that careful research and investigation, I finally had a front-row seat that allowed me to peer into the day-to-day activities of large, organized cybercriminal gangs operating out of Eastern Europe.

Over the course of several months, I was able to learn who these criminals were, where they worked, what they did in their free time, and who they were attacking—often before the victims themselves knew they had been robbed of hundreds of thousands of dollars, sometimes millions. The bank accounts at most small businesses and organizations are managed by regular men and women who are no match for organized cybercrime gangs, and I desperately wanted to continue spreading the word about this increasingly common and costly form of online robbery.

Moreover, I was beginning to understand that ChronoPay and Vrublevsky were very much the tip of the iceberg—that they were just the most visible figures in a largely Russian and Eastern European underground community whose members all seemed to know and rely upon one another.

So fourteen years after I joined the *Washington Post*, I was let go from the company with six months' severance, just enough time to plot my next career move. I remember feeling at the time that it was very important for me to hit the ground running on a new job on January 1, 2010. What that new job was to be, exactly, I wasn't sure of, though.

I discussed my termination with only a handful of family members and with two trusted sources, but no one else. So I was baffled when, less than a month later and well before my official termination date, I discovered a lengthy discussion thread on Crutop.nu titled "Krebs fired from the *Washington Post*," in which members took turns celebrating and jeering at the news.

"For those of you who don't know—he is the author of Security Fix at WP, who loved to write about Atrivo, McColo, EstDomains, UkrTeleGroup, [and] 3FN, and he is the one who helped shut them down," wrote the Crutop member who posted the thread. Other members greeted the news with cheers such as, "Thank you, Santa!" and "Santa got our letters!" Having something so personal and private exposed on a public forum run by some of the most active spammers that I'd been striving to expose was eerie and unnerving, but it also made me even more determined to continue my work.

I had anonymously registered the domain name KrebsOn Security.com just two weeks before that Crutop thread was posted, but hadn't yet decided whether to pursue a traditional position at another major news publication or to go it alone on a blog. After hearing from colleagues at other large media outlets who were being let go, forced to take unpaid leave, or reassigned to more advertising-friendly beats, I was not anxious to jump back into a position at a major newspaper or online publication. But the idea of going out on my own—and making a living at it—seemed daunting, even terrifying at times.

At the same time, a part of me was eager to succeed on my own terms and to build an audience based solely on my original reporting. When I read that Crutop thread, it struck me almost as a personal challenge and I decided to take it on. In an encouraging development, I soon heard from Russian readers who expressed disgust at that Crutop thread and were anxious to share documents that could prove the extent of ChronoPay's involvement in the cybercriminal underground. I suspected, but couldn't be sure at the time, that Vrublevsky's old business partner-turned-nemesis—Igor Gusev—was behind this ruse, but for the moment I didn't want to do anything to deter my sources from sharing what they knew.

"Do not be mistaken," one source pseudonymously named "Boris" warned in an email that promised the delivery of massive amounts of incriminating evidence of wrongdoing at ChronoPay. "These guys, and probably Vrublevsky, will come at you hard, and it may not be pretty."

But Boris and others were true to their promises and their warnings. The anonymous threats started just days after a virtual treasure trove of incriminating ChronoPay emails and documents fell into my lap. Any last hesitation I'd had about striking out on my own disappeared. It was time to get to work.

Chapter 3

THE PHARMA WARS

The morning of May 14, 2010, began with a rambling, disturbing email message waiting in my inbox. The anonymous writer had read my blog post about a public speaking engagement on cybercrime that I'd just completed in upstate New York. The message read:

Brian,

You are a wonderful puzzle. Your wife apparently allows You to behave like a teenager. I would like to see You grow up.

We love You. But, Your wife is right. It's time for You to put Your peculiar talent in the hands of professionals. The last report about You driving around upstate New York prompts me to send You this final plea before...

Your long suffering, but loving, wife should be empowered to make a contract with a professional person, (who might be a female but Your docile wife will eat her eyeballs on top of Your breakfast cereal before You come up from the basement if she makes moves on You).

So, why am I writing? Well, it's easy. I like what You do and many more would if they only knew about You. But, like many artists You think everyone sees what You see. We do not.

Therefore, the next move is up to You. I would start with Your wife. I would ask her what she thinks of this email.

Then I would engage an attorney. You'll need one when she falls "in love."

The message was textbook Vrublevsky: Malevolent, rambling, graphic, and full of mangled metaphors. It was the kind of screed I frequently saw coming from Vrublevsky's alleged "RedEye" identity on Crutop.nu—the Russian adult webmaster forum that he'd cofounded and that was an education center for spammers. As the U.S. Federal Trade Commission (FTC) described the forum in its takedown of hosting provider 3FN, Crutop "features a variety of discussion forums that focus on making money from spam."

Vrublevsky had earned a name for himself early on in the business by creating a network of adult websites that specialized in extreme and violent pornography, mostly videos featuring rape, incest, and bestiality. His name and ChronoPay's address are on the company registration records of "Red & Partners BV," which was a company Vrublevsky formed and was the parent firm of his adult webmaster affiliate program, according to legal documents obtained by this author from the government of the Netherlands. Also, as I noted in a 2009 story in the *Washington Post*, the websites for both ChronoPay.com and Red & Partners (re-partners.biz) shared the same domain name servers and Google Analytics code for tracking site visitors, though ChronoPay denied a connection between the two. Many of the webmasters on Crutop were affiliates that made money by reselling subscriptions to porn sites run by Vrublevsky and others on the forum.

But aside from the strange and somewhat threatening language, the message held few other clues to support my suspicion that Vrublevsky was the author. It was just a hunch, yet the timing was suspect.

Six months earlier, I'd decided to go it alone and start my own site—KrebsOnSecurity.com—a daily news blog dedicated to investigative reporting on cybercrime to increase public awareness and action against it. The email arrived just two days after I'd told Vrublevsky that I was preparing to publish a story based on cybercriminal allegations leveled against him by Ilya Ponomarev, a deputy of the Russian State Duma's high-tech development subcommittee. Ponomarev had sent a letter to Russian investigators, echoing many of the allegations in my earlier reporting on ChronoPay and Vrublevsky for the *Washington Post*.

Ponomarev's letter also included a new tidbit of information for me, which offered the first of many insights into the widespread corruption and backwardness of Russian politics. Incredibly, Vrublevsky—who according to multiple sources at this point ran one of the Internet's most notorious pharmaceutical spam programs, Rx-Promotion—had been selected as chairman of the anti-spam working group of the Russian Ministry of Telecom and Mass Communication, a body tapped by Russian President Dmitry Medvedev to advise the government on new laws to curb junk email. Essentially, Ponomarev wanted Vrublevsky gone.

When I contacted him for comment on Ponomarev's missive, Vrublevsky publicly denied being associated with Rx-Promotion or spam and then accused me of having been bribed by his enemies into creating negative press about him. He once again promised to sue me, and this time actually took steps to follow through on the threat. He had already begun the process by the time we spoke, but as I'd find out, his attorney and executives at ChronoPay eventually talked him out of it because he would have a slim chance of winning, the case could drag on for years, and he and ChronoPay would be vulnerable to having even more of their business dragged into the light of day if the case ever went to trial.

How did I find all of this out when Vrublevsky never said anything more than threatening to sue me? At this point, dozens of leaked emails began showing up in my inbox; they were between Vrublevsky and a Russian-speaking lawyer he'd hired from the Washington, DC, law firm of Duane Morris LLP. The emails would later show that to silence me, Vrublevsky had been fully prepared to pay more than $100,000 to bring a defamation case against me for my stories about his role in the rogue antivirus and pharmacy industries.

These internal emails were the first of many compromised materials (or *compromat*, as they're called in Russia) that I would receive over the course of a year from unnamed and anonymous hackers apparently bent on exposing ChronoPay and Vrublevsky. When I first began to receive these materials—usually via a link to an archive at a free file-sharing site—I considered the possibility that someone had forged emails and documents to make them appear stolen from ChronoPay. Eventually, however, the sheer volume, complexity, and interconnectedness of the records made it clear they were legitimate.

Months later, Vrublevsky himself would admit this same thing to me in a phone conversation. Unknown hackers or ChronoPay insiders had leaked huge caches of his firm's internal correspondence—tens of thousands of emails and accounting documents—as well as hundreds of hours of phone conversations that Vrublevsky recorded with others. The information painstakingly documented the breadth of ChronoPay's involvement in the rogue pharmacy and fake antivirus business endeavors. These required the creation of an elaborate network of shell companies and offshore bank accounts—all documented in well-organized Microsoft Excel spreadsheets, and in some cases described in Vrublevsky's own voice.

This cache of purloined documents contained not only evidence of wrongdoing by ChronoPay and its executives, but also intricate, sometimes lurid details about some of the most powerful people in the cybercrime underground.

It took many months to read through all of the materials, but more importantly to discover the most significant emails and documents. Part of the difficulty was that the ChronoPay employee email inboxes I'd been given offline access to were, ironically enough, laden with spam messages themselves, causing plenty of false positives when I searched them for specific terms that might expose ChronoPay's involvement in establishing shell companies and affiliate programs, and running spam operations.

Also, almost all of the missives were written in Russian, and specific phrases or proper nouns often had multiple permutations of their Cyrillic and transliterated Russian equivalents, or shorthands that required individual searches for each, or both.

Thankfully, I'd begun learning the language four years earlier on my own. In my work for the *Washington Post*, I had found myself spending an unusual amount of time on Russian-language underground forums that were not only hostile to Westerners, but which often chastised or banned members for the unforgivable sin of communicating in English. To overcome this obstacle, I checked out sixty hours' worth of Russian language instruction on CD from my local library. By 2008, I had finally mastered enough Russian to be able to read most forums without the aid of an online translation service. For an investigative reporter like me, this was vital to ensure I didn't misinterpret any of the information I was picking up there. Plus it made my research go a whole lot faster.

As I trolled through the documents, I discovered hundreds of emails between Vrublevsky and Stanislav Maltsev, a former investigator with the Russian Ministry of Internal Affairs. In 2007, Maltsev was responsible for investigating charges of illegal business activities levied against Vrublevsky. But in short order, Vrublevsky had hired Maltsev as his head of security, and the case against Vrublevsky quickly died on the vine.[6]

---

6. Vrublevsky claimed the charges were trumped up and nothing more than a legal shakedown orchestrated by his enemies, but the company that was being "shaken down" operated a virtual currency he created to help his webmasters and spammers get paid without leaving an official money trail through the Russian banking networks.

It also became clear that ChronoPay executives had tried in vain to isolate the company's "black" projects—the Rx-Promotion pharmacy spam program and its fake antivirus business, for example—from the company's more legitimate client base. The leaked ChronoPay emails show that in August 2010 cofounder Pavel Vrublevsky authorized a payment of 37,350 Russian rubles (about $1,200) for a multiuser license for an online project-development tracking and management service called MegaPlan.

ChronoPay employees used their MegaPlan accounts to track payment processing issues, customer order volumes, and advertising partnerships for these black programs. In a move straight out of the Quentin Tarantino film *Reservoir Dogs*, the employees adopted curious aliases such as "Mr. Kink," "Mr. Stranger," "Mr. Templar," and "Ms. Gandalfine."

However, in a classic failure of operational security, many of these employees had their MegaPlan messages and passwords automatically forwarded to their ChronoPay employee email accounts, which ended up in the corpus of emails that were leaked. An organizational chart featured on the ChronoPay MegaPlan homepage showed that the former cop Maltsev (a.k.a. "Mr. Heppner") had been appointed the deputy manager of Rx-Promotion, directly under the "big boss," Vrublevsky (a.k.a. RedEye).

Finally, I had the key that I'd been looking for. The MegaPlan accounts provided the single largest cache of information on the extent of ChronoPay's involvement in fostering the development of markets for rogue antivirus software, or "scareware." These are malicious programs that use misleading security prompts about nonexistent security threats on a victim's PC, and then hijack the computer until the victim either figures out a way to remove the malware or pays for a license to the bogus software.

These types of programs affect tens of millions of people around the world and are shockingly lucrative. Most PC users would be hard pressed to say they've never encountered one of these messages, and it's just the most visible sign that your computer has been hijacked by a remote spammer or other stealthier malware. (Whatever you do, don't ever click these messages! Try to get the malware removed immediately by an antivirus professional, or see the epilogue for tips on how to avoid making a bad situation like this worse.)

The leaked records show ChronoPay's high-risk or "black projects" division worked diligently to stay on the cutting edge of the scareware industry. In March 2010, the company began processing payments for icpp-online.com, an innovative scam site that stole victims' money by bullying them into paying a "pretrial settlement" to cover a "copyright-holder fine."

As security firm F-Secure noted at the time, victims of this scam were informed that an "Antipiracy Foundation scanner" had found pirated movie and music files on the victim's system, and that those who refused to pay $400 via a credit card transaction could face jail time and huge fines. The scheme was brilliant in its simplicity. Many people have, at some point, watched or listened to pirated content, so there was no reason for them to distrust this message. As a result, thousands were swindled.

Here's the kicker: for many years, scareware was a problem only for PC users who browsed the web with computers powered by Microsoft's Windows operating system. But in May 2011, scareware purveyors began targeting users of Apple's Mac OS X operating system for the first time. No one was safe from spam and malware attacks anymore.

The leaked ChronoPay internal documents would reveal the company's hand in this innovation as well. A few days after the first attacks surfaced, experienced Mac users on Apple support forums began reporting that new strains of the Mac malware were directing users to pay for the software via a domain called mac-defence.com. Others spotted fake Mac security software coming from macbookprotection.com. When I first looked at the registration records for those domains, I was not surprised to find the distinct fingerprint of ChronoPay.

The website registration records for both domains include the contact address of fc@mail-eye.com. The leaked ChronoPay documents show that ChronoPay owned the mail-eye.com domain and had paid for the virtual servers in Germany that ran it. The records also indicate that the fc@mail-eye.com address belonged to ChronoPay's financial controller, then an employee named Alexandra Volkova. One of the smoking guns had been found, and it was time to let the public know.

◆　　◆　　◆

After the Ponomarev story ran, I began hearing from Vrublevsky by phone at least once a day, often for no apparent reason. The calls came from a different mobile number almost every time. (When asked why his calls always appeared to come from a different Russian phone number, Vrublevsky nonchalantly replied that he currently had no fewer than nine mobile phones, and that this was a common tactic used by successful Russian businesses who wished to evade surveillance by meddlesome Russian government agents.)

At first, I thought he was being dramatic or overly paranoid; I would find out later he was very much the target of Russian government surveillance. "Gusev put in his blog the name of an FSB guy working on the Vrublevsky case," the ChronoPay CEO told me in one phone conversation, referring to himself in the third person. "They've been tapping my phone and know that I have ongoing communications with you."

I quickly discovered that this was a man who enjoyed the sound of his voice like no one else I'd ever encountered. Despite everything I knew about the guy—and the fact that he was often extraordinarily crass and derisive, and frequently outright insulting—I also found him to be disarmingly charming, funny, and likeable. He was just as likely to make fun of himself as he was of others, and he possessed a seemingly boundless supply of anecdotes about important Russian power brokers, politicians, and cybercrooks. Without prompting, Vrublevsky would excitedly segue from one colorful story to the other as if describing an elaborate soap opera, albeit one that never seemed to have a central plot or conclusion.

Moscow is eight hours ahead of the time zone in Washington, DC (Eastern), and that meant Vrublevsky would usually call me as his chauffeur was shuttling him from ChronoPay's offices to his home. In short, Pavel was frequently ready to unwind and be chatty right when I was getting ready to buckle down and start my workday. Most conversations ended with me hanging up on him after he refused to take a hint that I had more to do than to listen to him blather for hours on end.

Initially, I thought that the purpose of his phone conversations was to get me to publish something exonerating him of his wrongdoing, more and more of which I was discovering every day. In each of our conversations, Vrublevsky took great care to cast himself as an anti-cybercrime crusader determined to destroy the spam industry and ensure the arrest and conviction of all spammers.

Vrublevsky constantly intimated that I hadn't a clue about cybercrime, and there was no way to fully understand the nuances of the subject without making at least a token visit to Russia. In one conversation, he offered to fly me to Moscow so I could see firsthand that he was in fact one of the good guys.

"My proposition to you is to come to Moscow, and if you don't have money... I realize journalists are not such wealthy people in America... We're happy to pay for it," Vrublevsky said in a phone conversation on May 8, 2010.

When I politely declined his invitation, Vrublevsky laughed and said I was wrong to feel like I was being bribed or intimidated (which I did).

"It's quite funny that you think somehow when you fly to meet me in Moscow or ChronoPay offices that you are in any possible danger from me for being murdered," Vrublevsky said, pinpointing exactly what I was thinking. "Come to Moscow and see for yourself. Take your notebook, come to my office. Sit in front of me and look around. Because you're getting information which, to be honest, is not factual." (I would eventually do exactly as Vrublevsky urged, as we will see in "Chapter 9: Meeting in Moscow.")

After about a month of daily calls from Vrublevsky—sometimes twice a day—I realized that he was feeding me semi-reliable information about other cybercrooks in the hope that I would be diverted into researching and writing about them, instead of him.

The real trouble with these chat sessions—aside from their tendency to eat up half of my workday—was untangling the bits of truth and fact from Pavel's musings, paranoid conspiracy theories, and attempts to draw attention away from his own dealings. When I asked him point blank about my theory—that he was trying to turn the spotlight away from himself by regaling me with elaborate tales about rival businessmen in the Russian underground—Pavel momentarily dropped the phone as he burst out laughing for about a minute straight.

"You know, Brian, you surprise me sometimes. You really do. This is why I absolutely fucking love you," he said after picking up his mobile phone, still snorting and having fun at my expense. "Why do I say this? It's funny, sometimes I'm not really sure you are too bright. And then you go and say something like that. Dammit, Krebs, sometimes you're a lot fucking smarter than you sound."

But Vrublevsky also could be mercurial, prone to wild mood swings and bouts of mumbling or shouting profanities. Or sometimes the voice on the other end of the line sounded like a completely different person, the tone low and comparatively serene. Often, this was late at night when his three children and wife, Vera, were already in bed and he'd perhaps had a few drinks or something else to take the edge off.

In one marathon phone conversation shortly after I'd informed Vrublevsky about receiving the compromat, he was in one of his sullen moods and rather bluntly offered to pay me $30,000 to turn over all of the material that I'd been given. I'd told him about the leaked documents because I believed he already had a good idea of what information had been taken. Clearly, he was more interested in securing my future silence than in regaining control over the compromat. I politely declined the monetary offer and told him I was flattered but still planning to continue my investigations.

I soon realized that Vrublevsky had another, far bigger target in mind on this crusade to recapture ChronoPay's positive image: Igor Gusev, his former business partner in ChronoPay and now head of a pharmacy affiliate program that competed directly with Vrublevsky's Rx-Promotion. Vrublevsky was convinced (and, I think, accurately) that Gusev or one of Gusev's henchmen was responsible for leaking ChronoPay's internal emails and other incriminating documents.

Around the same time that the first batch of ChronoPay compromat was leaked, Adam Drake—a source in the anti-spam community in whom I'd confided some of my stories about Vrublevsky's strange phone calls—emailed to tell me about a bizarre message he'd just received. Drake's mysterious correspondent, who used the pseudonym "Despduck," said he had access to the database for GlavMed and SpamIt, sister programs that were responsible for a huge percentage of the world's spam problem. The "Desp" portion of the nickname was a play on the moniker chosen by Igor "Desp" Gusev, the man who cofounded ChronoPay with Vrublevsky in 2003 and went off on his own two years later to start SpamIt and GlavMed.

Drake wrote:

Brian,

Recently you posted about a Russian government investigation into the SpamIt operation ("Following the Money, Part II"— krebsonsecurity.com/2010/05/following-the-money-part-ii/).

I have a guy from Russia contacting me claiming to be a friend of a former member of the SpamIt-GlavMed affiliate group. He has a lot of information I want to share with you confidentially. I say this because I wanted your thoughts on it, and he makes claims about how some info for that story was handed to you, which I wanted your thoughts on.

He also claims to have quite a bit of raw data related to some of their gathering places which—if it seems legit—I will hand over to law enforcement. I've been working with a task force which includes members of Interpol and the FBI since last year investigating that group, so I haven't been able to post much publicly at all.

If any of this is not up your alley or within your range of interests, let me know, but I thought it might be. This same group is likely also behind the rash of rogue "antivirus" crap that's been making the rounds.

Hope you are otherwise well.

I immediately recognized Vrublevsky's hand in this ruse and asked Drake to forward a copy of the Despduck email. I could scarcely believe my eyes as I read the message, which looked as if someone had been taking dictation from Vrublevsky while he was regaling whoever would listen with one of his excitedly told, rambling stories. The letter went on for more than two thousand words and was full of elaborate theories of who was behind the attacks on ChronoPay, a company about which Despduck spoke positively glowingly.

I told Drake about my hunch that he also was being hounded by Vrublevsky, and he confided that a law-enforcement friend who was quite familiar with Vrublevsky and had also seen the Despduck emails had independently come to the same conclusion.

There was something else about Despduck's letters that I couldn't quite put my finger on. A week later, I went back and looked at my previous email correspondence with Vrublevsky, and compared it to the emails from "Despduck" that my anti-spam source was receiving. One commonality immediately jumped off of the screen in front of me. Both Despduck and Vrublevsky capitalized the letter *y* anytime they used the word "You" or "Your," regardless of the word's position in a sentence or how many times it was used. That capitalization pattern did not occur with any other words in the emails that shouldn't have been capitalized.

Then it occurred to me: What about that threatening "eyeballs" email I'd received just after calling Vrublevsky for a quote on the story about Ponomarev's allegations? Sure enough, I saw the same capital-ization pattern there. The pieces were starting to come together.

But why would Vrublevsky go to such pains to launch this multipronged campaign to simultaneously win me over and coerce me into cooperating with him? My anti-spam source provided the answer, sharing several emails sent by Despduck. They showed that Vrublevsky believed I had accepted money from his pharma-spam rival Gusev in exchange for writing stories about Vrublevsky's exploits. Vrublevsky also seemed convinced that I was in league with shadowy figures behind the Russian Business Network (RBN), the bulletproof hosting empire detailed in the first half of Chapter 2.[7]

Despduck wrote (again, with the *Y* capitalization in "You"):

1. Brian Krebs, believe it or not, was actually *paid* by RBN guys (by GlavMed mostly) to publish his research. All of his info is actually based on the fact that re-partners.biz had an office address of ChronoPay, which is bullshit, of course. Anyone can put any address anywhere.

2. Then Ilya Ponomarev (NOT a leading politician in Russia) wrote a letter to the cops in Russia trying to somehow fuck Vrublevsky based on Krebs info. A stupid attempt, probably just making it look like it can work to get more money from Desp. Obviously nothing happened because ChronoPay has an extremely strong image and brand in Russia. ChronoPay will soon sue Krebs, and Ponomarev has already changed his

---

7. While Vrublevsky acted as if he had nothing to do with RBN, the pharmacy spam websites and fake antivirus affiliate programs he ran took full advantage of hosting arrangements managed under the RBN banner.

opinion and sent another letter to the cops explaining he was not targeting Vrublevsky.

3. All this happened because Vrublevsky has a position with the Russian Government in fighting spam, and what's more important, in protecting Russian image abroad. Spammers hate him for that. I'll explain more when You have questions.

Once again, Despduck spoke glowingly of Vrublevsky as a cybercrime fighter who was being unjustly accused by the media and by his business rivals of orchestrating the nefarious activity he claimed to be battling. I was now more certain than ever that Despduck was Vrublevsky.

On July 12, 2010, an anonymous source with whom I'd be corresponding via email sent me another massive trove of compromat stolen from ChronoPay. My source, who used only the name "Boris" in our email exchanges, said he was sharing the data out of frustration with Russian authorities, who he said seemed to regard Vrublevsky as hardly worth the trouble of shaking down for bribes, to say nothing of investigating.

Brian,

This file contains *full* information about criminal activity of ChronoPay and personally Pavel Vrublevsky on legalizing out-of-law money [sic]. We've tried all methods accessible in Russia, but the absolute corruption of the Russian police brakes [sic] the criminal case and marks time. We hope you can effectively use this information in the struggle for the cleanliness of the Internet. The same file was transferred two weeks ago to the FBI.

Good luck,

Boris

The ChronoPay emails leaked by Boris—the "treasure trove of documents" referenced at the conclusion of Chapter 2—show that Vrublevsky hired a hacker named Nooder Tovreance to break into Gusev's SpamIt and steal the organization's payment and customer records. In one email exchange between the two, which begins April 8, 2010, and ends at the beginning of June, Tovreance offered to sell the database to Vrublevsky for $20,000, but said that he needed to break the file transfers up into multiple smaller chunks due to the size of the database.

The two ultimately settled on a price of $15,000, to be paid in WebMoney, a virtual currency that is popular in Russia and Eastern Europe. The first payment of $7,500 was to be made to a WebMoney purse specified by Tovreance in exchange for half of the files, with the remaining amount payable upon Vrublevsky's receipt of the entire database. Follow-up emails indicate that Vrublevsky paid the first $7,500, but welched on the second payment after receiving the database as promised. When I interviewed Tovreance, he confirmed that Vrublevsky had hired him to produce the GlavMed and SpamIt data, and that indeed Vrublevsky had stiffed him on half of the promised price.

◆   ◆   ◆

Roughly one week after miscreants leaked that ChronoPay compromat, Drake called with the news that Despduck had sent him a copy of the SpamIt and GlavMed database. By this time, I began to believe that just as Vrublevsky hid behind his "Despduck" identity in leaking the GlavMed-SpamIt customer database, Gusev was using the "Boris" identity to feed me the information stolen from ChronoPay.

The GlavMed-SpamIt database landed in my lap the day after I published on my blog the first breaking story about a new, exceedingly complex computer worm that appeared to have been weaponized for espionage. That blog post was the first widely read story about a piece of malware of unprecedented sophistication that would become known as "Stuxnet"—a computer worm that experts later discovered was a cyberweapon created by Israeli and U.S. intelligence agencies in a successful bid to delay Iran's nuclear ambitions.

But I filed the Stuxnet post just as I was leaving for a week-long vacation with my wife and mother in York, Maine, and I'd promised to give work a rest. While follow-up reporting on Stuxnet would take dozens of telephone interviews, delving into the scoop that my anti-spam source was handing me could be done without letting my family know I was back on the clock.

Drake set up an account for me on his web server and placed a copy of the SpamIt archive there. The file contained almost ten gigabytes worth of data. (To put that into perspective, if the SpamIt database was compiled into paperback books three inches wide, it would take a bookshelf roughly the length of a football field to hold them all.)

I was already overwhelmed with gigabytes of fascinating internal material from ChronoPay, and had to delete data from my Macbook's hard drive to accommodate the SpamIt archive. As I sat on the back deck of a coastal Maine vacation property with my laptop propped up on my knees, while listening to the roar of the ocean surf, I began to see the enormity of the task before me. I would need to make sense of raw intelligence from two of the largest sponsors of spam on the planet, in the process potentially incurring the wrath of the most powerful and vengeful cyber-criminals on earth.

Chapter 4

MEET THE BUYERS

T hough my ultimate goal was to unmask the botmasters who were getting paid to send most of the world's junk email, I knew it would take months, possibly years, of poring over the data coming in from the two competing rogue pharmacy programs. What I had discovered so far were small pieces of criminal activity here and there, so a lot more in-depth research and investigation would be required to build a watertight case against these guys and expose their malicious activities. I decided to focus my immediate efforts on reaching the people directly affected by these cybercriminals: customers who purchased and ingested pills from spam ads.

Almost all of us have gotten pill spam or pharma spam at some point in our lives—those emails that show up in our inboxes, spam filters, and junk folders, offering cheap prescription or enhancement drugs. It may be less than shocking that about 70 percent of the transactions made through rogue pharmacy websites advertised by Gusev's SpamIt and Vrublevsky's Rx-Promotion were for male-enhancement drugs like Viagra and Cialis. Even GlavMed customers who did not order drugs to treat erectile dysfunction (ED) usually received penis pills anyway. So confident were these pharmacies in the power of their ED formularies that they routinely included two to four free samples of these pills with every customer order.[8]

For those of us who would never dream of ordering from an unknown pharmacy, this might seem like an obvious and unnecessary gamble. Why not just use an ordinary pharmacy? Indeed, I was intensely curious to learn what motivated people to engage in this apparently risky activity, and whether they were happy with their purchases—or if they felt they'd gotten ripped off. I thought that if I interviewed enough of these buyers and found that overall they did not get what they expected, exposing this reaction could help reduce demand and eventually drive the spammers out of business.

Thanks to data leaks from both Rx-Promotion and GlavMed-SpamIt, I had the names, phone numbers, addresses, and credit card numbers of more than a million people who had bought spam-advertised drugs. Some of those orders were fairly recent, so I was eager to interview buyers who might still have some of the pills and could forward them to me for testing at a qualified lab to see what these consumers were really getting.

I purposefully avoided calling customers who sought out and paid for knockoff Viagra and Cialis, partly because I thought that those who had come to these fly-by-night pharmacies to purchase

---

8. Again, while leaked ChronoPay emails show otherwise, Vrublevsky denies co-owning Rx-Promotion, but admits that ChronoPay did process payments for the pharmacy program. Gusev has publicly denied running SpamIt, but again, the evidence suggests otherwise.

drugs for more serious ailments and conditions would have more interesting and sympathetic stories to tell that would help me get to the heart of this issue: who was purchasing these drugs and why? But I'd be dishonest if I said my reporting wasn't also influenced by an experience I had with an interviewee very early in the process of contacting buyers.

Just a few days after I began phoning people who had purchased medications from GlavMed, I dialed the phone number supplied by a male customer who'd ordered Viagra. His wife answered instead. She broke down in tears when I explained that her husband had purchased generic Cialis a few months prior. She was not aware of this fact and said she couldn't think of a reason on earth why he would have wanted it. After that mercifully short interview, I decided to avoid calling any other customer who had purchased only erectile dysfunction drugs.

Over two months, I called more than four hundred people who had purchased pills from SpamIt. Most of those I reached either hung up on me or declined to be interviewed. But I managed to interview at least forty-five buyers who ordered everything from heart medication to antidepressants and pills to treat thyroid conditions. I began to get a clearer picture of who these people were, what their motivations were, and how their actions affect us all, even those of us who don't open spam emails, let alone buy anything from them.

Many people—particularly anti-spam activists—take an understandably dim view of consumers who buy items advertised in junk email. After all, the argument goes, if people stopped buying from sites advertised via the spam that floods our inboxes every day, then the spam industry and many of its corresponding threats to our identities and security would probably be greatly diminished. But contrary to popular belief, most of the people buying from spam aren't idiots or crazy. The majority appear to be technologically unsophisticated people making rational (if potentially risky) choices based on one or a combination of several primary motivations:

- **Price and Affordability**: Those who bought drugs other than male enhancement pills almost universally said they responded to prescription drug spam either because they had no health insurance, or because the same drugs available under their health plans cost *two to five times* as much as the drugs offered via these legitimate-looking Canadian pharmacy sites. (In reality, the spammers were just borrowing the good reputation of legitimate Canadian pharmacies. As we'll see in Chapter 5, the drugs that each affiliate program shipped were manufactured mainly in India and China, and the websites selling the drugs were most often hosted on botted PCs that had been hacked by the spammers for use in sending junk email.)

- **Confidentiality**: The buyer wants to purchase specific drugs discreetly and quietly, either out of embarrassment or shyness, or because he or she feels compelled to hide something from a spouse or loved one. Most of the customers I interviewed broke down into two camps here—those who were self-treating venereal diseases, and those who were ordering impotence drugs to perform for a lover or spouse. Sadly, the order history suggests that some of these buyers repeatedly fit into both categories.

- **Convenience**: Ordering drugs online without a prescription and having them shipped to your door is extremely convenient. In addition, a great many buyers I spoke with said they were merely purchasing drugs they had been previously prescribed for a similar or related ailment. In effect, these people were self-prescribing and didn't see the need to pay for a doctor visit or to submit to the higher prices charged by their local pharmacies.

- **Recreation or Dependence**: Buyers in this category purchased mainly drugs whose use and sale have been restricted in the United States, usually because the drugs have the potential for abuse. These were primarily painkillers such as generic oxycodone, hydrocodone, and tramadol; weight-loss drugs like phentermine (a powerful stimulant); and sleeping pills like Soma and Lunesta. Perhaps because of the addictiveness of some of these drugs, this class of buyers tended to be the most loyal, profitable repeat customers.

Price

SpamIt customers were motivated to purchase drugs from spam for a variety of reasons, but the number one reason I heard was affordability—particularly among customers who were purchasing medications taken to treat chronic conditions.

It is no accident that most SpamIt customers live in the United States, the country with the highest prescription drug prices in the world. Prices for pharmaceuticals in the United States are substantially higher than those in Canada, India, the United Kingdom, and many other countries, in large part because those nations have enacted price controls on drugs. Consumers and insurers paid an average of $13.14 per prescription for the fifty most popular generic drugs in 2010. In 2014, they paid $62.10—a 373 percent increase. The price of name-brand drugs also has skyrocketed in recent years. A 2014 study by Bloomberg News found that price increases in the United States have far outpaced inflation since late 2007 for many brand-name drugs; the publication found seventy-four drug brands whose U.S. prices for at least one dosage increased 75 percent or more in the period.

Other factors that have increased the cost of prescription drugs include: a spike in demand for these drugs over the last decade; intense marketing to consumers and doctors of higher-priced brand-name drugs; drug manufacturers' attempts to recoup the substantial costs of research and development; and the costly dice game that is the process of bringing a new drug to market in the United States. According to a 2014 study by the Tufts Center for the Study of Drug Development, drug makers can expect to spend more than $2.5 billion during the decade or more it can take before winning approval to sell a new prescription medicine.

But there's more to it. In a landmark 2011 study on the economics of the rogue Internet pharmacy business, researchers at the University of California, San Diego (UCSD) figured out a way to view countless purchase records from online pill shops tied to EvaPharmacy, another rogue pharmacy affiliate program that competes directly with the likes of Rx-Promotion and SpamIt. The researchers found significant differences between the drug-selection habits of Americans and customers from Canada and Western Europe. The analysis divided the EvaPharmacy pills into two broad categories: lifestyle drugs—such as erectile dysfunction and human growth hormone pills—and non-lifestyle drugs, including those used to treat disorders including anxiety, sinus infections, high blood pressure, hair loss, cancer, and infertility.

The researchers discovered that U.S. customers selected non-lifestyle items 33 percent of the time. In contrast, Canadian and Western European customers almost always bought drugs in the lifestyle category—only 8 percent of the items placed in their shopping carts were non-lifestyle items. In other words, many more Americans were turning to these spam pharmacies for prescription drugs to treat critical medical conditions, not to increase their comfort or enjoyment of life.

"We surmise that this discrepancy may arise due to differences in health-care regimes; drugs easily justified to a physician may be fully covered under state health plans in Canada and Western Europe, leaving an external market only for lifestyle products," the researchers wrote. "Conversely, a subset of uninsured or underinsured customers in the United States may view spam-advertised, no-prescription-required pharmacies as a competitive market for meeting their medical needs."

Interestingly, dozens of SpamIt customers I interviewed said the pills they received were indistinguishable from the same drugs they had purchased from local pharmacies, except that the pills they ordered online cost far less. In fact, many customers were so satisfied with their orders that they went back to the same site month after month.

Henry Webb, a forty-two-year-old real estate agent from California, had been buying from online pharmacies for nearly three years when I first called him, though he said he had no idea who he was really buying from until I contacted him. Webb battled depression for much of his adult life, until about ten years ago when his doctor prescribed him Lexapro, a prescription antidepressant. For years, Webb paid close to $500 for a ninety-day supply of the drug.

And then one day he opened an unsolicited email that advertised Lexapro for almost one-quarter of that price. He's been ordering from a couple of different "Canadian pharmacy" sites ever since, and said he has yet to have a negative experience.

"The pills look exactly like the kind I paid five hundred dollars for at the drugstore—they're in the same blister pack and everything," Webb said. "The only comment I have is that it's sad we live in this country and have to look outside of the United States for affordable medicine."

Contacted a few months after that initial interview, Webb said he quit ordering online after he had bad experiences with some drugs that made him sick. Webb also experienced something that nearly all who purchase products advertised in spam will deal with at some point: incessant phone calls from aggressive online pharmacy merchants trying to refill his prescription or sell him other drugs.

"They won't leave me alone and have been calling several times a day," Webb said. "I can't change my number because it's attached to my business, but these guys do very devious stuff like spoof the caller ID so it looks like they're calling from my local area. So I pick up, because I have to be reachable for my real estate clients."

Exacerbating the pricing problem for consumers is the little-known but widespread practice among the major pharmaceutical manufacturers of paying generic rivals to delay the introduction of lower-cost medicines. According to the U.S. Federal Trade Commission (FTC), pharmaceutical companies struck an unprecedented number of these collusive deals in fiscal year 2010. The FTC found that the number of these deals skyrocketed more than 60 percent, from nineteen in FY 2009 to thirty-one in FY 2010. In 2013, branded and generic drug companies struck at least twenty-nine of these "pay for delay" agreements, with a combined annual U.S. sales of approximately $4.3 billion.

Craig S., a now-retired life insurance salesman from North Carolina, knows firsthand how it feels when a drugmaker or health insurer suddenly stops offering generics. Craig said his employer of twenty years previously offered a health-care plan with generous drug coverage benefits. Then a year prior to our interview, his employer dropped the insurance provider and pushed all employees into health-care savings accounts (HSAs), which his employer contributed a mere thousand dollars annually. Craig's doctor had long prescribed the name-brand drug Actos to help treat his type 2 diabetes, and Craig had been buying the generic version.

But he soon discovered that the generic version of Actos was not offered through the HSA program. Strangely enough, however, he was able to use his HSA credit card to buy a ninety-day supply from the GlavMed pill shop for $178 including shipping and handling.

"The drug my doctor wants me to take is $212 per month, and I told him that's just not going to happen," Craig said. "It costs me now about a third of what it would if I bought the brand-name version each month through my health plan."

When asked whether he's concerned about the quality, efficacy, and safety of the drugs he's purchasing from spammers, Craig said, "Not really." He said he still sees his doctor every ninety days, and that the drugs he's been ordering from GlavMed appear to be keeping his diabetes in check.

His chief concern is that the pills he's ordered may one day simply not arrive in the mail, noting that he had a close call once with an order that arrived a week later than it should have. But for now, the people supplying his drugs over the Internet appear to be getting their act together on the shipping. Craig said that every few months, when his prescription is about three weeks away from running out, he'll start getting phone calls from people with Indian accents, asking if he's ready for refills.

◆　　◆　　◆

Illinois resident "Steve" suspected his girlfriend had been cheating on him, but he didn't fully accept the news until the day he received some jolting news via text message.

"I needed meds due to cheating girlfriend syndrome," Steve explained sheepishly in our interview as to the reason for his purchase. "She texted me one day and basically told me she had gonorrhea and that I should get checked out, too."

It had been a tough month for Steve. Not only had his girlfriend slept with a coworker, dumped him, and stuck him with a (mercifully treatable) venereal disease, but his employer—an environmental testing firm—had just laid him off, and he had no health insurance.

"I could have had COBRA insurance but that's like three

hundred to four hundred dollars a month," Steve explained. "And when you've got no income, plus rent and a car payment and everything else, that's not really an option."

His ex-girlfriend helpfully texted the name of the drug her doctor had prescribed to clear it up—a full regimen of 500 milligram erythromycin tablets. So, Steve went online and searched for the drug and found exactly what he needed at a site claiming it was selling drugs from Canada. (The site Steve purchased from was actually hosted in China through GlavMed and the drugs shipped from India.) Seven days and sixty dollars later, Steve had received the antibiotics and was on his way to a VD-free existence.

Despite the circumstances that prompted his purchase, Steve said the overall experience with GlavMed was a positive one, and that he would buy from them again if he ever got another flare-up.

"Would I do it again? Sure. Why pay a copay and seventy-five dollars for a prescription when I can get it online for a lot less bother? I mean, I could have treated five people with [the number of pills] they sent me. So, for the price you can't beat what they're offering."

As the stories of these buyers show, a great many Americans turn to drugs marketed via spam because the alternative is several times more expensive, or because their insurance doesn't cover the drugs they've been prescribed. While Steve's positive experience with pills ordered for a single use or regimen seems to be fairly common, repeat buyers purchasing pills to treat chronic conditions are likely to encounter a bad batch of pills sooner or later.

As we'll see in Chapter 5, this is because spam-advertised pharmacies tend to get their cheap pills from dozens of different sources around the world, some of which appear to have little—if any—accountability for the safety and efficacy of their drugs. Inferior and poor-quality medications may only make the customer sick, as in Henry's case. In extreme cases, as we'll see in Chapter 5, substandard pills may send the customer to the hospital—or worse yet, to the morgue.

Confidentiality

A lawyer by profession, Washington, DC, resident "John" spent far too much time behind his desk and was looking for a quick and easy way to bulk up his muscles. After researching several online bodybuilding forums, he began taking some legally questionable steroids from one of the sites recommended by the seasoned meatheads. A few months and a short regimen of gym workouts later, the bulker pills had helped add several pounds of muscle to his lean frame.

But then one day in February 2010, John began to feel puffiness and sensitivity around his nipples. Worried that it may be a latent side effect from the bulker pills (and nervous about discussing his recent regimen of bulker pills with his doctor), John returned to the bodybuilder forums for advice from his fellow meatheads.

Forum members told him he was suffering from a steroid-induced case of gynecomastia, the development of abnormally large mammary glands in males that results in breast enlargement.

"The medical shorthand for the condition is pronounced 'guyno,' but most of the guys on the forums just call them 'bitch tits,'" John said. "The guys were telling me that if you don't get it fixed with medication, then you need plastic surgery to fix your chest and I didn't want to do that."

The cure for John's condition—according to his newfound friends on the forums—involved a regimen of additional drugs designed to counteract the hormones that cause guyno. Among them was a drug called "Femara," which is most often prescribed to treat postmenopausal early-stage breast cancer patients.

John searched the web and ended up buying a two-week regimen of 2.5 milligram Femara pills for $136 from a GlavMed site called elitepharmacy.com. He waited three weeks for the drugs, but they never arrived. So John canceled his order with GlavMed and ordered them from another online pharmacy that was not affiliated with GlavMed. (John recollects that the two sites looked nearly identical.) The original site apologized for the delay and credited his credit card with the amount he'd paid.

The drugs that he received from the second site showed up in a manila envelope addressed from India, but the pills themselves were sealed in a blister pack with the brand name Novartis seamlessly printed multiple times across the silver foil on top of the pills.

According to John, the pills looked like the real thing, and they reduced the tenderness and swelling in his nipples, effectively nipping his pouty man-boobs in the bud.

"I was a little leery of the whole thing at first, but it worked," John said. "I also thought I was wasting my time canceling my order. I sort of figured this was a shady operation…but they refunded my money."

John's experience highlights the lengths to which rogue pharma programs will go to ensure customer satisfaction. The goal here is not necessarily to keep the customer happy. Rather, the people running these operations will do next to anything to keep customers from initiating "chargebacks," a process in which the customer reverses the charges, claiming fraud or some other misdeed on the part of an online store. Merchants that receive too many chargebacks pay much higher processing fees and may eventually be fined or have their accounts closed, or both.

Data from GlavMed's customer database shows that the program had dozens of customer support personnel working round-the-clock via phone and online chat, responding to customer concerns or questions about existing orders.

Vishnevsky, the spammer discussed in Chapter 1 who worked with GlavMed-SpamIt to help bankroll the development of the Cutwail botnet, said in an interview via instant message that people who buy from pharma sites can always get their money back just by calling and lodging a complaint with the pharmacy program's 800 number.

"The bank will screw every merchant that has chargebacks [that are] more than 1 percent of total sales," Vishnevsky said. "So no one will risk to lose the [card processing account] by not returning money, and everyone who asks [the pharmacy affiliate program's] customer service department] for money back will get it."

Self-Prescribing

Kimberly from Virginia was a GlavMed buyer who self-prescribed but received a refund after complaining she was unhappy with her purchase. She and her husband were having trouble conceiving a child. He was frequently gone on long military deployments, and she was anxious to get pregnant before her husband left for another year-long stint abroad. A nurse by profession, Kimberly said she'd decided to order the fertility drug Clomid online because she knew that it was what a fertility doctor would prescribe.

"I basically knew how to use it and what I was supposed to do, and instead of having to pay a doctor tons of cash to explain something I already knew how to do, I opted to do it myself," Kimberly explained. "It's not like I just ordered from the first site that popped up. I looked around and saw one specific site pointed to by so many other sites."

A few weeks later, a brown envelope arrived via post, with markings from India on the package. The Clomid pills were in the familiar blister packaging, but she noticed they were stamped with an expiration date that had already passed. She insisted on a refund and received it without delay. Ironically, she discovered she was pregnant just a few days after receiving the refund—no pills necessary.

But she says her inbox has been inundated with spam ever since she ordered the drugs online, and she remains concerned that the people who run the online pharmacy are going to push fraudulent charges through to her credit card.

"They've spammed me a million times since then," Kimberly said. "I know that obviously wasn't the best idea for me to order these drugs online, but I was desperate at the time. I'm really glad I didn't take the medication. It probably would have hurt the baby I already had inside of me."

Vishnevsky confirmed that people are often inundated with spam after ordering from or responding to junk email offers. That's because addresses of known buyers are a valuable commodity frequently resold or simply stolen by other hackers and spammers. (Recall how Vishnevsky's own list of two billion email addresses was left on McColo's servers. That list was downloadable by anyone who happened to discover the correct link needed to grab the file.)

But Vishnevsky said it's a common misconception that ordering from online pharmacy sites will result in credit card fraud. None of the spammers for SpamIt, GlavMed, or any other pharmacy spam program allow affiliates to view customer card data, he said, because they want to keep that information for themselves.

"Only administrators of [the] pharma program would see that, and they have no benefit to getting fraud on [the] card, because [the] merchant would risk losing [their card processing] account" as a result of increased chargebacks and fraud claims, he said.

Dependence and Addiction

Most of the buyers I reached who fit into this category declined to be interviewed. Also, all of them had ordered from sites run by affiliates working for Vrublevsky's Rx-Promotion, which had carved out a niche as one of the few rogue pharmacy affiliate programs that marketed and sold painkillers, stimulants, and other substances whose distribution is heavily controlled by authorities in the United States and elsewhere. (Records show that GlavMed also offered controlled pills for the first two years of its existence, but it was no longer selling controlleds when I began this project.)

Goran was a forty-one-year-old former prisoner of war from Eastern Europe, now living in the United States, who badly injured his back almost twenty years ago. Doctors long ago stopped prescribing him hydrocodone, so he spends between $250 and $500 a month buying it off the Internet along with tramadol, even though doing so is a felony in his state. Records leaked from Rx-Promotion show that Goran made several purchases throughout 2010.

Goran told me he's been happy with his purchases so far, and that they work about as well as the drugs prescribed by his doctor to keep the pain at bay. He said the online drugs typically ship from Hong Kong and arrive in blister packs wrapped in a sealed ziplock bag.

Without the pain meds, he said, he'd be unable to manage his transportation business. "In this country, if you don't work, you know what you are?" he asked. "You're homeless."

Goran may be taking the pills for legitimate back pain, but I suspected many others were not. Interestingly, the GlavMed database shows telltale signs of abuse among customers who ordered controlled substances during the years that the affiliate program was selling them. I shared the GlavMed customer data with Gary Warner, director of research in computer forensics at the University of Alabama at Birmingham, who ran a series of queries on the database to see if any immediate patterns became clear.

"What we found is that if you were a GlavMed customer who made more than five orders, there was an 80 to 85 percent chance that you bought tramadol or Soma," Warner said. "The question is, were they buying it for personal use or for resale? These are pills that have a street value of about five dollars per pill, which means that if you ordered a bottle of these pills through GlavMed and sold them one by one, you could have made about $1,300 profit per bottle."

The UCSD researchers with whom I shared the Rx-Promotion sales data also found strong indications that a major driver of revenue for that rogue pharmacy was repeat customers. The team found that sales of painkillers and other drugs that are highly restricted in the United States produced 48 percent of all revenue for the Rx-Promotion program.

"The fact that such drugs are over-represented in both Rx-Promotion (and, for drugs like Soma and tramadol, in SpamIt) reinforces the hypothesis that abuse may be a substantial driver for this component of demand," the UCSD team wrote in a research paper on their findings.

For the most part, I was unable to learn firsthand from the people I interviewed about the efficacy and safety of the drugs they received from GlavMed or Rx-Promotion sites. Nearly everyone I spoke with promised to mail a pill or two from the packages they'd received, but only one interviewee actually followed through. That package contained both knockoff Viagra and another drug that were in the same bag and got crushed together and badly contaminated.

So while I'd gotten some good information on why people were ordering these drugs and perpetuating the spam problem, I decided that to make sense of the GlavMed and Rx-Promotion affiliate and client data, I needed help from Warner and several other prominent academic researchers with the capability and facilities to test these drugs. What I didn't know at the time was that these researchers had been trying to discover the same thing on their own, only to be stymied by miles of red tape and the pharmaceutical industry itself. I was also about to discover the much darker, more sinister consequences of these online drug buyers' choices.

Chapter 5

RUSSIAN ROULETTE

Less than twenty-four hours after Christmas 2006, Marcia Bergeron succumbed to poisons mixed into several medications she had ordered from a supposedly Canadian pharmacy online. Her body was discovered by a neighbor, and more than a hundred generic pills were found in her home, including a sedative, an antianxiety drug, and acetaminophen.

Bergeron, a fifty-seven-year-old resident of Quadra Island in British Columbia, Canada, had started losing her hair and experienced blurred vision in the days before her death. According to the coroner's report, "Mrs. Bergeron had been suffering from a range of symptoms. In emails to a friend, she described symptoms of ongoing nausea, diarrhea, aching joints, and other issues. Her friends locally were aware she was losing her hair and having vision problems. In the days immediately prior to her death, she was extremely fatigued and sick."

An autopsy report showed that Bergeron had been slowly poisoned by extremely hazardous chemicals included in the pills, which the Coroners Service of British Columbia said were ordered from an online pharmacy.

Toxicology tests indicated that many of the pills contained dangerously high levels of heavy metals that had probably been used as filler or were trace elements from a contaminated production facility. Among the chemicals included in the pills were uranium and lead, both of which can be lethal or severely damaging even in small doses.

It remains unclear which rogue Internet pharmacy program sponsored the site from which Bergeron ordered. Drugs purchased by GlavMed and other rogue pharmacy partnerships are marketed as if they come from pharmacies in Canada, which is world-renowned for its affordable medications. But most of the drugs from GlavMed appear to have been shipped from a half-dozen pharmacies or suppliers in India, a nation that is also now among the world's largest sources of legitimate branded and generic medications. The rest seem to have come from more than forty manufacturers and suppliers in China, India, and Pakistan, some of whom appeared to resell legitimate, branded drugs at bargain basement prices and some who didn't. The one that Bergeron used clearly didn't.

India has the brains, manpower, and infrastructure to manufacture huge quantities of pills each year, and it has fostered a booming, $10 billion-a-year pharmaceutical industry even though the country has routinely denied the patents for many drugs made by Western drugmakers.

As Vikas Bajaj and Andrew Pollack wrote for the *New York Times* in March 2012, India's conflict with Western drug companies over patents dates back to 1970, when the country stopped granting drug patents. It resumed granting them in 2005 as part of an agreement with the World Trade Organization, but the agreement was not retroactive to medicines created before 1995.

Since then, the *Times* notes, India has emerged as the world's pharmacy and, in recent decades, has been the largest provider of cheap, generic lifesaving medicines in poor countries across the globe. Western drugmakers have charged that by limiting drug patents in specific cases and fostering the development of inexpensive, generic knockoffs, the Indian government and the pharmaceutical industry there are stifling innovation and reducing profits that are essential to continued research and development on lifesaving drugs. The Indian drug companies say their practices ensure that poorer nations maintain affordable access to drugs for scourges like HIV and cancer.

Indeed, in one high-profile legal showdown, the Indian drugmakers faced off against Swiss pharmaceutical giant Novartis in a legal battle over whether Indian firms could continue to produce generic copies of Gleevec, a drug that provides effective treatment for some types of leukemia. As the *New York Times* notes, Gleevec can cost as much as $70,000 per year, while Indian generic versions have sold for about $2,500 a year. In late March 2013, the Indian Supreme Court ruled that the patent that Novartis sought for Gleevec did not represent a true invention.

The problem is that India's admirable, if self-serving fight to produce affordable generic drugs for the rest of the world does not address the safety and efficacy of these non-brand drugs. But to hear the U.S. pharmaceutical industry tell it, any prescription drugs produced outside the so-called "approved supply chain" are counterfeit at least, probably substandard, and quite possibly harmful or lethal. Whether or not that's always the case, the U.S. drugmakers are right about one thing: most drugs sold by rogue online pharmaceutical companies are not produced in regulated facilities—and therefore pose serious risks to anyone who decides to take them.

The statistics about the rogue pharmaceutical industry—and their implications for the health of its customers—are truly terrifying. According to the World Health Organization, approximately 8 percent of the bulk drugs imported into the United States are counterfeit, unapproved, or substandard, and 10 percent of global pharmaceutical commerce—or $21 billion— involves counterfeit drugs. A study led by the *International Journal of Clinical Practice* (*IJCP*) published in 2012 puts the number at more than three times that amount. The *IJCP* study estimates that global sales of counterfeit medicines doubled in the five years between 2005 and 2010, and now exceed $75 billion. The Alliance for Safe Online Pharmacies estimates that 30,000 to 40,000 active online drug sellers operate at any given time, and that only a fraction are legitimate.

Pharmaceutical giant Merck recently analyzed more than 2,500 Internet pharmacies and found that more than 80 percent of those sites were selling their drugs without requiring a prescription. Online pharmacies run by pharmacy affiliate networks like Rx-Promotion and GlavMed-SpamIt never asked customers to produce a prescription, although legitimate online pharmacies selling prescription drugs to Americans must by law require a prescription. What's more, Merck discovered that nearly six hundred of those pharmacies were selling the drugs at a price below the lowest wholesale average price available to any market anywhere, strongly indicating that the drugs were counterfeit—and very possibly unsafe.

Many people who bought from Rx-Promotion and SpamIt-affiliated online pharmacies expressed surprise at receiving their pills in packages showing that they were shipped directly from India and China. But according to a 2010 report from the U.S. Government Accountability Office (GAO), that's where the vast majority of drugs you buy from your corner drugstore are also produced. The GAO found that roughly 80 percent of the raw ingredients that go into all pharmaceuticals—including those peddled by rogue online pharmacies, approved online pharmacies, and even Main Street vendors like CVS and Walgreens—come from chemical factories based in India and China.

The problem isn't that these drugs are produced outside North America for U.S. and Canadian consumers. The issue is that it's unclear whether the suppliers that rogue pharmacy operations like SpamIt and Rx-Promotion use are supplying branded and generic medications to the supply chain for pills sold at legitimate and approved pharmacies in the United States and abroad—and, more importantly, whether the drugs they're creating are safe or not.

SpamIt pharmacies, for example, relied on pills bulk-shipped by at least forty different suppliers, but the vast majority of the medications sold via their spamvertized sites came from a half-dozen drop shippers in India and Hong Kong. According to information pieced together from the SpamIt affiliate database and the

Stupin online chats, the top suppliers for SpamIt included Sai Balaji Enterprises and Hemant Pharma (doing business as "Chinmay Overseas"), both from Mumbai, India. Other top suppliers for SpamIt included Trans Atlantic Corp., based in Hong Kong, and Shri Kethlaji Traders in Sumerpur, India.

The trouble is that the GlavMed-SpamIt order fulfillment system appears to have selected suppliers and drop shippers automatically based on which one recently bid the lowest for the class of drug the customer is seeking. The spam pharma companies have no idea whether these drugs are safe for consumer consumption—or whether they're even the real drugs or fake ones stuffed with potential poisons and toxins like what killed Marcia Bergeron.

In short, customers who order drugs from spam may be playing a dangerous game of Russian roulette.

Digging deeper, I discovered that GlavMed kept scrupulous records of customer service complaints and requests. Thousands of complaints from customers appeared in the leaked GlavMed database, yet relatively few of them pertained to the quality of the drugs that were delivered. Rather, most complaints were about delays in receiving the ordered drugs or were lodged by customers who received the wrong medications or were unhappy with how the drugs were packaged.

One exception was a transaction made by Deborah G., a resident of the United Kingdom. Deborah ordered weight-loss drugs and other items from pillaz.com—a site advertised by a spammer working for Igor Gusev's GlavMed affiliate program. According to the GlavMed customer complaint database, the pills that Deborah ordered sent her to the emergency room. The London resident described herself as a forty-three-year-old woman who weighed more than two hundred pounds but who had no allergies or current medications. In 2010, she paid $437.39 (not including shipping) for a veritable medicine cabinet of prescription drugs, including:

- One hundred eighty (20 milligram) tablets of the anti-obesity drug Acomplia.
- Sixty doses of Xenical, a drug that blocks the absorption of fat in certain foods.
- A three-month supply of Hoodia, an organic weight-loss supplement.
- Four tubes of acne-fighting tretinoin cream.

Not long after ingesting her new pills, Deborah fell into a deep depression and had to be admitted to the hospital after she began to feel sick to her stomach. Suspecting that the tablets she'd received from her online order may have been tainted, she brought the drugs to a lab to have them professionally tested.

"On testing, they discovered they were completely fake," Deborah said in her emailed complaint to GlavMed's customer support team. According to Deborah, the lab results revealed that some of the pills contained a variety of inactive and decidedly hostile ingredients, including poisons, cement, and talcum powder.

Deborah later lodged a threatening complaint at the site from which she'd ordered.

"I want ALL my money back. I will gladly post back the tablets, and no further action will be taken," she wrote in a comment included in the SpamIt database. "However if I do not receive this I will face no other option than to go to the police and all the customs authorities dealing with counterfeit drugs, and trust me, I will get you prosecuted. I will expect a full refund for all your poisons immediately."

Records show that the SpamIt-affiliated pharmacy site complied, posting a full refund to Deborah's credit card. Again, the last thing these rogue online pharmacies want is to be pulled onto the radar of law-enforcement authorities or to have unsatisfied customers issue chargebacks, which could endanger the online pharmacy's ability to take credit cards (which would kill its business) and could cause it to incur heavy fines.

Given the quantity of fake pharmaceuticals that flood markets in North America and Europe each year—and the potential brand damage and profit losses wrought by rogue pharmacies— one would think the powerful and influential pharma industry would use its might to show just how dangerous these drugs can be. Indeed, the story of Bergeron's death is almost always recited in some form whenever experts allied with the pharmaceutical industry talk about the need to eradicate rogue Internet pill shops.

Yet, neither the Food and Drug Administration (FDA) nor the giants of the pharmaceutical industry appear to have taken concrete steps to fight back against these rogue online competitors, though it'd be easy to show whether the drugs being offered through them contain harmful ingredients or at least dangerously low or high levels of the active ingredients compared to legitimate versions of their pills.

John Horton, president of LegitScript, a company that maintains a searchable database of thousands of approved and "rogue" pharmacy websites, said the FDA occasionally publishes the results of chemical testing done against dietary supplements and some prescription drugs bought from online pharmacies, but that few comprehensive studies have been conducted.

"It's fair to say that there's a dearth of testing," said Horton, a White House aide on drug policy issues during the administration of President George W. Bush, from 2002 to 2007. "I think one of the problems you run into is that these tests are expensive. Also, it's difficult to scientifically study and analyze the chemical composition of these drugs ordered from rogue pharmacies because those pharmacies constantly are switching suppliers."

According to LegitScript, there are more than 35,610 active Internet pharmacies, yet only 212 are approved and legitimate web pill shops. In other words, if you order from one, you have more than a 99 percent chance of using an illegitimate, unapproved website. The company ranks pharmacies as legitimate if they meet a set of criteria, including registration with the U.S. Drug Enforcement Agency and possession of a legitimate license to dispense drugs. But most importantly, the pill shop must ask for and receive a legitimate, doctor-ordered prescription before shipping prescription drugs to Americans.

To make matters worse, Horton said many of the 35,000-plus rogue online pharmacies rely on multiple suppliers, meaning that the quality and safety of the drugs they ship can shift from day to day as prices in the wholesale and drop-shipping markets fluctuate.

"Most of these pharmacy affiliate programs don't just have one supplier," Horton said. "Some of the bigger ones have dozens. So, just because a given drug from a specific pharmacy program tests as genuine one day doesn't mean it's going to be the same genuine drug the next time someone orders it."

But Horton believes perhaps the single biggest reason neither the FDA nor the pharmaceutical industry has put much effort into testing is that they're worried that such tests may show that the drugs being sold by many so-called rogue pharmacies are by and large chemically indistinguishable from those sold by approved pharmacies.

"Frankly it's sort of a double-edged sword," Horton said. "Let's say you test Rx-Promotion's drugs and they turn out to be real, to be chemically equivalent to the stuff you'd get from your local pharmacy. Does it then follow that by publishing those results, you are almost implicitly endorsing the site that sold those drugs?"

Thus, most of the work of testing pills sold by rogue pharmacies has fallen to academic researchers attempting to unearth data on the safety and efficacy of prescription medications ordered through spam. Stefan Savage, a professor in the systems and networking group at the University of California, San Diego (UCSD) led a research team that spent many months in 2011 making more than eight hundred test orders from pill shops advertised via junk email.

"The prevailing wisdom was that these pharma shops took your money and ripped off your credit card, and you never got jack," he said. "We wanted to know if you ordered from these stores whether you actually got anything, and if so, where it came from, who did the payment processing, all that stuff."

Savage said the group was surprised to learn that the drugs they purchased and tested all seemed to have the right active ingredients in roughly the correct amounts, but they weren't able to test the drugs for contaminants that may have introduced health risks for customers.

"For legal reasons we can't buy every drug, and we're not equipped to test everything," Savage said. "But in the drugs that we have tested, the right active ingredient has appeared in the right amount. So it really seems like from the standpoint of the people in this business and their communications with each other that they believe they're selling an equivalent product" to what consumers would otherwise get at a local drugstore, he said.

In 2012, Savage and his fellow UCSD researchers, along with researchers at the International Computer Science Institute and George Mason University, examined caches of data tracking the day-to-day finances of GlavMed, SpamIt, and Rx-Promotion. The result is perhaps the most detailed analysis yet of the business case for the malicious software and spam epidemics that persist to this day. They found that repeat customers are critical to making any rogue pharmacy business profitable. Repeat orders constituted 27 percent of average program revenue for GlavMed and 38 percent of that revenue for SpamIt. For Rx-Promotion, revenue from repeat orders was as much as 23 percent of overall revenue.

"This says a number of things, and one is that a lot of people who bought from these programs were satisfied," Savage said, noting, however, that many of the repeat customers were purchasing controlled and habit-forming prescription drugs, including painkillers. "Maybe the drugs they bought had a great placebo effect, but my guess is these are satisfied customers and they came back because of that."

◆   ◆   ◆

By far the most important question about the pills pimped by the spam business is the efficacy and safety of the drugs. I interviewed hundreds of U.S. residents who purchased prescription drugs from the pharmacy sites advertised through SpamIt, and received a panpoly of responses about the effectiveness of these pills. But none of those I interviewed could tell me about the safety of the drugs or their purity.

For that, I'd hoped to enlist the help of chemists and researchers. Gary Warner, director of research in computer forensics at the University of Alabama at Birmingham (UAB), had sought to conduct much of the same research, but ran into bureaucratic hurdles left and right. So not long after receiving a copy of the GlavMed-SpamIt data, I shared it with Warner. He, in turn, tried to get various pharmaceutical firms interested in using the data to open a broader, well-funded investigation into these rogue online pharmacies. But his efforts were met with little success.

The sprawling campus of UAB is also known as "the University that Ate Birmingham," and it's not hard to see why. The city of Birmingham is home to fewer than a quarter-million residents, and about one in ten are students at the university.

On the fourth floor of a nondescript brick building smack in the middle of the campus is the UAB computer forensics lab, where Warner spends eight to ten hours a day with a mix of undergraduate, graduate, and PhD students who, like me, seem to be infected by a passion for going after Internet bad guys.

Warner is standing in front of a floor-to-ceiling whiteboard that is covered with equations related to a mathematical algorithm that the computer lab's twentysomething geeks are trying to work out. He is gesturing at rows of computer servers and Mac OS X systems that line either side of the climate-controlled and tightly secured room, which is used in part by university students laboring under a grant from the Defense Advanced Research Projects Agency (DARPA) to create and study malicious software in a lab environment.

A complete and unabashed caffeine junkie, Warner is slurping from his third diet Mountain Dew of the day. He's talking excitedly about the dangers of ordering from unlicensed Internet pharmacies, irrespective of whether the pills themselves are real and chemically equivalent to pills that customers might otherwise purchase from a local pharmacy.

Part of the problem, Warner said, is that many unlicensed Internet pharmacies will happily ship a variety of drugs whose use has been banned or highly restricted in the United States because of the drugs' tendency to induce dangerous side effects—without offering any warnings or instructions on using the medications.

For example, pharmaceutical giant Roche decided to pull its anti-acne drug Accutane from the U.S. market after juries awarded millions of dollars in damages to former Accutane users. The drug has been strongly linked to birth defects among children born to women who took it while pregnant. As a result, the U.S. FDA in 2005 ordered that Accutane only be sold to women who sign a pledge saying they will submit to multiple pregnancy tests and practice at least two forms of birth control while on it. But Accutane is still available through rogue spam pharmacies.

This is another example of the risks people take when buying from these rogue pharmacies: they don't get vital information on the serious health hazards they could face in taking certain drugs in certain conditions or in combination with other drugs. Legitimate pharmacies, on the other hand, do their best to ensure that their customers understand these risks before giving them their prescriptions.

"Many of these rogue pharmacies are still advertising a number of discontinued, banned, or very restricted drugs," Warner said. "And they're definitely not passing on warnings about how these drugs should be used, even when there are strong conditions that would normally be impressed on the customer when ordering these drugs from regular pharmacies."

The most obvious example of a common risk introduced by pills dispensed from GlavMed and SpamIt pharmacies is the two to four free counterfeit Viagra or Cialis pills that were shipped with every order. The pills were stuffed into all orders, even those in which the customer had purchased drugs such as nitrates that could produce a deadly cocktail when taken with erectile dysfunction (ED) medications. Physicians have long warned against taking ED drugs in tandem with medicines designed to decrease high blood pressure, because doing so could lead to dangerously low blood pressure levels, a condition that often precipitates a heart attack.

The UAB computer forensics lab is the ideal location for testing drugs bought through spam. One floor below Warner's lair, Elizabeth Gardner, PhD, spends much of her time analyzing new "legal highs." These are mind-altering substances created with synthetic versions of chemical compounds whose use and distribution are restricted in the United States. Some of these legal highs are fairly benign, such as the "performance-boosting" pills sold at gas stations that hint at their supposed abilities to enhance a man's stamina in the bedroom.

"Most of these are just lots of caffeine and wishful thinking," Gardner quips.

On a Thursday afternoon in mid-June 2012, Gardner is looking at the chemical analysis of a local bath-salts sample. Bits of the drug are being fed into a large white box that resembles an oversized laserjet printer. The device is a mass spectrometer, a tool that this lab uses to search for and identify the active ingredients found in various controlled substances. Almost noiselessly, it automates the fetching and analysis of tiny glass vials filled with chemical samples that are fed into the machine's interior.

The machine produces data that are relayed to a nearby computer, which uses the information to plot a line graph that shows several distinct upward spikes.

"See these spikes here," Gardner says, pointing at two especially tall peaks in the graph. "These are the chemical markers for mephedrone, which is the active ingredient in these salts."

Despite our efforts, I was unable to get any of the online drug buyers to send me useful samples of the pills for testing in Gardner's lab. Not that it would have mattered: UAB couldn't get legal cover to do it anyway.

Incredibly, the UAB researchers have legal approval from federal regulators and law-enforcement agencies to test and handle highly controlled and illegal substances, such as cocaine, heroin, and a methamphetamine, but they had not yet received permission from the FDA and DEA to test pills ordered through junk email.

Part of the problem is that Congress changed the law in 2008, when it enacted the Ryan Haight Act, which makes it expressly illegal for anyone to order prescription drugs over the Internet without a prescription. In addition, even if an American has a valid prescription for a drug, it is illegal for him or her to order the drug from a pharmacy outside the United States and have it shipped back into the United States.

"We've kind of gotten it taken care of," Warner said. "We've got the memorandums of understanding in place and got the post office boxes all set up and the top-level approval at the university. But we still have this one tiny little administrative hurdle to get over." They still needed a green light from federal regulators.

Warner even had a regional bank on board to provide his researchers with prepaid cards that could be used to covertly buy drugs from GlavMed-SpamIt and Rx-Promotion.

"The bank was willing to put up the money to help fund our operations, but we still needed a government letterhead memo basically saying that no one was going to go to jail for this," Warner said. The university was slated to receive a grant from the FDA to conduct research on rogue pharmacies, but the grant would come with serious strings attached.

"They basically said that none of the money could be used to purchase drugs, and if any of the grant money is used to analyze drugs ordered from spam, then the grant will be withdrawn," Warner said. "What changed between when the FDA tentatively offered the grant and these conditions? Nobody can say. They just said, 'It's not legal for us to authorize you to buy drugs.' So the FDA Office of Compliance had to go back and revise the grant to only evaluate the websites in the spam emails, and we were no longer allowed to purchase the pills."

This was not the first time Warner and UAB were frustrated in their attempts to test pills ordered through spam to conduct their research. Not long before I'd shared the GlavMed data with him, Warner had a meeting with executives and fraud investigators from Pfizer. The pharmaceutical giant indicated it was interested in working with UAB on a study to analyze drugs purchased through rogue pharmacy affiliate programs. After all, counterfeit sales of its blockbuster drug—Viagra—accounted for more than 40 percent of the transactions from both Rx-Promotion and GlavMed.

But the funding for such a project would come with certain strings attached. "Pfizer said they wanted to work with us on this project as long as they had the right to shut the thing down if it turned out the drugs were real," Warner recalled. "Microsoft was talking with us and Pfizer about whether UAB and Microsoft could do something like a website such as pilldangers.org or something, and warn people of dangers of buying pills online. And my chemist said, 'Well, what if the drugs are real?'"

"In response, the Pfizer guy said, 'Well, then we wouldn't want to publish anything.' I told them that we're big on academic freedom and that we wouldn't be able to live with that condition," Warner recalled. "I told him that we'd want to be able to say, for example, 'Okay, so in 25 percent of pharmacy orders we got, we got the real thing.' They said, 'No, no, you can't do that. We only want you to publish about the fake pills.'"

Then, after Warner had received a copy of the GlavMed data, he had a chance to chat with another Warner—Mark Warner—the director of intelligence for Pfizer and a twenty-one-year veteran of the FBI. UAB's Warner said Pfizer's Warner called to discuss possible collaboration on mining the GlavMed data for information that U.S. law-enforcement officials could then present to Russian officials to help stop the tidal wave of spam affecting everyone.

"I got off the phone with him before I understood exactly who he was, but this guy acted like an old-school, knuckle-dragger cop," UAB's Warner recalled of the conversation. "He's a New Yorker, so it kind of went like this:

"'Well, Mistah Wahrnah, just listen to me. I've been doin' this a lot longer than you. And here's the way it's gonna go: the Russians aren't gonna do fuck all for us. What we need to do is find the spam affiliates who are in the United States and lock 'em up. Forget the Russians. We're never going to touch the Russians. The Russians are bulletproof. We can't touch 'em. So let's just find the guys who are in the U.S., put them in jail, and move on.'"

On the one hand, Pfizer's Warner had a point: according to most law-enforcement experts I interviewed for this book, there was almost no chance that the Russians *would* do "fuck all" about it. For starters, hackers in Russia are generally left alone as long as they do not prey on the country's own companies or citizens. But UAB's Warner said he was taken aback by such a response. After all, more than 40 percent of GlavMed's sales involved knockoff versions of Pfizer's blockbuster drug Viagra, so it would be in the pharma company's best interest to collaborate.

"I just couldn't believe the caveman mentality that this guy had,"

Warner recalled in a telephone interview. "I thought to myself, you know he may be a twenty-one-year veteran of the FBI, but it doesn't mean he knows jack about cybercrime. At the same time, counterfeit versions of his company's big moneymaker were by far the largest single drug that GlavMed sold. They're the ones in a perfect position to complain about pharmaceutical spam, but who knows? Maybe $100 million in counterfeit SpamIt and GlavMed profits is nothing to a company that makes tens of billions a year."

UAB's Warner said he began to feel despondent about having so much information on a massive criminal cybercrime conspiracy, while law enforcement seemed to have so little interest in running with the data cache.

"I had been participating in the FBI's pharmaceutical fraud working group, and I was horribly disappointed because hardly any of the big pharma companies came to the meetings," Warner said. "At least in the meetings I attended, there would be seven pharmaceutical companies at the table, and not a single one of them I'd ever heard of. Roche wasn't there, Bayer wasn't there, Pfizer wasn't there. Merck wasn't there. AstraZenica might have been at one of the meetings. But we couldn't get anyone interested."

That said, there may have been another reason that Pfizer was in no mood to help the FBI. Not long before Warner acquired the GlavMed-SpamIt data, the FBI wrapped up a criminal investigation into Pfizer for promoting off-label uses of its biggest selling drugs and for paying kickbacks to physicians to promote them. The government alleged that Pfizer sales reps made misleading marketing claims about uses for the firm's drugs. For example, reps allegedly were urged to instruct physicians on staging

conversations about prescribing Viagra for women who had difficulty reaching orgasm.

Pfizer denied the allegations but nevertheless agreed to a $2.3
billion settlement, at that time the single largest fraud settlement
ever collected by the U.S. Justice Department. The settlement
amount roughly equaled the revenues that Pfizer brings in each
year from sales of Viagra. It's no wonder the pharma giant didn't
want to draw the FBI into another investigation, even if this one
was to the pharmaceutical giant's benefit.

For its part, Pfizer has opted to pursue cases against spammers
and counterfeiters via civil lawsuits. Over the past five years, the
company has spent millions on investigation and legal fees to go
after purveyors of fake Viagra and other drugs. (Pfizer declined
repeated requests to be interviewed for this book.)

Warner was disappointed that he couldn't get permission to test
prescription drugs purchased from Rx-Promotion and GlavMed-
SpamIt. But he seemed genuinely hopeful that the customer
databases from both rogue pharmacy operations would be enough
to help bring down some of the world's biggest spammers and
botnet masters, nearly all of whom were working for one or both
of these affiliate programs and whose personal and financial data
were sprinkled throughout each affiliate program's leaked records.

The same anti-spam activist who had shared the GlavMed
database with me said he sent a copy of it to contacts at the FBI.
And for several weeks at the end of 2010, multiple law-enforcement
agencies fought to take the lead on the investigation. Ultimately,
the inquiry was determined to be best pursued as a trademark
infringement matter and was turned over to a multi-agency task

force of the U.S. Department of Homeland Security's Immigration and Customs Enforcement (ICE) bureau.

That task force, known as the National Intellectual Property Rights Coordination Center (NIPR), draws on civil and criminal investigative resources from at least twenty separate agencies, including the FBI, Interpol, the U.S. Postal Inspection Service, the National Aeronautics and Space Administration (NASA), and the Royal Canadian Mounted Police.

The investigation at NIPR was part of a broader push by the Obama administration to crack down on abuses of intellectual property rights online, including rogue pharmacy sales and the illegal trade in pirated movies, music, and software. Around that same time, administration officials were announcing the results of Operation Pangea, an annual international law-enforcement push led by Interpol and aimed at disrupting pharmaceutical crime. The week-long operation led to the shuttering of at least 290 rogue online pharmacies; the seizure of nearly 11,000 packages containing more than a million pills; and the arrest or investigation of at least seventy-six individuals connected with the pharma stores.

Many of the sites taken down in Operation Pangea were web storefronts advertised by spammers working for Vrublevsky's Rx-Promotion program. Just prior to the takedowns, the U.S. Food and Drug Administration sent a warning letter to Vrublevsky's partner—Yuri "Hellman" Kabayenkov—stating that the agency had identified 294 websites that were selling addictive, highly controlled prescription drugs such as painkillers without a prescription. It seemed U.S. authorities were finally starting to take a stand.

Rx-Promotion essentially shrugged. According to Vrublevsky, hardly anyone in the program noticed the takedowns, which ironically more or less equaled the average number of sites that disappeared each week as a result of regular cleanup efforts from anti-spam groups and web hosting firms.

"It was very funny to read the news and see that there was this huge, international operation that resulted in the closure of hundreds of illegal pharmacies on the Internet," Vrublevsky said. "And then you read spammer and hacker forums and see these guys asking each other, 'Dude, did you feel that?' and, 'Dude, did you notice that?' It didn't seem like anyone cared or really noticed."

Vrublevsky said that in the weeks prior to the operation, a group of U.S. firms—mainly copyright holders in the entertainment industry—had called a meeting with members of the Russian State Duma, the lower house of Russian parliament. That meeting was part of a campaign in Russia by the entertainment industry to crack down on music and movie piracy. The campaign's slogan was roughly translated, "Say No to a Thief!"

The leaked ChronoPay emails show that the company was quietly paying the salary of at least one member of the Russian Association for Electronic Communications (RAEC), an industry trade group. ChronoPay invoices indicate that the company paid a "monthly fee for public relations advice"—16,666.66 euros—to Dmitry Zakharov, then RAEC's public relations director. (This was yet another debt that Vrublevsky and ChronoPay would welch on. ChronoPay's internal email records are littered with emails from RAEC's debt collectors, who hounded ChronoPay officials to pay tens of thousands of euros in delinquent "consulting" fees, without success.) I sought comment from Mr. Zakharov about this apparent arrangement, but received no response. That was frustrating and ironic, in part because Zakharov left RAEC in 2010 and is now deputy director of the department of external communications for the Russian government's Ministry of Telecom and Mass Communications.

In a phone interview one month after Operation Pangea, Vrublevsky told me he contacted the RAEC leaders to make fun of them for participating in the copyright and trademark forum.

Unsurprisingly, the copyright owners—particularly from the movie industry—threatened RAEC members like Vkontakte (a Russian version of Facebook) and mail.ru (a webmail provider) that unless they removed all rights-infringing materials, law enforcement would get involved, Vrublevsky said. "I heard about this and called those RAEC dudes and said, 'Hey, how much brains do you need to have not to go to a meeting with rights holders called, 'Say No to a Thief?'"

Later in 2010, RAEC sent an official letter addressed to Victoria Espinel, the Obama administration's intellectual property enforcement coordinator. The letter—which also was sent to top officials at Google, Microsoft, the National Association of Boards of Pharmacy, and LegitScript—offered the Russian hi-tech industry's help with anti-spam efforts and with future initiatives aimed at stamping out rogue Internet pharmacies.

The letter claimed that the economic loss in Russia caused by spam was $450 million in 2009, and that as a result, Russia was hard at work crafting its own anti-spam laws. RAEC didn't mention that the man who cofounded the rogue Internet pharmacy targeted in the American government's recent Pangea effort was also in charge of the Russian government committee responsible for recommending ways to draw up those anti-spam laws.

RAEC officials closed the letter by offering to host a closed-circuit videoconference bridge with officials from the Obama administration and the technology industry, "during which we could discuss the available results of researches, the current matters, the initiatives, and opportunities for joint actions dedicated to the stabilization of [the] situation in the area of cybercrime in general, and in relation to the pharmaceutical spam in particular."

LegitScript President John Horton said his immediate reaction upon receiving a copy of the letter was to contact the FDA and Espinel.

"I said, 'I'm sure you guys know about what's going on with ChronoPay,' and it turns out they did," Horton said. "I also emailed Victoria [Espinel] and told her my informal suggestion was not to respond to the letter."

In mid-August 2010, Andrew J. Klein, President Obama's senior adviser for intellectual enforcement, invited leaders of the top Internet domain name registrars and registries to attend a three-hour meeting at the White House to discuss voluntary ways to shutter websites selling counterfeit prescription drugs.

The invitation was sent via email to dozens of executives and attorneys at some of the world's largest Internet companies, including Google, Microsoft, PayPal, Visa, and Yahoo! The recipients were invited to attend a meeting on September 29 with senior White House and Cabinet officials, including Victoria Espinel.

"The purpose of this meeting is to discuss illegal activity taking place over the Internet generally and, more specifically, voluntary protocols to address the illegal sale of counterfeit non-controlled prescription medications online," the invitation stated.

Multiple people who attended the event called it more of an ambush than a collaborative meeting of the minds to solve a tough problem, and said that Espinel essentially told attendees that they needed to work out a voluntary approach—or else.

"She basically got a bunch of big brand holders in the room to say, 'You guys need to do something about this or something will be done to you,'" UCSD's Savage said, recalling a conversation with an attendee.

Though few knew about it at the time, one of the firms invited—Google—was already under criminal investigation by the U.S. Justice Department for actively courting fake Canadian pharmacies—including many rogue Internet pharmacies created by SpamIt and Rx-Promotion—to advertise drugs for distribution in the United States.

The implications of this case were huge. One of the ways that affiliates for GlavMed promoted their pharmacy sites was by hacking websites. Affiliates would insert dozens of links and even entire web pages into hacked sites that redirected visitors to sites peddling knockoff prescription drugs. The more hacked legitimate sites that affiliates had pointing to their pharmacy stores, the greater their ranking would be in the major search engine results when consumers searched for specific drug names. This process—known in the underground as "black search engine optimization," or "black SEO" for short—was a major driver of pharmacy sales for affiliates of both Rx-Promotion and GlavMed-SpamIt.

It was bad enough that Google's search results were constantly being gamed by spammers. For Google to also be taking money from unregulated and potentially spammer-affiliated online pharmacies was beyond the pale. According to the Justice Department, Google was aware as early as 2003 that Canadian pharmacies were illegally shipping prescription drugs into the United States.

Google would later settle criminal charges in connection with the case and agree to pay a whopping $500 million in fines. One of the largest forfeitures ever paid to the Justice Department, the fine was intended to represent the company's advertising revenue from the Canadian pharmacies and the revenue the pharmacies received from American customers buying controlled drugs.

Less than two months after the White House meeting, Espinel stood at the podium in a press conference at the White House. Flanked by U.S. Attorney General Eric Holder and then Department of Homeland Security Secretary Janet Napolitano, Espinel announced the creation of a new nonprofit entity to battle rogue Internet pharmacies.

"A group of founding private-sector partners announced today that they will form a new nonprofit to work with each other and the U.S. government to rid the Internet of illegal Internet pharmacies," Espinel explained, naming the nonprofit members as American Express, eNom, GoDaddy, Google, MasterCard, Microsoft, Network Solutions, Neustar, PayPal, Visa, and Yahoo.

"This group of companies has taken an extraordinary and

unprecedented step to combat illegal online pharmacies," Espinel told a packed press room and CNN cameras. "We believe this will have a rapid and dramatic effect on illegal online pharmacies. This will change the rules of the road and make clear that legitimate companies will not interact with criminal actors."

There was only one problem with the whole announcement. Few at the companies named as members could remember having agreed to form such a nonprofit.

"Prior to that news conference, the participants from those companies had a roundtable conference call to talk about it, but nobody went into that meeting planning to agree to form that group," Warner said. "The people I spoke to who watched that announcement saying they'd agreed to form that group came out afterwards and were like, 'We did?'"

Eighteen months after the creation of the nonprofit that was first announced by Espinel at the White House gathering, the group had yet to hold its first meeting. At the same time, the NIPR case was being closed. The Pfizer security chief's warning would turn out to be eerily prescient. According to sources from two separate federal law-enforcement agencies who asked not to be identified because they were not authorized to speak on the record, the investigation into the core spammers and hackers employed by GlavMed and SpamIt was abandoned in part because most of the perpetrators were believed to be in Russia and former Soviet nations, countries that were typically less than cooperative with Western law-enforcement agencies seeking to apprehend cyber-criminals within their borders.

Given the lack of interest by federal regulators in methodically testing drugs ordered through these fly-by-night online pharmacies, it remains unclear whether the bulk of these drugs contain adequate amounts of the active ingredients without also mixing in harmful contaminants that could hurt or even kill people who ingest them.

This inaction appears to suit the pharmaceutical industry, which is wary of testing and getting results that might indicate that the vast majority of the prescription drugs ordered through spam are far cheaper and no less safe than the same pills ordered through a local pharmacy.

Unfortunately, the lack of objective data about the safety and efficacy of spam-ordered prescription drugs does little to dampen demand, while continuing to expose consumers to a dangerous game of Russian roulette.

Chapter 6

PARTNER(KA)S IN (DIS)ORGANIZED CRIME

T here's a famous quote from Sun Tzu's *The Art of War* that applies to my research and motivation for writing this book: "Know your enemy." Indeed, with some understanding of what motivates these spam pharmacies and their customers, it's time to look at how spam operations actually work. The driving force behind the success of programs like GlavMed and Rx-Promotion—and the engine that propels virtually every cybercriminal collaborative effort—is an arrangement known in Russia as the *partnerka*—literally, a "partnership." *Partnerkas* such as GlavMed and Rx-Promotion seek to match dodgy advertisers with businesses that are willing to purchase the web traffic that can be generated through spam.

Many legitimate businesses that are searching for more customers—principally small businesses based in Russia and Eastern Europe—will try to raise awareness of and demand for their products or services by hiring a spammer. While using hacked computers to send junk email is technically illegal in

Russia, many legitimate businesses there remain unaware or unafraid of this prohibition.

Indeed, as we'll see in Chapter 7, our "Virgil" in the spammer underworld—Cutwail botnet bankroller Igor Vishnevsky—got his start in spamming when his boss ordered him to figure out how to drive more traffic to his heating company's website.

In fact, when the Cutwail spam botnet is used to send spam to email addresses ending in ".ru," the messages very often include a Russian phone number where recipients can inquire about ordering spam advertisements for their own products and services.

"I've seen pretty much everything from e-cigarettes to office space to resorts advertised in this way," said Brett Stone-Gross, a University of California researcher who has studied the Cutwail botnet's operation for years.

In a typical spam partnerka, the individuals who run the operation—the sponsors—assume responsibility for coordinating and maintaining almost every aspect of the business, from the web content to customer service, to negotiating with suppliers and setting up the web servers and domain names needed to advertise the product for sale.

The only role of the spammers (sometimes referred to as "adverts" or "traffers") is to drive traffic to the websites where the goods advertised in the spam are sold, and they can walk away from the deal at any time. Spammers are typically paid commissions that equal 30 to 35 percent of the total sales generated by their traffic. It's a fairly lucrative business for them, provided their traffic actually generates paying customers.

This dynamic of partnerka systems allows the sponsors to

maintain a safe distance (in theory, at least) from the more illicit aspects of the spam business—which typically uses hacked PCs by the thousands to relay spam and to host pharmacy websites. The adverts benefit from the arrangement by being able to quickly unplug their traffic from one partnerka program in favor of another that may offer more attractive terms—such as higher commissions, better customer service, and greater product selection—that increase their likelihood of attracting customers through their spam. And there are multiple types of partnerships, including those that peddle replica watches, porn, knockoff designer handbags, and fake antivirus software as well as pharma spam. When spam emails show up in your inbox or get caught by your firewall, spam filter, or antivirus software, they're likely from one of these partnerkas.

Technology and security experts like to talk about these partnerkas as "organized cybercrime." But according to UCSD's Stefan Savage, partnerka systems are more accurately described as "disorganized crime"—that is, loosely affiliated networks of independent contractors, each of whom is essentially out to make a buck for himself and will only continue the partnership so long as it remains economically viable and competitive to do so.

"It's really a brilliant business model on both sides," said Savage, who has coauthored several long-term studies on various aspects of the partnerka economy, from spam to botnets. "On the affiliate side you don't need to learn about all the stuff like payment processing and fulfillment; you just have to figure out how to get traffic. Also, you have a great deal of flexibility—if one partnership goes offline or has better rates, you can move to someone else. So the partnerka model really offers incredible mobility to the affiliate, because they're not tied to anything."

Savage said the partnerka programs themselves benefit from the arrangement by not having to deal with the potential risks of being technically associated with botnets and other inventive yet potentially harmful (and legally murky) ways that their spammers may dream up to generate traffic.

"It's a win for the affiliate program because they don't need to make a bet on what's the best way to get traffic," he said. "The affiliate program says, 'Most of these guys [the spammers] are going to get screwed, but I don't care because I pay on a commission basis only. Someone is going to get this right, and when they do, I'll make money off of it.'"

As a result of the partnerka dynamic, most spammers also have no allegiance to any one pharmacy partnerka program. For example, almost all top spammers for both GlavMed and Rx-Promotion partnered with at least a half-dozen other pharmacy partnerkas, including EvaPharmacy, Bulker.biz, Rx-Partners, and Mailien. This dynamic presents perhaps the most frustrating problem of all for anti-spam crusaders trying to stem the flow of junk email. Much as squeezing an inflated balloon doesn't make the balloon any smaller but instead merely displaces the air into new bulges, anti-spam campaigns that succeed in shuttering one partnerka or a major component of that operation often result in the most successful affiliates simply shifting their spam traffic to competing partnerkas.

As Dmitry Samosseiko, a security expert with SophosLabs Canada, noted in his seminal paper, "The Partnerka—What Is It, and Why Should You Care?", all partnerkas are in strong competition with each other.

"Allegiance is earned through more generous commission rates, shorter 'hold' periods, support for a wider range of payment systems, higher quality promotional material, better support, etc.," Samosseiko wrote. Partnerkas typically place a one- to two-week hold on paying affiliate commissions to hedge against the possibility of having to pay all affiliates at the same time and to ensure that affiliates do not receive commissions for sales later reversed by credit card processors.

Samosseiko said partnerkas frequently use competitions and other gimmicks to attract more affiliates (spammers). "Many organize expensive parties for their members, send generous gifts for holidays, run lotteries where a top producer wins a luxury car, and the list goes on," he wrote.

These incentives also drive up the amount of email spam we receive. For example, in 2008, Stupin and Gusev—the founders and administrators of GlavMed and SpamIt—decided to sponsor a competition among their top spammers, with hefty cash prizes going to those adverts whose spam generated the greatest number of sales. Each participant was given a list with approximately 20,000 email addresses, and the contest began on July 4, 2008, Independence Day in the United States.

The first three finishers were awarded prizes of $1,000 to $3,000, and were bestowed with "Master of Inbox" status on Spamdot.biz, an exclusive forum owned by the SpamIt administrators. (The winner of that competition, a hacker nicknamed "Engel," was the Russian man allegedly behind the "Festi" spam botnet, an extremely virulent and powerful spam-spewing machine, as detailed in Chapter 7. Incidentally, Engel and his botnet would eventually catapult Vrublevsky and himself toward a dangerous collision with the law, as we'll see in Chapter 12.)

In their seminal paper, "PharmaLeaks: Understanding the Business of Online Pharmaceutical Affiliate Programs," researchers at the University of California, San Diego (UCSD), the International Computer Science Institute, and George Mason University examined caches of data tracking the day-to-day finances of GlavMed, SpamIt, and Rx-Promotion, which collectively over a four-year period processed more than $170 million worth of orders from customers seeking cheaper, more accessible, and more discreetly available drugs.

The result is perhaps the most detailed analysis yet of the business case for the malicious software and spam epidemics that persist to this day. The researchers concluded that spam—and all of its attendant ills—will remain a prevalent and pestilent problem because consumer demand for the products most frequently advertised through junk email remains constant.

"The market for spam-advertised drugs is not even close to being saturated," said UCSD professor Stefan Savage. "The number of new customers these programs got each day explains why people spam. Because sending spam to everyone on the planet gets you new customers on an ongoing basis, so it's not going away."

Affiliates understand this deeply, and like regional drug dealers who stake out huge swaths of online territory, they frequently squabble with one another out of jealousy or animosity, or in retribution for some perceived slight. These virtual turf wars can quickly become quite ugly and expensive for all involved. This is especially true when disputes break out between competing partnerkas, because most of the top affiliates are big-time spammers with extremely powerful botnets at their disposal.

Such disputes also are expensive because of the opportunity costs involved. The crippling attacks are carried out via botnets, by diverting resources that normally are used to send spam so that they instead send junk Internet traffic until the targeted website is overwhelmed and can no longer accommodate legitimate visitors (that is, potential buyers).

In their "PharmaLeaks" paper, the UCSD researchers discovered that just 10 percent of the highest-earning affiliates accounted for 75 to 90 percent of total program revenue across all three affiliate programs.

"Undermining the activities of just a handful of affiliates would have considerable effect on a program's bottom line," the researchers wrote.

The shadowy bosses at the head of various partnerka programs identified this weakness as an existential problem early on. To remedy it, the crime bosses sought to establish a virtual cartel for online pharmacy partnerkas that was designed to prevent inter-partnerka disputes, price wars, and affiliates stampeding from one pharmacy program to the next at a moment's notice. The partnerka bosses believed that such a deal would reduce overhead costs and episodic dips in overall spam volumes, and ultimately ensure a more consistent flow of junk email into inboxes everywhere.

To facilitate this, on September 4, 2007, Dmitry Stupin told his partner Igor Gusev that he would like to see SpamIt and GlavMed enter into a pharmacy cartel with other partnerka programs. A week later, Gusev arranged a meeting to discuss the idea with Leonid Kuvayev, a convicted spammer who was coadministrator of Rx-Partners, a competing pharmacy spam program.

Around that same time, Pavel Vrublevsky was reportedly setting up his own rogue pharmacy operation—Rx-Promotion—in conjunction with a coworker and longtime friend, Yuri "Hellman" Kabayenkov. Vrublevsky denies playing an active role in Rx-Promotion, but according to emails leaked from ChronoPay, Vrublevsky had a meeting with Rx-Partners' Leo Kuvayev and Kuvayev's partner—Vladislav Khokholkov—to discuss Rx-Promotion's participation in the still nascent cartel. In the leaked emails, Vrublevsky claims to have declined participating in the cartel, but said that Mailien, SpamIt, and another large program—EvaPharmacy—had agreed to set price controls on drugs and to cap affiliate commissions at 40 percent.

Chat logs that Russian investigators eventually seized from Stupin's computer suggest that the cartel worked assiduously to win over EvaPharmacy. Below is a transcript of a chat between Stupin and representatives of Eva (also known as "Bulker.biz"). Their chat has been translated from Russian into English.

> STUPIN: I don't like the conditions we give to adverts. Some of them demand 45 percent. We suffer from it because of low prices, plus some of them are asking to lower hold to one week. I want to straighten them up and pay more to myself than to them ;) We do not offer less than two-week hold

to anyone. Simply because of delays in payments from Shaman and the islands (off-shore), our account balances are going down.[9] I am not asking you about anything, just saying that you also can set a minimum hold to two weeks and then adverts will not have a choice, because we will offer similar conditions. I also think that it is going to be easier for you to pay with the hold time than without it, because if adverts raise production, you need to keep too much cash in banks. In summary, my utopia is a cartel agreement to lower advert commissions to 30 to 35 percent, similar to the payoffs of Western affiliation programs.

BULKER.BIZ: We also have two weeks of hold. However, we do exclude our best adverts [from that restriction]. You forced a lot of our adverts to switch to you by lowering your prices. Therefore, we have no other choice ;) To have an agreement is a great idea, yet for it to work, it needs to include Mailien and others. Otherwise, spammers will continue to run to them. Surely, 45 percent is just outrageous! The partnerka earns three times less because of that!

---

9.   The name "Shaman" in this chat conversation is a reference to the nickname of Nikolai Victorovich Illin, the forty-three-year-old computer whiz behind Gateline.net. Gateline was a credit card processor that SpamIt, GlavMed, Rx-Promotion, and other partnerkas apparently prized for its ability to process MasterCard transactions. Stupin and Gusev considered Shaman a key and equal partner in their business.

STUPIN: Yes, and the only argument for asking for 45 percent, is that Eva pays that much ;)

BULKER.BIZ: Some people pay even 50 percent and are killing the market even more. I also want to say that I know which advert you are talking about. He does not have a hold at all, but it does not mean that he costs us the entire balance every day.

STUPIN: I know, he told me everything.

BULKER.BIZ: Listen, we are willing to strike an agreement and to establish the same conditions with adverts, but only after we test new suppliers and are able to lower our prices to match or to be close to yours, only when our competitive conditions are similar.

According to Vishnevsky, who was active in the development of the Cutwail botnet, the findings by the UCSD researchers show that about a handful of affiliates generating the bulk of the revenue for partnerka programs are accurate. Vishnevsky said very few affiliates who did not already own significant spamming resources could expect to make much money because of the costs involved in creating those.

The most expensive part of any spamming operation is the process of procuring the bots used to relay junk email. Almost without exception, the top-earning affiliates ran their own very large botnets, crime machines that they used to send their own spam and that were rented out to other affiliates.

Vishnevsky said affiliates who rent botnet resources from other spammers frequently do so by purchasing "installs," or seeding a prearranged number of bots with an additional malicious program that sends spam for the affiliate. Affiliates who rent bots from fellow affiliates often will pay for those resources by simply diverting a share of their commissions on each sale from spam generated by the rented bots. Very often, Vishnevsky said, botmasters would demand up to 50 percent of an affiliate customer's commissions.

But a proper spam-spewing network consists of much more than just bots. If we compare a spam network to a factory, the bots can be thought of as the machinery responsible for assembling the component parts of the product for sale. And a spam botnet is only as effective as the software that directs the day-to-day activities of that machinery. Modern PCs are extremely powerful systems, but they can quickly become overwhelmed if too many operations are demanded of them simultaneously. Decent spam software distributes the workload across thousands of infected machines, ensuring that individual PCs aren't being overpowered by more work than they can handle.

At the same time, good spam software is responsible for keeping track of how many emails were successfully delivered and how many recipients clicked through to the advertised site. The software also is expected to automatically delete or "scrub" from spam lists any email addresses that are no longer active or that refuse to accept incoming email. Spammers often "spoof" or fake the address in the "From:" section of a junk email, and when spam messages are sent to inactive inboxes, the messages frequently bounce back not to the spammers but to the unwitting person whose email address was used to spoof the email's origin! (No doubt you may have been on the receiving end of one of these from a friend, colleague, or relative whose email account was hacked or spoofed.) Emails that bounce like this prompt confused and concerned Internet users to complain to their Internet or email providers, or both, which in turn may enact more stringent measures to block such wayward messages in the future.

Finally, an affiliate who doesn't already have decent email lists will have to buy them from someone else, if he cannot write his own program to continuously harvest new email addresses from random websites.

According to Vishnevsky, an affiliate can expect to spend 20 to 30 percent of his income on renting software and email lists.

"It should not be surprising that most spammers do not make much money if they have to rent all of these things," he said.

It's impossible to say how much organizations worldwide spend fighting junk email sent by the likes of affiliates of Rx-Promotion, GlavMed, and SpamIt, but it is almost certainly many, many times more than the profits eked out by the administrators and founders of those programs.

What's mind-boggling is that when the UCSD researchers calculated the direct and indirect costs of these programs during an eleven-month period between May 2009 and April 2010, they found that the net profit for these programs was about 20 percent of gross revenue.

"What's fascinating about all this is that at the end of the day, we're not talking about all that much money," said UCSD's Savage. "These guys running the pharma programs are not Donald Trumps, yet their activity is going to have real and substantial financial impact on the day-to-day lives of tens of millions of people. In other words, for these guys to make modest riches, we need a multibillion-dollar security industry to deal with them."

Savage and his research team also had a chance to review many of the leaked chats between Gusev and his business partner Stupin, and said the conversations were replete with examples of how these guys were constantly looking for ways to add value to their consumer offerings. Guys like the SpamIt administrators succeeded because they understood their core market: selling discreetly delivered and affordable products—from online porn to penis pills—that many adults would be ashamed to buy otherwise.

At one point, the chats show that Stupin and Gusev considered using their spam infrastructure to promote a far more question-able consumer product: penis-extending devices.

"This is by far the funniest conversation in the whole collec-tion," Savage recalled. "It's basically Gusev fighting with Stupin over whether or not they should add penis-extender devices to their online shops. Gusev is totally into the idea. He's like, 'Yeah, Americans really want to add inches,' but Stupin is unconvinced. And that's the thing I try to explain to people [based on] all of our research into this bizarre underground economy.

"The pharma and spam guys don't fundamentally think of themselves as criminals at all. I think their mental model is that they're selling a quality product to an audience that is demanding it. Yes, there may be some laws in their way, but those laws are tools of a Western power structure and bourgeois intellectual-property bullcrap, and it's just The Man getting in the way of their marketplace."

◆   ◆   ◆

If Savage is correct—that partnerkas represent "disorganized cybercrime"—then the role of creating and maintaining order from all of this criminal chaos falls to the cybercrime forums. These are online communities where most spammers, scammers, and fraudsters meet, transact, earn, and maintain a "trustworthy" reputation in the underground.

Cybercrime forums serve a number of core purposes. For starters, they offer relatively unknown and novice criminals an opportunity to establish a reputation as a trusted, reliable vendor or buyer of services. If these newbies wish to construct a new cybercrime operation—such as a spam botnet—but lack the knowledge or resources to build up a particular component of that business, they can simply purchase the missing components or information from other members. Or, they can turn to senior members and self-help tutorials on these forums for pointers and questions.

In this way, crime forums almost universally help lower the barriers to entry for would-be cybercriminals. Crime forums also offer crooks with disparate skills a place to market and test their services and wares, and in turn, to buy ill-gotten goods and services from others.

There are forums dedicated to almost every major language and specialization of cybercrime, but most crime forums are either in

Russian or English. Likewise, most are built upon a similar structure of a main homepage with links to sub-forums dedicated to a broad array of cybercrime specialties, including: spam; online banking fraud; bank account "cashout" schemes; malicious software development; identity theft; credit card fraud; confidence scams; and black SEO, or techniques to fraudulently manipulate a site's rankings in Google and other Internet search engines.

Even forums dedicated to a specific form of cybercrime—such as spam—tend to model themselves on this same sub-forum structure. In 2011, researchers at the University of California, Santa Barbara, and Ruhr-University Bochum in Germany published an in-depth analysis of the Cutwail botnet, "The Underground Economy of Spam: A Botmaster's Perspective of Coordinating Large-Scale Spam Campaigns." In the course of their investigation, the researchers acquired the back-end database of the now-defunct crime forum Spamdot.biz, a closely guarded cybercrime community, and ultimately agreed to share the site's complete information with me for research for this book. In 2007, Spamdot came under the ownership of Igor Gusev and Dmitry Stupin, the coadministrators of the sister pharmacy partnerkas GlavMed and SpamIt.

It was clear from this material that while Spamdot counted among its members some of the world's most established and successful spammers, it also included dozens of members whose primary specialty was offering ancillary cybercrime services, from providing bulletproof web hosting and the mass registration of domain names, to selling huge email spam lists and software to help spammers "scrub" their existing lists of dead addresses and those used by anti-spam activists and security firms.

These activists frequently seed the Internet with dummy email addresses in the hopes that spammers will find and spam the addresses. Both vigilantes and security firms then use the spam sent to these dummy addresses to collect samples of the latest malicious software or phishing scams being distributed via junk email. These help gauge the size and location of major spam botnets, and from there, these anti-spammers can generally improve the performance of spam filters. But since these activities eventually tend to cut into the profitability and stability of any spamming operation, more experienced spammers recognize the long-term value in scrubbing their distribution lists of these decoy addresses. It's a constant game of cat and mouse.

Sub-forums tend to be moderated by established cybercrooks who are proficient in their respective specialization. It is not unusual to see the same cybercriminal acting as the moderator of the same sub-forum across multiple, distinct cybercrime forums. For example, an infamous Russian fraudster known as "Severa" acts or has acted as the moderator of the spam sub-forum on at least four different major cybercrime forums, including Spamdot. As will be further described in "Chapter 7: Meet the Spammers," Severa is the author of some of the most prolific and "successful" spam botnets that have ever been created. As a result, Severa knows virtually everyone of consequence in the spam industry and has a broad cross-section of knowledge about the topic that makes him ideally suited to moderate discussion forums dedicated to the subject.

Actors such as Severa are the living "glue" holding these cybercrime communities together. They possess a wealth of knowledge about their industry and are adept at connecting novices with more experienced members looking for partners or subcontractors. As such, core miscreants like Severa present attractive targets for law-enforcement officials, since taking them out can often destabilize the fraud ecosystem.

Many crime forums—particularly new, fledgling forums—allow open registration, accepting all comers. But forums populated by some of the most experienced and connected cybercrooks tend to erect various hurdles for new members designed to screen out useful and talented hackers from hangers-on or, worse, possible law-enforcement officials attempting to infiltrate and gather evidence of these spammers' illicit activities. To create these safeguards, most established crime forums require new applicants to list at least two existing and trusted forum members as references or "vouches," signaling that one or more existing members of the forum can vouch for the applicant's skills and integrity and have invited the novice to apply for membership.

New applicants generally also must proffer a nonrefundable deposit, usually in the form of a digital currency such as WebMoney or bitcoins. Assuming the applicant's references confirm that members know him and can vouch for his skills, the applicant is granted limited access to the forum, which he can then use to introduce himself to the broader community, plead his case for membership, and list any unique talents that his full membership would bring to the forum.

Existing members may use this trial period to haze or verbally abuse the applicant, or to test his knowledge of programming, hacking, or skill sets related to his claimed area of interest or speciality. This weeds out the weakest novices. In the end, however, many forums are democratic, leaving the approval of an appli- cant's permanent membership to a vote in which all established members may—but are not required to—participate.

So what's the incentive to join these forums and why are they so popular among spammers? Much like a castle once provided its inhabitants with protection from marauding raiders and bandits, crime forums offer full members a modicum of protection (or at least cause of action) against getting ripped off. Fraudsters are particularly vulnerable to being cheated out on their own because they lack the ability to report being victimized to local authorities. After all, the transactions in which they engage are in most cases illegal. To combat any such "ripping" activity, forums enforce a strict code of ethics so that members caught trying to cheat fellow members are quickly ostracized or banned.

For starters, most established forums will offer an escrow service—a small percentage of the transaction cost—that will hold the buyer's funds until he is satisfied that the seller upheld his part of the bargain. Legitimate and longtime forum members tend to insist on the use of escrow for all transactions, while cheapskates and less experienced members eschew this offering at their own risk.

Much like the online auction house eBay encouraging users to leave positive or negative feedback based on the quality of the transactions they conduct with other members, a fraud forum member's standing is governed in part by the number of reputa- tion or "rep" points he has accrued during his time on the forum. Members can earn rep points simply by being regular, active participants in various forums' discussion threads—essentially sharing their knowledge and experience on a range of computer crime topics. The rep points are awarded or subtracted by established forum members and moderators who have earned the right to bestow or revoke such status indicators.

This system is remarkably effective at regulating the criminal acts of these crooks against each other. Aleksey Mikhaylov, a native Russian and information security expert who has exhaustively reviewed the documents, chats, and other material leaked from the Spamdot forum, said that the threat of a single negative post on the forum prompts these guys to amicably resolve issues worth tens of thousands of dollars. Access to the forum and their "standing" there preoccupies all of them. Without the protection and accountability afforded by these criminal havens, spammers, scammers, and other online ne'er-do-wells are at much greater risk of getting fleeced by their contemporaries.

Members judged by forum administrators as guilty of multiple or serious forum rule infractions may be assigned the rank of "deer," or even the more serious "ripper" label. A deer marker usually is an indicator of a new member who has violated the forum rules by accident, or because he isn't yet familiar enough with them. Forum members who earn a deer status tend to be considered clueless newbies, their status alerting fellow forum members that dealing with them might be more trouble than it's worth.

Rippers are those who have been shown to have "ripped" someone off by failing to consummate a previously agreed-upon transaction—either by refusing to pay for a service or good, or by neglecting to deliver on these as promised. The aggrieved party must demonstrate to forum administrators that he or she was ripped, typically by starting a discussion thread in a sub-forum called "blacklist." Very often this means posting lengthy online chat records of a previous conversation that document the alleged infraction. Interestingly, these self-reported records can often present invaluable evidence and intelligence to undercover law-enforcement officials and security researchers who frequently lurk on underground crime forums.

Although the average crime forum has many members—sometimes tens of thousands—most of the more active forums exist to make money for the administrators, the subforum leaders, and those selling turnkey services or solutions to the rest of the community. The top sellers pay to have their sales threads made into "stickies" so that the sales pitches stay at the top of their respective sub-forums and are thus more likely to be to read by people seeking help in those cybercrime specializations. Depending on the forum, these stickies are sold annually or monthly, and range in price from a hundred to thousands of dollars per month.

Over the past few years, the number of new cybercrime forums has skyrocketed, illustrating a burgeoning demand for criminal services and a robust competition among them for customers. And while many new crime communities disappear or fizzle out shortly after their creation, others are now more than a decade old, suggesting that the cybercrime industry is quite mature, each marketplace with its own unique means of self-policing, networking, and rapid information sharing.

Attempts by anti-spam activists to shutter the more mature of these cybercrime communities—usually by applying pressure to their hosting providers or domain registrars, or both—ultimately backfire. The forums simply transfer their domains to another, more bulletproof and insulated hosting provider, often enacting more stringent security measures in the process that more carefully screen new and existing members for signs of lurkers, law-enforcement officials, and researchers.

But there's hope: Some of the most successful efforts at tackling the spam and malware epidemics have focused on identifying and apprehending the world's top spammers and dismantling their crime machines, as we'll see in the next chapter and in "Chapter 11: Takedown."

Chapter 7

MEET THE SPAMMERS

Igor Vishnevsky wouldn't have known where or how to get started in the spamming business had it not been for the connections he made spending countless hours on several major cybercrime forums at the time. At nineteen years old, he enrolled at a university in Moscow and had dreams of landing a job as a programmer at a legitimate company. But soon enough, the money dried up.

"I studied three years, and then my parents stopped paying for my education because they didn't have money," Vishnevsky said in an interview.

What little Vishnevsky knew of computers dated back to his time as a teenager, when his parents bought him a Sinclair ZX Spectrum, an early home computer that was among the first mainstream home computers sold in Europe. In his early years, Vishnevsky taught himself everything from BASIC to more complex assembly programming languages. Later, he acquired a secondhand PC and learned PASCAL, a programming language designed to teach students how to devise more complex software programs.

The clever young hacker was making between $200 and $300 per month creating porn websites as part of an affiliate program run by Vrublevsky's Crutop.nu. But that was hardly enough to live on in Moscow, so he took a job at a local company that sold heating and air-conditioning equipment and services. Little did he know that would lead to spamming.

One day his boss asked for help in advertising the company's services via some less-than-legitimate means.

"One time, my boss ordered spam from someone and told me that it was cool and that I should find out how to send spam myself," Vishnevsky recalled. "Of course, I told him that spam was bad, blah, blah, blah, but he told me that we had a lack of orders and I have to do that [in order to drum up more business]."

Vishnevsky's research for his boss into the spam industry led him to Carderplanet.com, which at the time was an extremely popular Russian language cybercrime forum. Carderplanet drew thousands of members from around the world who traded knowledge and tips on everything from running spam botnets to cashing out hacked bank and credit card accounts.

Founded in Ukraine in 2001, Carderplanet.com was the most brazen collection of carders (crooks who traffic in stolen credit cards) hackers, and cyberthieves the Internet had ever seen. As Joe Menn writes in his book, *Fatal System Error*, there was virtually no enforcement of computer intrusion laws in Ukraine, so the group felt secure enough to organize parties and to advertise their hacking services on the larger Internet. Carderplanet would come to be the mold out of which nearly every future crime forum would be modeled, with sub-forums for every imaginable form of computer crime specialization.

It was on Carderplanet that Vishnevsky was introduced to Vardan Kushnir, a thirty-five-year-old notorious spammer who ran the American Language Center (ALC), a legitimate business in Moscow that taught English to Russian nationals. Kushnir offered to help get Vishnevsky started in spamming if he would agree, in turn, to use some of his resources to send junk email advertising the services of the ALC.

"He offered me money enough to rent servers, and soon I was making four times as much as the climate company was paying," Vishnevsky said. "But I continued to work there because I was not sure that spam was a stable source of money. Within a couple of months I was already quite good with spam."

Through spamming for his mentor Kushnir, Vishnevsky was introduced to Dmitry "Gugle" Nechvolod.

"Gugle was Vardan's friend, and he was always coming to him discussing different shit," Vishnevsky said. "At some point, I started to communicate with [Gugle], too."

But Vishnevsky's real break came after his spamming mentor was suddenly and brutally murdered. One morning, Kushnir's mother found her son's bloodied corpse on her bathroom floor, his skull bashed in. As detailed in a 2007 story in Wired.com, Kushnir's spam operation sent more than twenty-five million unsolicited junk messages each day, most of them pimping the ALC's services and sent to Russian inboxes. According to Wired and Vishnevsky, Kushnir's blatant and repeated disregard for complaints about spam pimping the ALC may have been a primary contributor to his murder.

Undeterred by Kushnir's gruesome death, Vishnevsky and Gugle pooled their resources and started their own spam business.

By October 2011, I decided there was enough information in the leaked SpamIt and Rx-Promotion data to begin identifying and profiling the world's top spammers, and by extension those responsible for building and maintaining the largest spam botnets. Buried within the gigabytes of internal ChronoPay documents was a Microsoft Excel spreadsheet innocuously titled "Registration data" that would become the Rosetta Stone for identifying many of these miscreants.

When I compared the information in this spreadsheet with other earnings and contact information I'd already gathered from the leaked SpamIt data, it was clear that for unknown reasons, someone at ChronoPay had compiled this list about the most active spammers. Most of the spammers for both Rx-Promotion and SpamIt were paid via WebMoney, which, as mentioned, is a virtual currency like PayPal that is popular in Russia and Eastern Europe and widely used in the hacker underground.

WebMoney accounts can be set up under pseudonyms or as merchant accounts, or they can be formally attested. The latter two types of accounts require the applicant to show a copy of his passport at an authorized WebMoney location prior to obtaining attestation for that account. This account information is not listed publicly by WebMoney, but it appears that a ChronoPay employee paid an insider at WebMoney to divulge the name and other contact information tied to each account used by top SpamIt affiliates. As it turns out, many of those individuals also spammed for Rx-Promotion.

Of the 163 WebMoney accounts listed in that spreadsheet, roughly one-third of them were formally attested or were merchant accounts. The data included in the spreadsheet showed the affiliate's WebMoney ID, name, address, phone number, date of birth, email address, passport number, and the street address of the government office that issued the passport.

Many of these WebMoney accounts had been set up years before their owners began spamming or participating in any cybercrime activity. But one in particular caught my eye. Among the attested accounts detailed in the spreadsheet was a WebMoney purse created in January 2002 to a user who provided the account alias "Software Seller." This account was credited with more than $175,000 for promoting pharmacy websites for SpamIt. That was where I would start.

Gugle

It took many weeks of digging through countless leaked chat records between this user—who used the nickname "Gugle" on both ICQ instant message chat and as a nickname on Spamdot. biz—and the administrators of the SpamIt pharmacy partnerka. Ultimately, I was able to determine that this was the same individual who ran the Cutwail botnet, easily the largest and most active spam botnet at the time. (It remains quite active.)

The spreadsheet entry for the corresponding WebMoney ID next to the botmaster named Gugle listed a Dmitry Sergeyvich Nechvolod, born July 9, 1983, and living in Moscow. When I saw Nechvolod's information in that document, something in it reminded me of a conversation that I'd had with Vrublevsky earlier in the year. I didn't realize the significance of that discussion at the time, because I didn't quite understand Gugle's role then.

It was late 2010, and Vrublevsky had just called me and was excitedly relaying some intelligence that he'd gleaned from his network of law-enforcement contacts. He'd received word that cybercrime investigators with the U.S. National Aeronautics and Space Administration (NASA) were coming to Moscow to meet with Russian FSB agents. The NASA officials, who have guns and badges and just as much investigative authority as other U.S. law-enforcement agencies, were coming to discuss cooperating with Russian authorities over an investigation into Nechvolod.

By that time, NASA investigators had connected the dots between Nechvolod and Gugle, and had been building a criminal case against him for allegedly infecting countless NASA computers with Cutwail malware.

"The Americans came to Moscow trying to find the Cutwail owner, who goes by the nickname 'Gugle,'" Vrublevsky told me excitedly and proudly in a phone interview, speaking of a man who was among the top spammers for both Rx-Promotion and SpamIt. "They got his nickname and even his real name correct, but they were never able to catch him. Honestly, I think someone warned him. You know, Brian, the corruption level in Russian law enforcement related to cybercrime is really quite high."

I'm still not sure why Vrublevsky told me all of this. Perhaps it was to brag that he was so well-connected to Russian cyber law-enforcement officers that he could help save one of Rx-Promotion's best spammers from being delivered into the arms of American federal agents. I believe Vrublevsky also wanted the NASA investigators to know he'd played them for fools. After all, these same NASA investigators had convinced the U.S. Federal Trade Commission to unplug the bulletproof hosting provider 3FN, a disconnection that caused much trouble and expense for Vrublevsky and his network of extreme adult webmasters, and fake antivirus and spam peddlers.

According to a source who helped work that investigation with NASA, Vrublevsky had been given advance notice of the visit by corrupt FSB agents. Days before the scheduled meeting between NASA and the FSB, Nechvolod fled Russia for Ukraine.

"Gugle and Pavel were business partners and friends," said my law-enforcement source at NASA, speaking on condition of anonymity because he was not authorized to discuss the case. "It was Pavel who tipped off Gugle that [NASA] was meeting with the FSB about Cutwail. Gugle is reportedly in Ukraine now, lying low."

According to the website of Russian software firm Digital Infinity Developers Group, Nechvolod was part of a team of elite programmers that could be hired out for jobs at diginf.ru. The Diginf Team page on that site (now defunct) listed Dmitry Nechvolod as an "administrator of UNIX-based systems," an "administrator of Cisco routers," and "a specialist in information security software." Between Nechvolod's expertise and that of his team, it is clear from reviewing their résumés that this group of programmers could hack their way in or around virtually any communications or security system.

Nechvolod's cadre maintained a core version of the Cutwail

bot code and rented it out to other miscreants on underground forums, where the spamming system was known as "0bulk Psyche Evolution."

In many ways, Nechvolod is the poster child for the modern cybercriminal, a profession not unlike drug dealing in that it generates a constant stream of cash. Those illicit funds need to be either laundered by investing in properties or other hard assets, or spent. Nechvolod, like many of his peers, preferred to splurge on a lavish and fast lifestyle of fast cars, fast girls, nice clothes, and drugs, Vishnevsky said.

"He always dressed very nice, and when he wrecked his $100,000 Lexus sedan, he went and bought a brand-new BMW," Vishnevsky said.

By 2008, Nechvolod's spam business was booming. His Cutwail botnet had grown to more than 125,000 infected computers and was able to blast out sixteen billion spam messages daily. Soon enough, his company's growth forced him to find and hire several new programmers. To give you a sense of what he was looking for, below is an ad that he posted to Crutop.nu, seeking a talented programmer experienced in building web applications.

Job type: local office in Moscow (benefits package included), full-time (9 hours per day, 5 days a week).

REQUIREMENTS:
- Excellent knowledge of Perl and PHP
- Excellent knowledge of SQL

- Knowledge of AJAX, JavaScript
- The ability to quickly write scripts without bugs
- At least 22 years of age
- Responsibility

The salary for a probationary period $1.5K (1 month), after—$2K +.

A full-time salary—with benefits—and opportunities for advancement. What enterprising young coder could ask for more? And while $23,500 a year would be a very good salary for a junior programmer living in Moscow, it was an absolute dream for coders from the countryside who could convince the boss to let them telecommute. Nechvolod's job offer is yet another illustration of how cybercrime businesses in some parts of the world are in direct competition with many legitimate companies in the search for talented programmers.

Cosma

The records leaked from both GlavMed-SpamIt and Rx-Promotion show that one of both partnerkas' most successful spammers was a hacker who used a variety of nicknames, including "Cosma," "Tarelka," "Bird," and "Adv1." Cosma, as we'll call him here for simplicity's sake, and all of his affiliated accounts with SpamIt earned more than $3 million in commissions over three years with the pharmacy program.

His spam machine was the Rustock botnet, a malware strain

that was first unleashed onto the Internet in 2006. The botnet's name was derived from its initial purpose: to help perpetrate a form of securities fraud known as "pump-and-dump" stock scams. In such schemes, fraudsters buy up a bunch of low-priced micro-cap stock (the prices usually vary from a fraction of a penny to a few cents per share), blast out millions of spam emails touting the stock as a hot buy, and then dump their shares as soon as the share price ticks up from all the suckers buying into the scam.

In 2007, researchers began noticing that PCs infected with Rustock had started sending pharmacy spam in addition to pump-and-dump emails. Experts at Dell SecureWorks estimated around that time that Rustock had infected more than 150,000 PCs and was capable of spewing as many as thirty billion spam messages per day.

The emergence of pharmacy spam from Rustock coincides with the time that Cosma signed up as an affiliate with SpamIt. Those same three affiliate names that the Rustock botmaster used with SpamIt—Cosma2k, Bird, and Adv1—also were registered using the same ICQ account at Vrublevsky's Rx-Promotion. Leaked ChronoPay data shows that these three accounts collectively earned approximately $200,000 in commissions by promoting pharmacy websites for Rx-Promotion in 2010.

In several chats, Cosma muses on what he should do with tens of thousands of compromised but otherwise idle PCs under his control. Throughout the discussions between Stupin and Cosma, it is clear Cosma had access to internal SpamIt resources that other spammers did not, and that he had at least some say in the direction of the business.

In one conversation, dated October 14, 2008, Cosma tells Stupin that he's decided to dial back his public image a few notches after attracting unwanted attention from other crooks. Cosma tells Stupin he was mugged and held hostage by thugs who'd targeted him because of his late-model Porsche Cayenne, a sport utility vehicle that costs considerably more than $100,000 in Moscow. After being roughed up by his captors, Cosma relinquished the keys to his Porsche. Cosma laments to Stupin that as a result of that incident, he decided to replace his stolen Cayenne with a less flashy BMW 530xi.

Cosma left behind a number of clues about his real-life identity. He registered with the SpamIt program using the email address ger-mes@ger-mes.ru. That website disappeared in 2010, but a cached copy of the site shows that its homepage previously featured some very interesting information. It included a job résumé for a Belarusian-educated programmer underneath a picture of a brown-haired young man holding a mug. Above the image was the name "Sergeev, Dmitri A." At the very top of the page was a simple message: "I want to work in Google." Beneath the résumé is the author's email address, followed by the message, "Waiting for your job!"

If the thugs who stole Cosma's Porsche had known who he was, they might have handed him over to Microsoft. In July 2011, Microsoft offered a standing $250,000 reward for information leading to the arrest and conviction of the Rustock botmaster. Cosma remains at large.

Severa

Cosma ran his stock spam business in tandem with that of another cybercrook, a hacker who uses the nickname "Severa." This spammer was named as a defendant in an indictment handed down by a U.S. federal court in 2007 as a major partner of Alan Ralsky, an American spammer who was convicted in 2009 of paying Severa and other spammers to promote the pump-and-dump stock scams. But while Severa was indicted, he was never arrested, and his case is still pending. Partially, this is because he appears to still be in Russia, a country that traditionally hasn't extradited alleged cybercriminals to stand trial in the United States or Europe.

Severa's spam machine was powered by a sophisticated computer worm known as "Waledac." This contagion first surfaced in April 2008, but many experts believe that Waledac was merely an update to the Storm worm, the engine behind a massive spam botnet that first surfaced in 2007.

Waledac and Storm were major distributors of pharmaceutical and malware spam. At its peak, Waledac was responsible for sending 1.5 billion junk emails per day. According to Microsoft, in one month alone approximately 651 million spam emails attributable to Waledac were directed to Hotmail accounts, including offers and scams related to online pharmacies, imitation goods, jobs, penny stocks, and more. The Storm worm botnet also sent billions of messages daily and infected an estimated one million computers worldwide.

Both Waledac and Storm were hugely innovative because they each included self-defense mechanisms designed specifically to stymie security researchers who might try to dismantle the crime machines. Traditional botnets are controlled by Internet servers that can be shuttered just like McColo or Atrivo. But Waledac and Storm sent updates and other instructions via a peer-to-peer communications system not unlike popular music and file-sharing services. The beauty of this approach is that even if security researchers or law-enforcement officials manage to seize the botnet's back-end control servers and clean up huge numbers of infected PCs, the botnets could respawn themselves by relaying software updates from one infected PC to another.

According to SpamIt records, Severa brought in revenues of $438,000 and earned commissions of $145,000 sending spam advertising for rogue online pharmacy sites over a three-year period. He also was a moderator of Spamdot.biz.

Severa made more money renting his botnet to other spammers. For $200, vetted users could hire his botnet to send one million pieces of spam. Junk email campaigns touting employment or "money mule" scams cost $300 per million, and phishing emails could be blasted out through Severa's botnet for the bargain price of $500 per million.

There is ample evidence in the leaked SpamIt chats that Severa controlled the Waledac spam botnet. On August 27, 2009, Severa sent a private message to a Spamdot.biz user named "IP-server." Those communications show that the latter had sold Severa access to so-called "bulletproof hosting" services that would stand up to repeated abuse claims from other Internet service providers (ISPs). The messages indicate that Severa transacted with IP-server to purchase dedicated servers used to control the operations of the Waledac botnet.

In the private message, Severa wrote to IP-server (translated from Russian): "Hello, writing to your ICQ, you are not responding. One of the servers has been down for 5 hours. The one ending on .171. What's the problem, is it coming up or not, and when?" Severa then pasted an error message sent by the problematic web server. IP-server must have resolved the outage, because the Internet address that Severa was complaining about—193.27.246.171— would be flagged a day later by malware analysts and tagged as a control server for the Waledac botnet.

The federal indictment lists Severa's name as "Peter Severa," but this last name may be a pseudonym. According to anti-spam activists at Spamhaus.org, Severa's real name is Peter Levashov.[10]

Why should anyone care who Severa really is? Much like his close associate—Cosma, the Rustock botmaster—Severa may also have a $250,000 bounty on his head. The Conficker worm, a global contagion launched in 2009 that quickly spread to an estimated nine to fifteen million computers worldwide, prompted an unprecedented international response from security experts. This group of experts, dubbed the "Conficker Cabal," sought in vain to corral the spread of the worm.

But despite infecting huge numbers of Microsoft Windows systems, Conficker was never once used to send spam. In fact, the only thing that Conficker-infected systems ever did was download

---

10.   I contacted Severa using the instant messenger address that he provides on multiple cybercrime forums on which he is a global moderator for discussions about junk email and spam services. The person answering messages on that address said he didn't know any Severa, that he'd never used botnets for mass mailing campaigns, and that he only conducted small, targeted email campaigns for clients.

and spread a new version of the Waledac botnet. Later that year, Microsoft announced it was offering a $250,000 reward for information leading to the arrest and conviction of the Conficker author(s). Some security experts believe this proves a link between Severa and Conficker.

Severa and Cosma had met one another several times in their years together in the stock spamming business, and they appear to have known each other intimately enough to be on a first-name basis. Included in the archived Spamdot.biz records that were leaked to me is a series of private messages exchanged between Cosma and Severa on May 25 and May 26, 2010. In it, Severa refers to Cosma as "Dimas," a familiar form of "Dmitri." Likewise, Cosma addresses Severa as "Petka," a common Russian diminutive of "Peter."

Both Severa and Cosma remain free and quite active in the spam and malware scene. Severa is still the spam subforum administrator on several underground forums, pimping his spam services, remarkably under most of the same prices he offered them for in 2008. The spam botnets that Severa maintains continue to inundate inboxes with junk email promoting fly-by-night products and spreading malicious software.

GeRa

According to the leaked SpamIt data, the second most successful affiliate in the program was a member nicknamed "GeRa." Over a three-year period, GeRa's advertisements and those of his referrals resulted in at least 80,000 sales of knockoff pharmaceuticals, brought SpamIt revenues of in excess of $6 million, and earned him and his pals more than $2.7 million.

A variety of data suggest that GeRa is the lead hacker behind Grum, a spam botnet that could send more than eighteen billion emails a day prior to its takedown in 2012.

GeRa and Stupin chatted online by ICQ almost every day, usually because GeRa was complaining that some portion of his spamming infrastructure wasn't working properly. In fact, Stupin would remark that GeRa was by far the most bothersome of all the program's top spammers, telling a fellow SpamIt administrator that "neither Docent [Mega-D botmaster] nor Cosma [Rustock botmaster] can compare with him in terms of trouble with hosting providers."

Several of the leaked Stupin chats show GeRa pointing out issues with specific Internet addresses that would later be flagged as control servers for the Grum botnet. For example, in a chat with Stupin on June 11, 2008, GeRa posts a link to the address 206.51.234.136. Then after checking the server, he proceeds to tell Stupin how many infected PCs were phoning home to that address at the time. That same server has long been identified as a Grum botnet controller.

By this time, Grum had grown to such an established threat that it was named in the "Top Spam Botnets Exposed" paper released by Dell SecureWorks researcher Joe Stewart. On April 13, 2008—just five days after Stewart's analysis was released—GeRa would post a link to it into a chat with Stupin, saying "Haha, I am also on the list!"

The chats between GeRa and Stupin show that at some point GeRa defected from working with SpamIt to spam for

Rx-Promotion. Researchers from the University of California, San Diego (UCSD) who studied the leaked Rx-Promotion affiliate data noted that all Rx-Promotion pharmacy sites included a "site_id" in their source code, which uniquely identified the store for later assigning advertising commissions. The researchers discovered that whenever Grum advertised an Rx-Promotion site, this identifier was always the same: 1811. According to the leaked Rx-Promotion database, that affiliate ID belongs to a user named "gera."

"It doesn't prove that GeRa owned Grum," said Stefan Savage, a professor in the systems and networking group at UCSD and coauthor of the study. "But it does show that when Grum advertised for Rx-Promotion, it was for sites where commissions were paid to someone whose nickname was 'GeRa.'"

According to payment records leaked from GlavMed and Rx-Promotion, GeRa received commission payments for all of those accounts to a WebMoney purse with the ID number 112024718270. According to a source who has the ability to look up identity information attached to WebMoney accounts, that purse was set up in 2006 by someone who walked into a WebMoney office in Moscow and presented a Russian passport. The name on the passport was that of a twenty-six-year-old named Nikolai Alekseevich Kostogryz. (My attempts to contact Kostogryz to confirm if GeRa was indeed him or if his identity had been stolen were unsuccessful.)

Stupin's chat records and GeRa's private messages on Spamdot. biz reveal a belligerent, argumentative hacker who seemed to be perpetually angry about getting screwed over by someone. GeRa had a long-running feud with FTPFire, a SpamIt member that he referred to the program. In one of his conversations with Stupin, GeRa stated that he wanted to find the guy and "take care" of him in "the Italian way." He told Stupin that he had some police officers on his payroll and had asked them to locate FTPFire.

GeRa also said he was robbed of $30,000 when a rogue antivirus partnerka he was working with folded. That criminal outfit, called BakaSoftware, was in the scareware racket, inundating victims with increasingly alarmist warnings about security threats and viruses on his or her PC. These warnings would continue until the victim either paid to license mostly useless security software or figured out a way to remove the invasive program.[11]

Although it is unclear if GeRa is still active in the spam scene, his contribution to the junk email world lives on. The source code for his Grum botnet has been sold to several other spammers who have apparently modified it for their own purposes and are currently using it to blast junk email.

Engel

Few botmasters were as angry and as vindictive as "Engel," the nickname chosen by the convicted Russian spammer named Igor A. Artimovich, and his brother, Dmitry. Engel allegedly maintained the Festi botnet and, for a time, spammed for both Rx-Promotion and SpamIt. But in 2009, a series of incidents and altercations between himself and the SpamIt administrators would turn him forever against the SpamIt program and make him a

---

11. It's worth noting that BakaSoftware's core credit-card processor was ChronoPay.

close ally of Pavel Vrublevsky. Ironically, that alliance would eventually lead to Vrublevsky's and Rx-Promotion's undoing.[12]

First spotted in autumn 2009, Festi quickly became a potent threat on the botnet scene. According to ESET, a Slovakian antivirus and security firm, Festi was at the time among the most powerful and active botnets for sending spam and for launching distributed denial of service (DDoS) attacks. A vocal and often combative member on the Spamdot.biz forum, Engel referred to his botnet as "Topol Mailer." That moniker was an oblique reference to the Russian-made intercontinental ballistic missile known as Topol-M, an apt nickname for a botnet that once delivered a third of all spam to inboxes around the globe, but principally to Americans.

Engel's profile on Spamdot.biz listed his email address as "support@id-search.org." That domain is no longer online, but archive.org reveals that Engel used it as the home base for a bot whose sole purpose was to harvest email addresses from billions of web pages. Engel claimed publicly that the bot was nothing more than a research project, but he bragged privately to Spamdot members that his search bot could scour hundreds of sites simultaneously and quickly collect "hundreds of megabytes" of email lists.

Early in his work for SpamIt, Engel began to suspect that Gusev and Stupin were "shaving" his commissions—essentially not paying him all of the money that he was due from pharmaceutical

---

12. According to the *New York Times* in 2013, Artimovich does not deny going by the nickname Engel, but he does deny using botnets or sending spam, and says he was only hired by ChronoPay to help the company build an antivirus product.

sales at sites that he had promoted using spam sent from the Festi botnet. SpamIt's Gusev and Stupin denied that they were shaving commissions—and they were truthful in their denial—but private chats leaked by Stupin show this was only a half-truth.

Those chats show that the Cutwail botmaster Gugle (Dmitry Nechvolod) had somehow hijacked portions of Festi's traffic and diverted the spam destined for Engel's pharmacy sites to his own pill shops. Gusev and Stupin were aware of this activity, but seemed unwilling to do much about it—mainly because they intensely disliked Engel and already suspected that he was too closely allied with Vrublevsky.

By 2009, Engel became so embittered over continued allegations of being shortchanged on commissions that he began using the Spamdot.biz forum to aggressively promote his own new pharmacy partnerka and forum—Spamplanet.net. In short order, he succeeded in luring away several top botmasters, including Cosma, the Rustock botmaster.

Gusev and Stupin decided this activity, combined with Engel's increasingly public and combative allegations of shaving, were unacceptable, and banned Engel from their forum. When the SpamIt administrators ignored Engel's demands to re-enable his account, Engel used the Festi botnet to launch a long series of crushing DDoS attacks against SpamIt and its network of pill-shop sites, decreasing revenue for everyone in the partnerka.

The spammers profiled in this chapter were in charge of building and maintaining some of the world's most powerful and disruptive spam botnets, and as a result are or were responsible for a huge chunk of the junk email sent globally each day. Collectively, their spam botnets have infected tens of millions of computers over the years, and gobbled up personal and financial data from countless consumers in the process.

Individually, these junk email artists earned a few million dollars for their efforts, yet they've forced businesses and consumers to spend hundreds of millions more shoring up digital defenses to fight their daily glut of crimeware.

But these spammers were mere vassals and barons in charge of warring fiefdoms. The real authors of this economic asymmetry—the kingpins who created the pharmacy partnerkas—used the spammers like so many pawns in a high-stakes game of chess, a costly conflict that denizens of the digital underground would soon dub the "Pharma Wars."

Chapter 8

OLD FRIENDS,
BITTER ENEMIES

I n early summer 2008, SpamIt co-owner Igor "Desp" Gusev, then twenty-seven, was vacationing with his young wife and infant daughter in Marbella, on the picturesque coast of southern Spain. He'd just been offered a job as a civil servant in Russia, as an aide to an official at the Russian government's Ministry of Economic Development, but he was ambivalent about leaving Spain and accepting the position.

At that time, SpamIt and GlavMed had emerged as the largest rogue Internet pharmacy program on the planet and had attracted nearly all of the world's top spammers. Both programs had just reached what would be the peak of their earning power and were bringing in almost $6 million in revenue each month.

Despite the success of his spam venture, Gusev was thinking strongly about taking the government job and leaving his life as a cybercrime boss far behind. The subject hadn't come up yet with his business partner, Dmitry Stupin, but Gusev had to break the news at some point. The two had built GlavMed and SpamIt from nothing into a thriving business, but lately bitterness had arisen between them. Gusev was anxious for a more meaningful, legitimate, and stable life with his family. Stupin, meanwhile, was growing increasingly resentful that Gusev was constantly traveling and leaving him to wrangle with the day-to-day challenges of running a business that relied principally on criminals.

The following exchange, from a chat log between Gusev and Stupin recorded in summer 2008 and translated into English by native Russian speaker Aleksey Mikhaylov, illustrates the simmering resentment that Stupin felt at being left behind. It also includes a theme that ran through many of their conversations: Stupin was forever dreaming up new ways to make money, while Gusev seemed to yearn for a more respectable—if also more routine way of life.

> GUSEV: I like it in Spain very much :) However, all the fun is shadowed by the future "job"; we'll see what kind of shithole this is.

> STUPIN: What kind of "job"? What are you talking about?

> GUSEV: I am going to join the Ministry of Economic Development as an assistant to the vice minister.

> STUPIN: Hmm…have you finally decided to do it? If you think thoroughly, and invest your time and efforts into what we already have, we can raise

profits up to two to three times, which translates to several extra millions of dollars per year just for you.

GUSEV: Surely, if your goal is to make money :) It's too long to explain in writing. Let's have lunch in Moscow sometime and I will explain to you why I want to take this job. However, here is short version: it is not the main thing to make money in our country. The most important thing is to retain it, multiply it, to ensure that nobody is going to seize it. Our main source of income now is a semi-legal business. If they want to bring us down, they will do it as easy as 1–2–3. It's not going to be easy to escape from it, even with the two or three political connections I have now. The main goal is not to lose what we already have and not allow us to be brought down.

STUPIN: When it comes to not losing—simply buy real estate abroad. It is more "mobile" than you think. If the shit hits the fan, we can maintain everything with the efforts of four to five people. Everyone else—they are only for business development.

GUSEV: I am not talking about money. This is about business itself. If you and I get into trouble, all this "mobility" will disappear. Therefore, I want to make it so that it would not be easy to cause problems for you and me. You have to admit that the business is not going to sustain itself without you and me. Andrey, Margo, Sashka, Stratos will not be able to do it by themselves.

STUPIN: I have a feeling lately that I am talking to a wall. Am I getting on your nerves?

GUSEV: No, why do you think so?

STUPIN: Your behavior is different. There is no more communication.

GUSEV: It is not too different for me. I write something and do not get any replies. You just write "okay" from time to time :)

STUPIN: I do not consider you a "worker" anymore, a person to work with. I constantly communicate with Andrey and Sashka, and I discuss everything with them. You are either absent, or you are doing nothing (as it appears to me). It does not get on my nerves or irritate me. I just no longer consider you a person I need to or can work with.

GUSEV: As far as the job, you have had full authority for a long time. It is more efficient this way.

STUPIN: It is more convenient for me not to

communicate with you much, because otherwise I start wondering why we need you at all. It is going to be better if you start doing something, or else I will continue to discuss stuff with you less and less.

GUSEV: You know, thanks for being frank with me, but I have not given you an opportunity to rise to a partner from a simple programmer just so that in the future you'd tell me that I was no longer necessary. You would have been a lead developer in some major company with the salary of five to seven thousand, and you would not have been able to buy your house in Turkey if we did not meet together at that time, and if I had not have allowed you to manage the company. Think about it at your leisure. Money blinds people and gives false feelings of total power.

STUPIN: Did I say that you've become unnecessary? That was your own thought. If you had thought a bit further, you'd understand that *I* was the reason that everything was working so reliably and so thoroughly, only because of my becoming the person you allowed me to become.

GUSEV: Let's talk tonight. I will cool off a little.

STUPIN: No problem. I have no issues.

But this feud would have to wait while a more pressing concern came to the fore. While Gusev was still in southern Spain, he received a flood of urgent messages from a friend named Alexey, a hacker upon whom he relied for intelligence about law-enforcement interest in spammer activity.

> LEHA: Hey. Are you there? I've been looking for you.

> GUSEV: Sorry, have been in Spain with the family.

> LEHA: There is something bad that you need to know. Just listen to what I have to say, and then draw your own conclusions.

Leha explained that a few nights prior, he ran into Yuri "Hellman" Kabayenkov, Vrublevsky's fifty-fifty partner in Rx-Promotion. As happened more often than not, Kabayenkov was drunk, and on this night in particular Leha heard him bragging about his role in bribing the local police into opening a criminal investigation into Gusev's business.

> LEHA: So I happened to run into drunken Hellman last week. And either just to brag, or just because he's a stupid moron, he spilled his guts. He asked, "Have you stayed in touch with Desp (Gusev)?" This was definitely a loaded question. I immediately said, "Why do you ask?"

Hellman hinted that "right-thinking people" would start thinking about distancing themselves from Gusev, and that he himself had seen the paperwork for the case, which specified that Gusev was to be accused of money laundering.

GUSEV: What are they trying to pin on me?

LEHA: The article in the criminal code that deals with legalization of proceeds from crime. I'm not sure whether the criminal case actually exists yet or not, I'm just relaying what I heard. I myself am shocked by such stupid behavior. Obviously, Pasha [Pavel Vrublevsky] was the one who initiated this, but the fact that Hellman got himself into this is especially ridiculous.

GUSEV: Thanks, Leha. You warned me in time.

LEHA: Hellman wanted to buy a car. If you remember, he bragged about this at my birthday party... But at some point he said that he had to delay the purchase, because he needed lots of money for something. And now, while he's drunk, he let it spill exactly what he needed the money for.

GUSEV: Do you by any chance know the prosecutor's office that is in charge of the case?

LEHA: I have no idea which prosecutor's office or who initiated the case. I'm not even sure the case exists. I didn't see it.

GUSEV: But what reason does Hellman have to pay for my criminal case? What did I do to him?

LEHA: It's total nonsense. I have no idea what reason he might have. I asked him and his response was, "But why not?" Pasha [referring to Vrublevsky] is a fucking asshole. To do this kind of bullshit is way too much.

GUSEV: The funny thing is, he still owes me money.

LEHA: So much bragging. He says that police colonels and generals are working for him on these things. Hellman has also picked up on this crap. Says that he has everything under control.

GUSEV: If you can try to find out which prosecutor's office is handling the case, it will make finding it a lot easier.

LEHA: I have a very fucking bad feeling about this, Igor. Do you have any way to solve this problem?

GUSEV: I will start working on this now. I'm not 100

percent sure, but I will ask some very serious people
for help. As you know, a 100 percent guarantee of
solving all problems is not given even by God.

And so began the Pharma Wars, a long-running, public, and
ultimately very costly grudge match between the proprietors of
the world's largest pharmacy partnerkas then—a feud that would
forever change the course of the spam industry. The investigation
that Vrublevsky and Hellman allegedly purchased against Gusev
and his business would set in motion a damaging series of events
that would find the two men competing to see who could spend
more money bribing officials to help ruin the other.

And they would both succeed.

Gusev believes that Vrublevsky and Hellman paid for the
criminal case against him because they suspected him of being
responsible for a recent financial catastrophe that wiped out more
than $7 million in funds belonging to one of their businesses. The
lost money was being held in escrow for some of Russia's most
accomplished hackers, and the resulting fallout from the money's
disappearance quickly made RedEye (Vrublevsky) a persona non
grata among adult webmasters and spammers alike.

In a telephone interview, Gusev said the trouble with Vrublevsky
started shortly after the latter was the victim of a corporate raid
that led to the looting of millions of dollars that Vrublevsky reportedly owed to Russian adult webmasters. Many Western readers are
no doubt familiar with the concept of a conventional corporate
raid—also known as a hostile takeover—which involves buying a
sizable interest in a company and then using the resulting voting

rights to enact changes such as replacing top executives or liqui-
dating the company.

In Russia, however, the hostile takeover is all too frequently a
violent event, and can just as often happen via bribed judges or politicians as at the point of a gun. According to *Knowledge@Wharton*, a
publication from the Wharton business school, *a staggering 70,000*
Russian companies each year become targets of raider attacks.

"In the mid-1990s, reports of AK-47 wielding masked men
storming the headquarters of up-and-coming companies, seizing
assets, and forcing owners to sign a variety of property transfer documents were all too common," wrote the five members
of the 2010 class of Wharton's Lauder Institute who authored
the article.

"Since the [Russian] financial default of 1999, however, tactics
of raiders and their agents have become much more sophisticated.
These days, the most common scenario involves an interested
party placing an order with a raiding team for the takeover of a
target company. Raiders typically start by acquiring a minority
share in the target firm and using this share to initiate frivo-
lous lawsuits against the target. The raiders then use a complex
game of legal arbitrage to compromise the company's operations
and drastically devalue its stock. These actions result in possible
bankruptcy and almost certain takeover by the raider."

The business entity targeted in the raid against Vrublevsky was
Fethard Finance, a now-defunct virtual currency system of which
Vrublevsky was a majority shareholder. Through a legal entity he
founded called "Red & Partners," Vrublevsky developed a network
of extreme porn sites. The online forum that Vrublevsky (a.k.a.

"RedEye")[13] founded—Crutop.nu—was the perfect spot for marketing the Red & Partners sites to Russian adult webmasters, who could earn commissions for selling monthly memberships to the sites. (Recall that our "Virgil" in this spammer netherworld—Vishnevsky—earned a tidy living as a young man advertising Crutop-affiliate websites.) When these webmaster affiliates got paid, they were compensated not in dollars or Russian rubles, but in credits with Fethard's virtual currency, which quickly caught on as an accepted form of payment for goods and services in the Russian cyber underground.

Fethard and Vrublevsky's porn empire seemed to be humming along nicely until September 2007, when Vrublevsky—or rather the Crutop administrator RedEye—broke the news to more than eight thousand Russian adult webmasters who had money tied up with the virtual currency: Fethard had been the latest victim of a corporate raid and was flat broke.

According to Gusev, the brains behind the raid was Mikhail Zhilenkov, the husband of Maria Okulova, the granddaughter of the first president of Russia, Boris Yeltsin. Interestingly, Okulova's father, Valery Okulov, is the former CEO of Aeroflot—Russia's largest airline, and a company that would soon radically change the direction of Vrublevsky's life.

"In 2007, the Fethard system had two main shareholders: Pavel and Zhilenkov, who is a well-known raider and has some good connections in police and [Russian FSB]," Gusev recalled in a phone

---

13.   Note that Vrublevsky denies being RedEye, and speaks of RedEye always as "Mr. RedEye," which is a bit of a joke. Gusev's blog about Pavel is called redeye-blog.com.

interview. Indeed, Alexander Khinshtein, a journalist for the Russian news magazine *Moskovsky Komsomolets*, has detailed the exploits of RostInvest, a Zhilenkov investment firm implicated in a number of raider scandals throughout the latter half of the last decade.

Gusev believes Vrublevsky's lust for power and the desire to be associated with anyone who had it blinded his former business partner to what lay ahead. Zhilenkov used his sway as a 50 percent shareholder in the company to take control of the day-to-day management of Fethard. And that gave Zhilenkov direct access to all the Fethard affiliate accounts.

On September 12, 2007, Vrublevsky was sucker-punched twice. The first blow was learning that virtually all of the funds in the Fethard accounts had been drained and funneled to various banks offshore. The second was discovering that Russian police had opened a criminal investigation into him and Fethard, calling it an illegal banking system.

"Pavel either didn't see or didn't worry about that side of Zhilenkov, because he was strutting around like a turkey cock and boasting about getting such a bigwig as his new partner, and all of the connections and power it would bring him," Gusev said in an interview with this author.

The raid against Fethard was an important event because Vrublevsky became convinced it was orchestrated by Gusev. (Gusev vehemently denies he had anything to do with it—a claim I've come to believe.) Determined to strike back at his perceived aggressor, Vrublevsky began scheming with the aforementioned cofounder of Rx-Promotion—Yuri "Hellman" Kabayenkov—to get a criminal investigation into Gusev started.

"Zhilenkov was the originator of this case," Gusev said. "It was a warning from Zhilenkov to Pavel not to try to get the money back. Zhilenkov made it very clear that if Pavel intended to try to get the money back that was stolen from Fethard, he will have even more problems, and the criminal case would move forward. But all along, Pavel has wrongly suspected that I was somehow involved in this."

It's not hard to see why. In many ways, Gusev and Vrublevsky could not be more different. Gusev is thoughtful, erudite, deliberate, self-deprecating, and miserly. In contrast, Vrublevsky is vulgar, impulsive, loquacious, self-aggrandizing, and a spendthrift. Gusev is a self-described "golden boy" who grew up in a wealthy family—his grandfather was a minister of construction and building in the former Soviet Union—and he received a classical education at one of Russia's top schools. Vrublevsky, who looks at least ten years older than his real age—in his midthirties—had a bit less sheltered upbringing and was tossed out of several schools as a young man.

Gusev said he got his start in the Internet industry in 1998, when a local businessman hired him to create a website for a sports memorabilia business. Gusev learned as much as he could about HTML and web programming, and earned two hundred dollars for his efforts. Not long after that, he decided he could make much more money in the porn business, so he hired a programmer to help him make software that collects lists of top porn sites used in so-called "circle jerk" operations.

"CJs, as they're called, are a kind of system in which different sites hosting many porn images redirect viewers who click on an image from one site to another," Gusev said. "The idea behind the CJ is that you are redirected so many times that finally you are so tired of looking for the content that you actually click on one of the sponsor ads and purchase a subscription. It is a system designed to wear people down, and it worked quite well, at least for a while. But I can tell you this much: this was a trick first tried in the United States. It was not invented in Russia!"

Gusev and Vrublevsky first met as a consequence of their common links to pornography of the rather extreme variety. In 1998, Gusev was administrator of a Russian online forum that catered to webmasters who marketed films and images involving bestiality and sex with farm animals. Vrublevsky's market, which he served through his Red & Partners holding company, were those who enjoyed viewing violent pornography, mainly pictures and short films depicting rape or other forms of forced sex, incest, and sodomy.[14]

Gusev was able to profit from the business because he owned a credit-card billing firm called Digital Internet Billing, or "DiBill" for short. The billing firm relied on connections to the Dutch banking system, where, according to Gusev, a sizable portion of the market for his company's product happily resided.

One day, Gusev received an instant message from Vrublevsky, asking to meet and to discuss combining their efforts and creating a consolidated payment processing company to service the

---

14.   Vrublevsky denies even being associated with the parent company that owns all these
      sites, even though incorporation records put it at the same address in the Netherlands that
      ChronoPay used in its registration documents. What's more, the Red & Partners website
      was for many months hosted on Internet address space assigned to ChronoPay by European
      Internet address authorities.

booming porn industry that had sprouted up virtually overnight with the broad adoption of the commercial Internet in the West.

"We spoke several times in Moscow, and he was seeming so enthusiastic and so motivated about this new business, ChronoPay, and he offered me to join him," Gusev said. "I thought for this time it could be a very good step in my career. I wish I had been a bit smarter and refused his proposal."

In 2003, they made it official. Red & Partners teamed up with Gusev's firm DPNet to form a new corporation in the Netherlands, and ChronoPay was born. Among the investors was Vladimir Tsastsin, the chief executive of an Estonian Internet domain name registrar called EstDomains. Tsastsin and Vrublevsky would become fast friends, and for the next five years, Tsastsin's EstDomains would become the most popular domain registrar among Russian webmasters (particularly those pushing spam and malware).[15]

For a short while, Gusev and Vrublevsky worked side by side in the same office. But after less than a year, both men were bickering

---

15. Tsastsin dismissed as "rubbish" claims that EstDomains was courting spammers and malware purveyors. Nevertheless, his company's business would later be stripped of its ability to issue new domain names by Internet regulators, after a report in the *Washington Post* exposed that he had been convicted in Estonia of conspiracy to commit credit-card fraud, money laundering, and forgery, among other offenses. EstDomains ceased to exist after that incident, but Tsastsin and six other associates allegedly continued their illegal schemes. In 2011, he was arrested by Estonian authorities in an international law-enforcement operation aimed at dismantling the DNSChanger Trojan. This huge botnet had infected more than four million PCs worldwide with malware that hijacked search results, shut down security software, and earned Tsastsin and his business partners more than $14 million. Tsastsin and his colleagues were charged with wire fraud and money laundering, but in late 2013, they were acquitted by an Estonian court. As of this writing, the men are awaiting extradition from Estonia to stand trial in the United States on cyberfraud charges.

constantly about the direction that the firm should take. After a protracted disagreement over who should be allowed to buy Gusev's shares in ChronoPay, Gusev sold DPNet to a Russian businessman named Leonid Mikhailovich Terekhov and went off to start work on establishing GlavMed and SpamIt.

"We were sitting in one office just opposite each other, and I guess because of this we should be considered some kind of friends or business partners," Gusev said in a 2011 interview. "But it worked only for [the] first five or six months. After that, we started having some problems communicating with each other. The problem was that I wasn't supporting his decisions and he wasn't supporting my decisions."

Meanwhile, something strange was brewing at ChronoPay. The company had begun to attract legitimate businesses—not just porn sites, but brand-name companies in Russia that were eager to help customers find alternative ways to pay for their goods. Few working-class Russians used or even had credit cards at the time, and while there was a growing desire for ecommerce, surprisingly few companies doing business in Russia were willing and able to help consumers use their bank accounts to pay for things online.

By 2006, ChronoPay had attracted as clients a number of Russia's top brands, including Russian mobile providers MTS and Skylink, and even more Western-oriented nonprofit organizations, such as the World Wildlife Fund. Millions of Russians could suddenly pay their heating or telephone bills online, or purchase concert and airline tickets, all via ChronoPay.

In securing these bigger, legitimate clients, Vrublevsky may have been ensuring that black and gray businesses would have sustained access to banking systems that would be willing to process riskier transactions, such as online pharmacy purchases and credit card transactions related to extortionist sales of rogue antivirus software, Gusev said.

"The main reason ChronoPay was so successful for so long in all of these gray and black businesses is that they have had a pool of white clients whose business was covering up these gray and black dealings," Gusev said. "They were using that to win better processing rates from the [acquiring banks], because they would say, 'We'll bring you millions of dollars in transactions from some of the largest Russian companies, and all you have to do is help us process these other things.'"

Stefan Savage, the University of California, San Diego professor who made hundreds of legal drug purchases through pharmacies run by GlavMed, Rx-Promotion, and dozens of other partnerkas said ChronoPay wasn't really a credit card processor, but rather a marketer and reseller of payment services (known in the business as a payment service provider or PSP).

"They didn't have their own bank relationships, but they worked with other companies that had that relationship. They had lots of deals with other people to help get money through," Savage said. "They were representing on behalf of clients, fake clients who were selling drugs via different banks, and they would round-robin their Rx-Promotion business through front companies that they created. And later, when the banks would figure out what was going on, ChronoPay would deny all knowledge of what its front companies were doing."

In other words, ChronoPay and Vrublevsky were instrumental

in establishing the organizational, legal, and technical cover that spammers needed to be able to accept credit card numbers for the pills they were pimping. ChronoPay and Vrublevsky also used these same obfuscation techniques to hide their integral role in the processing of tens of millions of dollars in credit card payments from Americans and Europeans who were victimized by scareware scams. As we'll see in "Chapter 9: Meeting in Moscow," Vrublevsky claims that his relation to scareware scams was merely as an advisor who helped these operations set up the front companies and payment systems to help make the whole operation appear aboveboard to the credit card companies.

According to Savage, the service that ChronoPay provided is known in the industry as "factoring." The company would take multiple clients, load them up with credit card processing, and then map their transactions into accounts on behalf of shell companies that they had, companies that they'd represented to the banks as being the true customer. And then Vrublevsky and other ChronoPay employees involved would simply pay these clients out of their own pockets.

In short, dodgy organizations turned to ChronoPay primarily when they had few other options.

"They were willing to take on and manage all of these really shady customers that were not going to be taken as customers by anyone else," Savage said. "There were lots of games being played with several banking partners, and ChronoPay was very good at playing these games."

Those partnerships—principally with financial institutions in the former Soviet republics of Azerbaijan, Georgia, and

Latvia—were the primary contributor to ChronoPay's dominance in processing transactions for rogue Internet pharmacies and scareware scams behind the company's legitimate front. Thankfully for Vrublevsky and Gusev, this activity was largely eclipsed for a while by the much higher volumes of transactions coming from comparatively legitimate Russian companies.

"ChronoPay is a unique company from one point of view, because it is famous in Russia for [its association with] big-name brands in that country," Gusev said in a 2010 interview. "But everyone knows who is the owner of the company and what he did before this company and what he does right now."

◆　　◆　　◆

Two years after Vrublevsky and Gusev parted ways as cofounders of ChronoPay, Gusev had become successful in his own right. GlavMed and SpamIt were pulling in millions of dollars a month and employing some of the smartest computer programmers that Moscow had to offer.

Not to be outdone by his rival, in 2007, Vrublevsky and Hellman would launch Rx-Promotion, seeking to lure away many of the top spammers from SpamIt. Rx-Promotion was entering an already crowded field including some two dozen other rogue pharmacy partnerkas. But from the start, Rx-Promotion would have an advantage over its competitors. It would specialize in offering highly restricted and addictive prescription medications—such as hydrocodone and Valium—to any and all customers, regardless of whether the customers had a doctor-approved prescription.

Gusev said GlavMed initially offered controlled medications as well, but that it decided early on that the market for these pills was too volatile and risky.

"When GlavMed started operations in 2006, there were some controlled substances, but we didn't understand what we were getting into then," Gusev said. "A couple of years later, we made some strategic decisions not to have any connection to controlleds. After all, there is not serious damage for health if you are selling Viagra. But controlleds...if you selling these over the Internet, you are most often selling to drug-addicted people. And honestly, I don't want to be some kind of drug dealer."

Gusev's timeline doesn't quite match up to the records leaked from SpamIt and GlavMed, which show that these two partnerkas continued to sell some controlled prescription drugs until at least mid-2009.

◆ ◆ ◆

All indications suggest that—despite Vrublevsky's early warning of the political and legal machinations set against him—Gusev underestimated his former partner's resolve, or else could not find properly connected allies in Russia's political and legal apparatus to derail the slowly building criminal case targeting him and his businesses. For one thing, Gusev did not start taking precautions to outflank Vrublevsky until the beginning of 2010, when he finally accepted that he was under investigation by Russian FSB agents, and that investigators were seeking to paint him as "Spammer #1 in Russia."

The case against Gusev coincided with a push by Russia's then-President Dmitry Medvedev to attract foreign investment for "Skolkovo." The project was an ambitious technology park being built outside Moscow that is intended to serve as a Russian version of Silicon Valley, America's biggest incubator of high-tech innovation. The Skolkovo project gained momentum in March 2010, after Internet hardware maker Cisco Systems Inc. pledged $1 billion to the project, and Silicon Valley venture capital firm Bessemer Venture Partners promised investments worth $20 million over two years.

But Medvedev and other leaders knew that if they were going to succeed in attracting more investment from Western nations, they would need to tidy up Russia's reputation for being lax in pursuing cybercriminals within its borders. Gusev was the perfect sacrificial goat to start with. He was to be the first high-profile cybercrime target of the National Anti-Corruption Committee, a body aimed at helping state agencies and ministries cleanse themselves of corrupt officials who often turned a blind eye to crime in exchange for bribes or "donations."

As if to validate the anti-corruption committee's choice, Gusev's first response to counter the criminal case being aggressively waged against him was to attempt to bribe public officials into delaying his case, feeding him details about its progress, and running interference on his behalf.

On January 9, 2010, Gusev reached out to GlavMed-SpamIt coadministrator Dmitry Stupin, via online chat to discuss options for avoiding or delaying his prosecution. Gusev told Stupin that he might be able to purchase protection from the charges by funneling money to key Russian politicians who have influence over investigators.

Specifically, Gusev suggested purchasing a sponsorship of the Volleyball Federation of Russia. The price tag for this is an official sponsorship fee of 10 million rubles (about $350,000), plus $150,000 in cash. The official head of the federation, Nikolai Patrushev, is a powerful man in Russian law enforcement. Patrushev was director of the Russian FSB, the successor organization to the KGB, from 1999 to 2008. He has been secretary of the Security Council of Russia since 2008.

According to Gusev, it is typical for Russian sport leagues and charities to be used as vehicles for funneling money into the pockets of policymakers.

"In Russia, sports is not really a business. It's a way of getting business settled," Gusev said in a telephone interview. "I have one friend who is a pretty famous hockey player. One time he told me that in [the] hockey league, there are only two teams who might earn something, while the other teams have only losses. Sport in Russia is some kind of…from one point of view one can meet some new faces and start some relationship for the future, and from other point of view you can get some kind of protection. That's because all leagues—basketball, football, hockey, whatever—all have persons from the government who are somehow controlling them."

The phenomenon Gusev describes is well documented. One example comes from a book by Lennart Dahlgren, former head of the Russian division of Swedish furniture maker IKEA. In *Despite Absurdity: How I Conquered Russia While It Conquered Me,*

Dahlgren writes of having to pay bribes of 30 million rubles ($1 million) to Russian charities that helped funnel money to bureaucrats and top officials.

In May 2011, Gusev told me in a telephone interview that he was a paid sponsor of the Russian volleyball league, hoping to persuade someone to stop the criminal case against him. Gusev was convinced, and other leaked documents appear to confirm his suspicions, that law-enforcement interest in his activities was paid for by Pavel Vrublevsky, his former business partner turned competitor.

Indeed, in late 2010, Vrublevsky secured a sponsorship of the Russian Basketball Federation for ChronoPay. The basketball federation is headed by Sergei Ivanov, a former KGB officer who was tapped by Russian President Vladimir Putin as deputy prime minister of Russia. In fact, ChronoPay used ties to Ivanov as an advertisement for its success and power. In a series of photographs of ChronoPay executives on the company's blog is a picture of Vrublevsky and Ivanov standing in the front row at a basketball game cheering on their team, both men in business suits and smiling broadly.

It remains unclear how much Vrublevsky had to pay to secure that sponsorship, but several clues suggest it was more than $1 million. A story in a March 2011 print edition of the Russian daily *Kommersant* stated that the basketball federation's budget was increased to approximately $6 million due to contributions from sponsors—ChronoPay, Russian investment group VTB, and Russian automaker Sollers. In that article, Ivanov is quoted as saying that VTB contributed more than half of the budget, and that the other half was contributed by ChronoPay and Sollers.

"If Pavel wants me to be named the World's Number One Spammer, he pay lots of money to get that name for me, but you know I never tried to do any research to find out who actually was the number one spammer," Gusev said. He was referring to a then-just-released paper by the UCSD researchers, who found that spammers working for Rx-Promotion blasted out more than twice the amount of spam of any other program, including SpamIt.

"I thought it should be the owners of the largest botnets, and I thought most of them were working with SpamIt," Gusev said. "But this research shows that 25 percent of spam was for Rx-Promotion sites. It's very difficult for Pavel, even with all this information and money and influence, to persuade people that the bigger problem is not with him."

Chat records from late January 2010 show that Gusev and Stupin sent initial "donations" of $210,000 and $115,000 from their company, Despmedia, to the Volleyball federation. In another online chat a month later, Gusev tells Stupin that their total expenses for bribes sent to Russian law-enforcement officials exceed $400,000.

In a conversation dated February 19, 2010, Gusev reports that he just paid $20,000—$5,000 to a middleman and $15,000 to someone from the Prosecutor General's Office, the law-enforcement body that was investigating him—for information and for "delaying" his case. In the same chat log, Gusev says that he has found someone—a very able man, a lawyer and *reshalshik* (problem-solver)—who can provide a "complete set of services" to deal with the "RedEye problem."

Gusev secured promises from this man that a donation in

the proper amount would virtually ensure the incarceration of Vrublevsky and the destruction of his various shady businesses. But the price tag for this assurance was steep—$1.5 million.

Gusev says he has met a reshalshik and asks Stupin for advice on how to deal with the guy in addition to the $1.5 million. This fixer's price is that Gusev and Stupin must agree to help an old, mutual acquaintance start a competing rogue Internet pharmacy program.

"I found a person who is willing to help me in this situation with RedEye," Gusev writes. "This guy has a proven scheme, because he is a very strong lawyer. A real fixer-upper. For his service, along with very large sum of money, he is asking for something in return—he is asking to help his friend—a very famous webmaster, who faced a similar problem to the one we are facing, and who was saved by that person. This 'friend' is not doing anything right now. This lawyer is asking us to help him with establishing an online pharmacy program. I am not happy about the idea of creating more competition, but out of all the people I talked to, only this guy offered a structured solution to the problem, giving us hope."

Gusev then goes on to talk about the volleyball federation sponsorship, which is code for funneling money to corrupt FSB agents to run interference. He says: "People from the volleyball association can and will cover us, using their FSB connections, but they can do very little with the Prosecutor's Office. They can only prolong the legal proceedings. They will also not be able to prosecute Red. The person who we are asked to help is my old acquaintance—Pet—the owner of лолного [this is a colloquial term—pronounced "loll-nah-vah"—referring to Lolita or child porn sites]—which handles billing through billcards." Gusev is almost certainly talking here about Evgeny "Pet" Petrovsky, the Belarusian owner of the Sunbill/BillCards payment processing firm who was kidnapped by Loginov's gang in Chapter 2.

After Gusev breaks the news that this fixer-upper lawyer is charging $1.5 million plus a personal favor, Stupin exclaimed, "Oh, my god! What does he promise for that?"

"He promises that Red would remain in prison and would not be able to buy his way out," Gusev answered. "Plus, he is going to lose a large portion of his business and will be left with no money to fight the war."

In a telephone interview in mid-2011, Gusev explained his actions thusly: "All that I wanted was to speak with someone from FSB [who] was making this [case] for Pavel, and to persuade them to stop all this conflict before it's too late," he said. "Unfortunately, this didn't help me very much."

In summer 2010, tens of thousands of emails and internal documents would be leaked from ChronoPay by unknown insiders or attackers who had hacked into the company's network—offering countless examples of the sort of activity that Vrublevsky had denied orchestrating for years.

When I asked Gusev whether he'd been responsible for the incident, he denied it, but then allowed that his involvement was a logical assumption, given the war of attrition that had earlier caught him flat-footed.

"Pavel has one year of advantage on me because I wasn't really expecting that he would make all these things public about me and our business," Gusev said. "Now, I am some kind of cybercriminal, and he is some kind of cybercriminal. The most logical decision is for us to solve this quietly, but he wants to harm me so desperately that he is making decisions without understanding the consequences."

Convinced that Gusev had been behind the leak of ChronoPay documents and emails, Vrublevsky paid a local hacker to break into and leak the SpamIt and GlavMed customer database.

The following chat log is dated August 28, 2010, just days after SpamIt's internal database found its way to U.S. law-enforcement agencies. In this conversation, Stupin and Gusev discuss whether to close SpamIt.

> GUSEV: It looks like I am in deep shit. Red gave our database to Americans.

> STUPIN: To which Americans?

> GUSEV: I can't tell exactly, yet. Probably to FBI or Secret Service. Have you read on Krebs's blog about the meeting at the White House regarding illegal pharmacy problems on the Internet?

> STUPIN: No.

> GUSEV: krebsonsecurity.com/2010/08/white-house -calls-meeting-on-rogue-online-pharmacies

> STUPIN: Maybe you return back to Russia?

GUSEV: I am planning to do that. I am really worried now.

GUSEV: Do you think "closing down" will help? Just realize: they have our ENTIRE database... There are 900,000 records. What are we going to do with those? For conviction and 5-year jail time, it is only necessary to prove 1 transaction! What is the worst? They combine the sentences and it is possible to get 5 life sentences.

GUSEV: I also think we need to shut the operations down, because it's an absolute disaster!

GUSEV: Regarding closing down—I think we need to shut down SpamIt first. In a month or 1/2 month—GlavMed.

Gusev and Stupin would close SpamIt.com in late September 2010, replacing the Spamdot.biz homepage with the following message to affiliates:

Because of the numerous negative events that happened last year and the risen attention to our affiliate program, we've decided to stop accepting the traffic starting 1.10.2010 [October 1, 2010]. We find the decision the most appropriate in this situation. It provides avoiding the sudden work stop which leads to the program collapse and not paying your profit.

In our case the whole profit will be paid normally. All possible frauds are excluded. Please transfer your traffic to other affiliate programs by 1.10.2010.

Thank you for your cooperation! We appreciate your trust very much!

Immediately after SpamIt's closure, the volume of junk email sent worldwide dropped noticeably—20 to 40 percent, depending on estimates—as spammers employed by the program sought to move their traffic to other partnerships that might pay for their services. Experts who tracked the top spam botnets used to promote SpamIt's "Canadian" pharmacy sites quickly noticed that most of the major botnets—including Grum, Rustock, and Cutwail—essentially were parked in neutral for several weeks as the botmasters tried to figure out new ways to earn a living from their crime machines.

Thanks to a *New York Times* story that—according to the leaked ChronoPay emails—was sourced in part by outreach from the public relations staff of the Russian Association of Electronic Communications (RAEC), Gusev had become the world's biggest spammer, even though Gusev claims that he was never a spammer in the conventional sense. By the time Moscow police searched his apartment, Gusev had already fled Russia with his wife and young daughter, reportedly headed for Spain.

But Gusev wasn't going to go down without a fight. In November, he launched redeye-blog.com, a website that he used to publicly catalog Vrublevsky's colorful past, even hiring a native English speaker to translate the blog for Western audiences. It didn't take long for Vrublevsky's many enemies to follow suit, airing RedEye's dirty laundry by posting comments on the blog. Hundreds of adult webmasters with long memories of Vrublevsky's wrongs against them began using the blog to chronicle the millions of dollars Vrublevsky still owed them from the Fethard disaster.

"Moscow is a good place to stay when you have money and good friends who can help you with your problems," Gusev said in a phone interview in November 2010. "I'm trying to ruin his ChronoPay because if he will not have money, he will hopefully stop all these things."

Not long after that interview with Gusev, Vrublevsky finally acknowledged that the Pharma Wars, as many were calling their feud, had progressed beyond the point of return. Rather, Vrublevsky said wryly, neither side appeared to be deterred by "mutual assured destruction." Here he was referring to a doctrine of military strategy in which both sides in a nuclear arms race are discouraged from launching a first strike based on the certainty that the aggressor's action will trigger an equivalent response.

"The problem is that Gusev is not trying to hit me with his weapons, but he is trying to scare me," Vrublevsky said in one of his many phone calls to this author. "His claim that he is staying abroad forever—this all is bullshit targeted to his webmasters, and of course it all sounds like a James Bond story, but nobody hides like this. In reality, Gusev is waiting for me to call him up and say, 'Okay, man, let's stop this war.' But there's nothing in that ChronoPay compromat that can make me stop or is able to save him now. It's just a way he thinks he'll be able to blackmail me every few months, and nothing else."

Meanwhile, consumers all over the world were enjoying a

brief reprieve from the barrage of spam email and the malware it carried with it that threatened to infect their computers and steal their identities. The spam email empire teetered on the brink of collapse. When asked whether he was worried that his efforts to embarrass and inconvenience Vrublevsky might further damage an industry that he'd helped to build and that had made him quite wealthy, Gusev told me it was a risk he had to take.

"At least we will both lose lots of time, power, and money, and no one will be a winner here," Gusev said, speaking by phone from an undisclosed location abroad. "I am still making some reports to continue this conflict with only one reason. Because if I stop now, in one or two years Pavel will find the possibility to hit me again on something else, and I don't want to [allow] him that."

I believed Gusev when he told me facts about his life, his business, and his conflict with Pavel. He may not have always told me the whole truth, but I had little reason to doubt his version of events. In contrast, Vrublevsky often lied to me or stretched the truth well beyond believability in our interviews. Even so, he'd promised to be more forthcoming if I met him on his own turf, and I was anxious to hear his side of the story. It was time to renew my passport.

Chapter 9

MEETING IN MOSCOW

T
he frozen Moscow River crunched and groaned as it churned
beneath the twin engines propelling our sleek, modern icebreaker cruise ship at a steady clip. On the far shore, the
formidable and beautiful edifice of the Kremlin towered over the
frosted black water. An open door behind me flooded the bracing
night air with the cacophony of pulsing Russian pop music, clink-
ing glasses, and the din of flatware on plates.

February is hardly the warmest month for a trip to Russia, but a
press tour invitation in 2011 from Russian security firm Kaspersky
Lab proved too timely to pass up. I wanted to surprise Vrublevsky—
and I wasn't sure he'd be a free man much longer—so I jumped at
the invitation.

I'd been studying the Russian language and culture—and its seedy
underbelly of cybercrime—for more than five years, and visiting the
country had long been a dream of mine. But I let few people know
that I was going to visit and told no one my real reason for making
the trip: to meet Pavel Vrublevsky in Moscow, and tentatively Igor

Gusev on a side trip to Europe (which I never followed through with). I had an idea at the time that their feud would make an interesting story, and I was anxious to meet each man face to face.

I had wanted to meet the infamous cybercrooks then because I believed this might be my one chance to interview them in person without prison guards present. I was preparing to run a series of articles documenting the Pharma Wars between Gusev and Vrublevsky, because between the two of them, they were responsible for probably 75 percent of the spam on the planet. I was certain neither man would want to talk to me much after that series started.

"Brian! Come, the performance is starting," bellowed a broadly grinning and waving Eugene Kaspersky, barely audible over the ship's powerful turbines and the crackling river ice. Following him through the door leading from the stern of the boat into the main hall, I nearly crashed into a troupe of young men in baby blue jumpsuits turning cartwheels and performing a traditional Russian folk dance on the wooden dance floor between the bar and the dinner tables.

The icebreaker cruise with Kaspersky took place the day before I was to depart from Moscow. After dinner was served, Kaspersky and I each enjoyed glasses of ice cold Russian vodka, and he began telling me about his cryptography work for a former Soviet institute in the 1980s that was sponsored by the Russian Ministry of Defense and the KGB (then the Russian equivalent of the U.S. Federal Bureau of Investigation).

It also emerged that we both got interested in computer security after getting hacked. Eugene became obsessed with viruses after finding malware on his computer in 1991. I started learning all I could about computers and Internet security a decade later, when my home network was overrun by the "li0n worm," a contagion unleashed by a now-famous Chinese hacker that locked me out of my systems and trashed several servers.

As I watched the dancers careen from one corner of the ship to the other, my thoughts wandered back to the day I'd arrived in Moscow and immediately sought an audience with Vrublevsky. I hadn't slept a wink since my meeting with the notorious cybercrime figure, and I kept replaying the day's events in my head.

My flight to Moscow was routed through John F. Kennedy International Airport in New York, where I ran into Paul Roberts, a security journalist and analyst who had recently begun working for Kaspersky. Roberts was joining the press tour as well.

I had never been to Russia, but as we approached Sheremetyevo International Airport, I could see that Moscow was up to that point exactly how I'd pictured it: overcast, cold, snowy, and windy.

Waiting for the plane to touch down, I was suddenly struck by how little I had actually done to prepare for my trip, and for the first time, I was a bit scared. Prior to my departure, a family member who'd been in the foreign service had given me some unsolicited advice on ways to ensure my safety while in Moscow. Much of his wisdom was common sense, such as "arrange all meetings in public spaces," "travel nowhere alone," and "avoid getting into cars with unfamiliar people." Nevertheless, I was stunned at how soon after arriving in Moscow I would be forced to ignore all of that advice.

Roberts and I were supposed to have a car waiting at the airport to take us to our hotel, but high winds had delayed the departure of our flight from New York. When we arrived in Russia, the hired car was nowhere to be found.

As we stepped out of the main terminal and onto the slushy sidewalk, we were immediately pegged as Americans and accosted by perhaps a half-dozen men offering us "cheap" cab rides from the airport. Unfortunately, our hotel was about thirty kilometers from the airport, and the trip would be anything but cheap.

Very soon after we walked out of the terminal, I began to feel queasy, enough so that I thought for sure I was going to lose my breakfast all over the cabbies who were constantly in my face and having trouble taking "no" for an answer. I retreated to a snow-covered metal bench to catch my breath and steady myself. The cabbies seemed to sense that they might regret getting too close and mercifully left me alone for a couple of minutes. Presently, Roberts ambled in my direction after scouting the length of the airport curb for any signs of our prearranged pickup.

"I'm not really crazy about the idea either, but it looks like we may have to hire one of these guys," he said, squinting through the driving snowfall.

Five minutes later, we were crammed into the back of a black, compact Russian-made automobile, racing through the soggy streets and swerving around the slower traffic crowding onto Leningradskoye Shosse, the main highway from the airport into central Moscow. I took this opportunity to try out my prepaid wireless Internet service. Because I rarely use unsecured public Wi-Fi and was even less interested in doing so in Moscow, I wanted to avoid being at the mercy of coffee shop or hotel wireless services while in Moscow. So I had arranged to purchase Internet access in advance via a company called XCom Global. The company's service will ship you a USB dongle just prior to your departure, which in theory should allow you to have 3G wireless Internet access more or less anywhere in the city of your choosing.

As I plugged the dongle into my Macbook in the back of the cab, however, I was dismayed to find that it was impossible to keep a signal for more than a few seconds at a time. I thought perhaps this was because we were hurtling down the highway at 120 kilometers per hour, but I later found the service was just as unreliable when seated at a coffee shop near our hotel smack in the middle of downtown Moscow. What few plans I had made in advance of my trip were rapidly falling apart.

Forty-five minutes and the equivalent of $170 later, Roberts and I exited the cab and checked in to the Marriott Grand Hotel on Tverskaya Street, the broad commercial thoroughfare that runs from Red Square through central Moscow. At the front desk, an attractive young woman behind the counter requested my passport. When I produced the passport, she took it, curtly told me I could come by and pick it up later in the day, and then disappeared into a back office.

I didn't much care for the idea of relinquishing my passport, but I also didn't have many other options. My unease soon turned to dread. I had been there all of five hours when I was alarmed by a Google news alert that I'd set up to monitor Internet postings that featured my name. The alert linked to a brief message posted to the Russian blogging service LiveJournal that broadcast my precise location. The posting read: "American cybersecurity blogger Brian Krebs is now in Russia, staying at the Moscow Marriott Grand."

I ran upstairs and bolted the door to my spacious hotel room, immediately beginning to wonder if I had made a huge miscalculation in coming to Russia. Eventually, I convinced myself otherwise, reminding myself that this interview was crucial to wrap up all the work I had been doing to expose these spammers. Within a few hours I finally got up enough nerve to call Vrublevsky. When I tried the third cell phone number I had for him, Vrublevsky answered.

"Duuuuuuuuddddde!" he bellowed into the phone. "It's 7 a.m. where you are. Who died?"

I informed Vrublevsky that I was in fact in his time zone, and that we should meet as soon as possible. After another long "Duuuuuuuuuddde!" Vrublevsky promised to send a car if I would wait in the hotel lobby. He told me he'd be sending along with the driver his receptionist, named Vera. He proceeded to describe Vera as this grossly overweight, unattractive older lady but, hey, she spoke English and knew how to deal with Westerners, so she was coming, he said.

Fifteen minutes later, I was seated in the lobby, nervously waiting for Vera and watching incoming guests as they stomped off snow and trudged through the hotel's revolving door. Sitting there nursing a cup of hot tea, I found it difficult to avoid staring at a gorgeous, slender, dark-haired young woman standing nervously just beside the door, clad in skintight jeans and a puffy white coat. After a while of unsuccessfully trying not to look in her direction, I had trouble ignoring the fact that she was also trying not to stare at me.

After about five minutes of this dance, the young woman came over and asked if my name was Brian. I was momentarily alarmed (I knew next to no one in Moscow at this point) until she told me her name was Vera, and I suddenly remembered with a smile why I could trust almost nothing of what comes out of Vrublevsky's mouth.

The joke continued when, after enduring about twenty minutes of creeping Moscow rush-hour traffic to travel a couple of miles, we arrived at ChronoPay's offices and I ran into the same girl clad in different clothes. It turns out that Vera has a twin sister who also works at the company.

Vrublevsky was feeling especially punchy that evening, and he was clearly excited by my surprise visit. True to form, almost immediately upon my arrival he launched into an elaborate tale. Apparently, someone had arranged a police raid on the Rx-Promotion Gold Party, a gathering held four nights earlier at Moscow's Golden Palace. The normally boozy and bawdy event is thrown for all Rx-Promotion affiliates—those several hundred individuals who pimp Rx-Promotion pharmacy sites. The top affiliate was to win an actual one-kilogram bar of gold, while other leading pill-pushers would win iPads and iPhones.

Unfortunately for the Rx-Promotion affiliates, the party was broken up when several busloads of men in ski masks and machine guns stormed the party and began interrogating the revelers. Vrublevsky claims the men were sent on behalf of the drug enforcement authorities, but according to several of those in attendance who posted on various Russian forums about the experience, the police appear to have used the raid as a pretense to match Rx-Promotion affiliates' online identities to real faces and names. I privately decide that Vrublevsky's version of the story is unlikely, but I'm unwilling to interrupt his narration in case it offends him and he decides to show me the door—or worse.

Vrublevsky never showed at his own party. As he explains it, the day before the gathering his wife inexplicably pleaded with him to go on an emergency vacation to the Maldives. What's more, someone had the presence of mind to take down all Rx-Promotion logos from the rented party space hours before the police arrived.

"The whole Russian Internet knew there was supposed to be an Rx-Promotion party in Moscow, and obviously everyone would expect logotypes of Rx-Promotion," Vrublevsky tells me, chain-smoking Marlboros in his company's cramped boardroom, which features an enormous, outdated map of the world flanked by swords and a giant red Soviet-era flag.

"And for some reason," he continued, speaking about himself in the third person, "everyone expected Mr. Vrublevsky would show up there. Obviously, Mr. Vrublevsky would probably not be able to control every motherfucker with a cell-phone camera around. And for that reason, Mr. Vrublevsky decided not to be there. At the same time, someone else decided to remove all of the Rx-Promotion logos around.

"Mr. Vrublevsky flies to the Maldives to have a one-week vacation. He then gets a phone call that there are five buses of special forces from Russian DEA going to that party, closing down Golden Palace and two nearby cafes, just for the reason that there are too many special forces and dogs and cameras. Getting in there just to find out some very stupid shit: there is no Mr. Vrublevsky, no logotype, absolutely nothing to shoot on their video."

The story about how police raided the Rx-Promotion party to dig up dirt on its founders and affiliates was certainly amusing, but it appears to have simply been one of nine such casino raids and nearly one hundred "gambling den" raids that were conducted in 2011 by a new anti-gambling sheriff of Moscow, Anatoly Andreev.

After relating this seemingly random anecdote to me, Vrublevsky asks Vera to bring us some coffee and we make some small talk about the Moscow traffic and about the man stomping above us, shoveling huge mounds of snow off the building's roof. I ask Vrublevsky a bit about his family, and he says with a knowing smile and a sardonic laugh that his father worked for many years as a researcher at Nycomed, a large European pharmaceutical company.

I ask him about the origin of the sword that flanks the Soviet flag standing behind my chair. Vrublevsky tells me a long story about how it was presented to him by the leader of the capital of Dagestan, whom he describes as a close personal friend. He doesn't tell me the guy's name, only that he was—at least at one time—mayor of Makhachkala. According to the *Moscow Times*, that person is likely Said Amirov, a four-time mayor who is said to have survived more than fifteen assassination attempts and is paralyzed from the waist down. In July 2014, a Russian court found Amirov guilty of planning a terrorist act, sentencing him to ten years in a maximum-security prison. Amirov also was found guilty of illegal weapons possession, so it's pretty funny that he gave Vrublevsky a sword.

"It turns out that the main dude I was with there, his uncle was the mayor of [Dagestan's capital city] Makhachkala," Vrublevsky recalled. "This mayor guy is the most blown-up guy in the world. This mayor dude has been blown up like thirteen fucking times. They didn't kill him—he's in a wheelchair. But once the local terrorist groups blew up a whole neighborhood just to try to kill him. Not just one building, but the whole neighborhood."

Vrublevsky dodges direct questions about why he was in the turbulent mountainous Russian republic, a mostly Muslim region that borders Georgia and the breakaway regions of Chechnya. But it is likely that Vrublevsky passed through the region on a side trip from Baku, Azerbaijan. The leaked ChronoPay emails show that executives visited Baku on several occasions to keep up relations with Bank Standard, an Azerbaijani financial institution that processed huge volumes of payments for ChronoPay's rogue antivirus programs and Rx-Promotion's pharmacy sites.

I change the subject and ask Vrublevsky if he'd discovered who was responsible for leaking ChronoPay's internal documents.

He responds, "The leak was done from within the company, from within the IT department. They realized they were going to get caught stealing money. So, first they disrupted [the] internal accounting system, which made this compromat useless for law enforcement, because we simply don't have any accounting database. It was destroyed before [the] compromat went out."

I push a manila folder full of printed emails across the table toward Vrublevsky. "Well, whoever it was also sent about 30,000 internal ChronoPay emails. This was part of the original package they had sent me of ChronoPay email from the beginning of 2009 through the middle of 2010."

Vrublevsky lazily leafs through a few of the pages, shrugs, and then shoves the folder back across the table. "I'm not surprised at all."

I'm not deterred by his vagueness. "It's a pretty rich collection of documents. You might find it interesting. There is a lot of damning stuff in there, and none of it too flattering about you or ChronoPay. But I guess you've already seen most of those emails."

"Could be. There are a lot of 'buts' there."

I persist. "Buts or no, the documents show me that you haven't been truthful with me at all, Pavel."

"Oh? On what?" he asks vaguely.

"On a lot of things. For starters, remember the first story I wrote about ChronoPay? The rogue antivirus piece back in 2009? You said you didn't have anything to do with that industry."

"Yeah, so what's the story?"

"You tell me! As far as I can tell, the story is that you guys set up an entire cybercrime industry and paid for the domains and processing for it."

"Yeah, so what? I've told you about this before: this is what all processors do, and nobody is able to disclose this to you for a very simple reason. It violates Visa and MasterCard rules. Visa and MasterCard know everyone is doing this, but by rules it's illegal. When you register merchant IDs, this is part of the service you provide. Plus you do customer support which is related to that."

Finishing his coffee and lighting another cigarette, Vrublevsky refers to my 2009 *Washington Post* story that drew multiple connections between him and ChronoPay and the rogue antivirus industry.

I couldn't believe my ears; Vrublevsky had admitted that many of the companies which ChronoPay claimed to represent as clients were in fact set up and run by ChronoPay employees.

"Here's your mistake. By the time which correlates with your story, we did not know too much about spyware. But that company which you tracked was not used for spyware only. It was used for a bunch of shit. You can go and dig into Wirecard and Visa Iceland

and you'll find the same shit. The reason is when you open a merchant ID, you need to register it to a company, and that company should have a rock-solid look from [the] outside, like a legitimate website, et cetera. So most payment service providers, you basically register the companies yourself and monitor it from the inside."

I counter, "You also never told me that ChronoPay was the processor for Rx-Promotion…"

"No, you're right. I didn't."

"But it's true, isn't it?"

"Yes. Well, it used to be, anyway."[16]

I was floored. "What do you mean? Not anymore? As of when?"

"My friend, if I was able to tell you that, I would be fucking happy to."

"That's it? What's the deal there, Pavel? You know I've come a long way at great personal risk to interview you here in person. It's really not nice to be like this." I knew I was running a risk in challenging him but I needed answers.

Laughing again, he answers, "We dropped them as a client. It's quite simple."

"Rx-Promotion? When?"

"September of 2010. So I have had…a half-fucking-year to do nice legitimate business decisions."

---

16. Finally, we were getting somewhere. Vrublevsky's admission that his company was in fact closely involved in working with Rx-Promotion confirmed what was obvious from looking at several years' worth of leaked ChronoPay emails and spreadsheets. In one of our marathon phone conversations prior to my visiting him in Moscow, Vrublevsky effectively acknowledged that the leaked documents and emails were legitimate when he grudgingly admitted to me that it would have been hard for even the Russian FSB to have faked as many documents as were leaked in the ChronoPay breach.

Vrublevsky makes a call and, speaking in Russian to Vera, asks her to bring us some more coffee.

I press on. "The people who released the documents about your company have a lot of information about your operations."

"They used to steal money from within here, obviously they do. But they're not going to get anywhere with this."

"Why not?"

"You see, compromat is not enough to fuck someone. You also need to have the possibility to prove something, and to do that, you need to know how it works. The people who released this information made a lot of mistakes. I spread information around quite carefully. You can see basically who was the one spreading the information, not from the information itself, but the information that surrounds it. You know what they don't know. You can figure out quite simply who was doing this based on what he knows and what he doesn't."

Beautiful Vera, nervously smiling at us both and somehow sensing the conversation has turned more intense, steps gingerly into the conference room, sets cups of coffee before us both, and quickly leaves. I'm baffled by Vrublevsky's response, but I don't want to interrupt him. "Okay," I said. "Go on."

"Brian, there is one other thing not related to this exactly, a thing that surprises me."

"What's that, Pavel?"

"When it comes to me...why is it again that you expect me to be truthful? Please remind me."

I was a bit taken aback by how he cleverly turned the conversation back on me. "Call me old-fashioned. I guess when I ask a direct question, I expect an honest answer."

"Ahahaha. A lot of people expect that. But coming back to the subject, I don't see Rx-Promotion or much of this other shit in the compromat to be much of a problem. And I'll tell you why: I really don't violate too many laws."

At this comment, I laugh so hard and so involuntarily that the coffee I just sipped almost comes spraying out my nose. It is all I can do to keep the coffee from spilling all over my suit and the board-room table. We both share a nice laugh that helps defuse the tension.

Nevertheless, I could see that this was not going to be a fruitful line of inquiry. So I tried changing tack and pulled some printed ChronoPay emails out of my briefcase.

"I want to get your reaction to this ChronoPay internal email sent by ChronoPay's chief of security, Vladimir Stepkov, dated March 16, 2010 with the subject, 'Rx-promotion2 total earnings.' It appears to describe your co-ownership of Rx-Promotion with Yuri 'Hellman' Kabayenkov. It reads: 'Men, our beloved Kisilev gave the data on the cost of tech support. Pavel and Hellman divide all in half, and…'"

Interrupting my recitation, Vrublevsky is clearly annoyed and no longer smiling. "Whoa, whoa, Brian, whoa, wait! I have no fucking idea what's going on here! I can't really get too much into discussions between other people and me. So if you drop the scary questions shit, please, perhaps it's better to move into normal talk."

I remain silent for a few minutes. Vrublevsky continues, smirking again and lighting another Marlboro before the one he was just smoking has been extinguished. I decide an awkward silence may prompt him to divulge more. But he isn't having any of it.

"I'm not going to get deep into this Rx-Promotion shit, and you're not going to figure out much of this for yourself. Same goes for spyware. I'm doing much better research when it comes to Gusev. Like the cops say, the best way to find out is when a person says it himself. This is not something I want to talk about. But I made you promises before to give you truthful answers to some questions. Not of course on all of them, but some."

"I see. Well, just do me a favor, will you? Just let me know when you want to start doing that."

We talked for more than three hours, and my additional direct questions elicited equally evasive and nonsensical responses from Vrublevsky. Exhausted, I finally packed up my things and thanked him for making time for me. On the way out, Vrublevsky showed me around the building that ChronoPay's offices were housed in, which according to him was an edifice of historic value.

As we descended the stairs to the parking garage, he pointed out a door directly one floor below the entrance to ChronoPay's office. On the door was a sign that read, "Russian Association of Electronic Communications." RAEC is a lobbying firm whose principal organizer, according to leaked ChronoPay documents, was being paid a monthly salary by ChronoPay. This was the same RAEC that had taken the lead in the campaign to organize Western media coverage of the criminal charges against Gusev as the "#1 spammer in Russia."

I left Russia two days later, after declining two more invitations from Vrublevsky to meet. Our meeting had annoyed and unnerved me. I had spent the previous eight months listening to him lie to me over the phone about various topics, but to see him do it so flagrantly and openly to my face was aggravating and left me extremely uneasy around him.

I didn't expect much from Vrublevsky, so I wasn't terribly surprised when he stonewalled me at our interview. He did, however, confirm several important pieces of information. ChronoPay was deeply involved in not only processing payments for fake antivirus companies and the pharmacy affiliate partnerka Rx-Promotion, but it was primarily responsible for creating and fostering these enterprises.

Vrublevsky's overconfidence in his claim that he really doesn't break too many laws turned out to be misplaced. Four months after our visit, Russian federal investigators issued an arrest warrant for him in connection with a massive cyberattack on ChronoPay's top competitor, a Russian payment processing company called Assist. Vrublevsky was later arrested, tried, found guilty, and sentenced to a two-and-a-half-year stint in a Russian penal colony. In May 2014, barely a year into his sentence, he was inexplicably released from prison.

Despite my disappointment over my visit with Vrublevsky, it did help me piece together a more complete picture of this fraud ecosystem—and that had always been my goal. At this point, I'd interviewed dozens of buyers who helped to perpetuate the spam problem, and I'd tracked down some of the world's most notorious spammers. It was time to press forward and dive into the trenches with the spam fighters on the front lines of this incessant, borderless war.

Chapter 10

THE ANTIS

F ew subjects so predictably rile the spam and cybercrime community as much as discussions about "antis"—the underground's derisive term for anti-spam vigilantes who act alone or in concert with other antis to hobble or take down the large-scale junk email operations plaguing us. The leaked online chats between Stupin and hundreds of bulk emailers who worked for SpamIt reveal that when affiliates weren't busy spamming, they were using their bot armies to bludgeon someone or something offline that threatened to kill their criminal operations. Very often, rival spammers would turn their digital armaments on one another. But their favorite targets were antis, whom the spammers perceived as a real and present threat to their business models— and rightfully so.

By the third quarter of 2013, nearly 70 percent of all email sent daily was unsolicited bulk email relayed via spam botnets. To give you a sense of how massive the spam problem is, miscreants like those working for SpamIt and other spam partnerkas were sending *an estimated eighty-five billion junk messages every day.* According to InternetWorldStats.com, more than three billion people were using the Internet as of June 2014, which means that spammers were sending approximately twenty-eight junk emails for every Internet user each day.

Some of the anti-spam tactics came from independent activists, such as members of InboxRevenge.com, a forum dedicated to exposing spammers by reporting spam domains to registrars and calling attention to spam-friendly bulletproof hosting providers. One of the most active InboxRevenge members was Adam Drake, the same anti-spam activist to whom Vrublevsky initially leaked the SpamIt database to undermine his archrival Gusev.

Ironically, in order to take down the spammers, Drake and his merry band of vigilantes had to use their adversaries' own techniques. They built a series of automated tools designed to place phony orders for drugs at dozens of spam-advertised websites simultaneously. These order-stuffing programs would place rapid-fire orders for pills using fake identities and made-up credit card details. The idea was to flood the spam partner-kas' databases with so much junk that they would be forced to manually verify each order. In some cases, the order-stuffing programs slowed the pill websites to a crawl, blocking interested buyers from making purchases.

"We sent on average 20,000 to 30,000 'orders' to their spamvertized domains every day," Drake recalled of the initiative they began in 2007. In response, the spam partnerkas built increasingly sophisticated fraud detection systems that behaved much like the spam filters they detested, but for bogus orders. Those systems "scored" each order on the likelihood that it was fake by looking for a combination of qualities about an order that flagged it as high risk. In the process, Drake said, the spammers ended up declining or canceling a great many orders from legitimate buyers. "Clearly we cost them some money."

Indeed, SpamIt and GlavMed's order-checking system routinely red-flagged purchases that were even mildly suspect. A review of the customer order record leaked from those sister partnerkas shows that thousands of orders were held or denied based on the slightest whiff of a fake order. For example, many orders were declined for the following reason, which accompanied thousands of orders in the SpamIt customer service system:

"This order is slightly riskier because the phone number supplied by the user is not located within the zip code of the billing address for the credit card."

According to Vishnevsky—our "Virgil" in the spammer underworld and the guy who helped to bankroll the development of the Cutwail spam botnet—the anti-fraud measures also served to keep in check spam affiliates who tried to generate fake sales and commissions using stolen credit cards. Such fraud activity would not only result in commissions for phony sales, but would ultimately bring unwanted attention to the partnerka's credit card processing systems, which would incur hefty fines if the number of credit card chargebacks exceeded a certain threshold (usually 1 percent of overall sales).

SpamIt administrators also took elaborate steps to ensure that anti-spam groups and activists could not easily take down the pharmacy websites being advertised via spam. The SpamIt folks used hacked PCs to help obfuscate the real location of the pill-shop sites, employing a circuitous method known as "fast-flux" hosting. This method, the virtual equivalent of the classic street-corner scam known as "three-card monte," involves rapidly changing the locations of the website so that no one site is used long enough to be isolated and shut down.

Under a fast-flux setup, the customer clicking a link in a spam email might reach a different site or Internet address if he or she clicked the link again a few seconds later. Potential customers of these pill shops would not notice anything different, except perhaps a short delay.

SpamIt's curators also kept a close eye out for fraud investigators from MasterCard, Visa, and the major pharmaceutical firms. The SpamIt database shows that they routinely added these Internet addresses and email addresses to a database of customers that were blocked from placing orders on the pharmacy sites.

Botmasters like Gugle and Cosma worked diligently to ensure maximum inbox deliverability of their emails and were constantly changing their approaches to evade new protections being added to anti-spam software and hardware. This glut of spam became so overwhelming that many network security professionals in charge of defending corporate networks were forced to supplement their hardware and software-based anti-spam tools with spam "black-lists" (also called "blocklists").

At its most basic, a spam blacklist is a record of Internet address ranges that are most frequently seen as sources of spam. Generally, Internet addresses on blacklists fall into one of two categories: they are at networks and Internet service providers (ISPs) that have earned a reputation for turning a blind eye to spammers on their networks—like Atrivo and McColo Corp.—or they are individual malware-infected, spam-spewing "zombie" PCs.

The most widely used blacklists were run by ad-hoc and secretive organizations with funny names, like Spamhaus, SURBL, and URIBL (the *BL* in these acronyms stand for "blacklist"). Companies trying to block spam for tens of thousands of employees routinely incorporate these blacklists into spam filters, blocking the delivery of email sent from any of the listed Internet addresses. Not infrequently, innocent, non-spamming networks would get lumped into these blacklists along with the bad actors. But most organizations were all too willing to accept that some legitimate email would not get through if it meant being able to stem the surging daily tide of junk messages.

For its part, the spam community was less than amused by these self-appointed guardians of the inbox, and maintained that antis had no right to decide which emails Internet users should and should not be able to receive. In 2011, a copy of Spamdot.biz, an extremely secretive forum frequented by most of the world's top spammers, was made available to several law-enforcement agencies and this author. The forum postings show that as far back as 2005, spammers began organizing and executing large-scale Internet attacks aimed at punishing and intimidating anti-spam activists.

Among the most destructive and blistering of such campaigns was one of the largest cyberattacks in the history of the Internet waged against a remarkably effective anti-spam start-up called Blue Security Inc. The company had devised an elegant approach to stopping spam destined for more than half a million users of its Blue Frog software. The program would simply fire off a reply to the sender's network, asking the spammer to stop delivering junk email to its users.

But because those sorts of requests tended to go ignored, Blue Security took them to the next level. It bombarded the spammers with requests from all 522,000 of its customers at the same time. That led to a flood of Internet traffic so heavy that it disrupted the spammers' ability to send emails to other recipients—a crippling effect that caused a handful of known spammers to comply with the requests.

But after a short while, key members of the spam underground declared they'd had enough and said it was time for Blue Security to be wiped off the face of the Internet. According to a lengthy discussion thread on Spamdot.biz, at least a dozen top spammers spent weeks and more than $15,000 marshaling their forces for an all-out surprise attack on Blue Security's customers.

Spamdot members had discovered that the Blue Frog software contained a critical weakness: spammers who wished to comply with Blue Frog removal requests were given a free tool that allowed them to clean their lists of Blue Frog user email addresses. While Blue Security took pains to encrypt the user email addresses included in that tool, it was easy for spammers to identify which email addresses on their spam distribution lists belonged to Blue Frog users. All the spammer needed to do was compare their unaltered spam email lists with those scrubbed by Blue Security's tool. The addresses that were missing from the spammer's scrubbed distribution lists were all Blue Security users.

The assault on Blue Security began with a threatening email sent to most of the 522,000 Blue Frog users. The message below was pasted for review and later edited by several Spamdot forum members before being emailed to the Blue Frog community:

You are being emailed because you are a user of Blue Security's well-known software "Blue Frog."

Today, the Blue Security database became known to the worst spammers worldwide. Within 48 hours, the database will be published on the Internet, and your email address will be open to them all. After this, you will see the spam sent to your mailbox increase 10 to 20 fold.

Blue Security was illegally attacking email marketers, and doing so with your help. Many websites have been targeted and hit, including non-spam sites. Blue Security's software has been fully analyzed and contains an abundance of malicious code. This includes: ability to send mass mail to users; the ability to attack websites with distributed denial of service attacks (DDoS); the ability to open hidden doors on any machine on which it is running; and a hidden auto-update code function, which can install anything on your computer and open it up to anyone.

Blue Security lists a USA address as their place of business, whereas their main office is in Tel Aviv. Blue Security is run by a few Russian-born Jews, who have previously been spamming themselves. When all is said and done, they will be able to run, hide, and change their identities, leaving you to take the fall. YOU CANNOT PARTICIPATE IN ILLEGAL ACTIVITIES and expect to get away with it. This email ensures that you are well aware of the situation. Soon, you will be found guilty of computer crimes such as DDoS attacking of websites, conspiracy, and sending mass unsolicited bulk email messages for everything from Viagra to porn, as long as you continue to run Blue Frog.

They do not take money for downloading their software, they do not take money for removing emails from their lists, and they have no visible revenue stream. What they DO have is 500,000 computers sitting there awaiting their next command. What are they doing now?

1. Using your computer to send spam?

2. Using your computer to attack competitor websites?

3. Phishing through your files for your identity and banking information?

If you think you can merely change your email address and be safe while still running Blue Frog, you are in for a big surprise. This is just the beginning...

An unusually active member of the Spamdot forum, a user who adopted the nickname "BoT," laid out a devious plan for an attack on Blue Security that would turn the company's own anti-spam service against its users. The strategy was simple and elegant. The spammers would register dozens of domain names, all of which would redirect visitors back to a single website that the spammers controlled. Then, the miscreants would spam Blue

Security's entire user base, and sit back and wait for the inevitable wave of Unsubscribe requests to come in. When the removal requests started flowing back to that single website, the spammers would simply change the site's settings so that all incoming traffic got redirected to Blue Security's homepage, effectively causing the company's own anti-spam technology to attack itself.

"This way they either get screwed in the ass by their own weapon or get abuse complaints," BoT explained in a Spamdot forum posting just prior to the attack. "Even better, would be to redirect the traffic to the websites of CNN, BBC, Reuters, and such, and those sites will start writing that the Internet is turned into a battle because of the 'blue froglings.'"

On May 1, 2006, the spam community unleashed a series of increasingly amplified attacks on Blue Security's Internet servers, immediately blocking legitimate users from visiting the company's site. Blue Security hadn't yet been made aware that it was being targeted, but company officials knew customers were having difficulties reaching the firm's website. At some point, the decision was made to redirect traffic destined for its unreachable homepage to a company blog, which included a message to Blue Frog users acknowledging the problem.

Blue Security's blog was hosted at a blogging service run by Six Apart Ltd., a San Francisco-based company that runs millions of websites through its TypePad service. (Six Apart would later be bought by Russian blogging giant LiveJournal.ru.) The result of this redirection meant that Six Apart's blog service then received the brunt of the attack, and that thousands of web logs hosted there also went down. The denial-of-service assault also shut down operations for roughly twelve hours at Tucows Inc., a Toronto-based Internet services company that helped manage Blue Security's site. Tucows CEO Elliot Noss called the attack "by far the largest the company had ever seen," and said that only a handful of companies have the infrastructure in place to withstand such an assault, much less a more powerful one.

"This attack really was like trying to take out a mosquito with an atomic bomb," Noss said.

Not long after that, Blue Security CEO Eran Reshef received an email from one of the spammers who had previously agreed to stop spamming Blue Security's users—telling him how to get in touch with the person in charge of the attack.

The message provided a link to a pharmacy website that was being promoted by spammers at the time and instructed Reshef to view the HTML source of the page. Within it, he would find an ICQ number. ICQ, or I-Seek-You, is an instant message technology that was immensely popular in the cybercrime community at the time.

Blue Security's team downloaded a copy of the pharmacy site homepage and then opened it in an HTML editor to make sure it was not booby-trapped with malicious code. They then located the hidden message: "preved, stuchis v asku 299650295," or "hello, add ICQ #299650295."

Soon after Reshef sent a chat request to that ICQ number, someone using the name "Pharmamaster" replied. Pharmamaster was taunting and not at all interested in bargaining.

Tue May 02 16:30:57 2006

[16:02] BLUESECURITY: Do you want to discuss now a friendly resolution to the current situation? We are aware of your concerns, but as I told you before, and unlike what you think, we don't want to affect your business. We are not a common anti-spam company.

[16:07] PHARMAMASTER: You started with me and my people and my staff, so you shall get hurt first and feel who we are. And when I'm sure you got the point of who we are, then we can talk. Bluesecurity .com is down now but how about we keep all your systems down for a few months?

Reshef declined to be interviewed about the specifics of the attack. But a source who helped the company respond to the onslaught said Reshef also received threats against his family.

"The level of the attack was so bad that I remember being in a meeting with Eran and the other guys," said the source, speaking on the condition of anonymity. "The other stuff that was going on was a personal attack where Eran was getting pictures of his children at a playground sent to him—pictures he'd never seen before."

The attacks continued for more than two weeks, with increasing intensity. At one point, the attackers began emailing Blue Security employees, saying that they had 70 percent of the Blue Frog email user base and offering $50,000 for the remaining 30 percent to any employee willing to turn over the company's internal data.

On May 14, the management of Blue Security met with the FBI to discuss their options, but this was more a formality than anything. Two days later, Reshef and Blue Security would wave the white flag. The *Washington Post* ran a front-page story by this author on May 17, observing that the company had acknowledged defeat. Blue Security had received more than $4 million in venture capital funding, but its benefactors had decided it was time to throw in the towel.

That story quoted Todd Underwood, then chief of operations and security for Renesys Corp., a company that monitors Internet connectivity. Underwood called the attack "unsurprising but sad."

"When the company's founders first approached the broader anti-spam community and asked them what they thought of Blue Security's business model, everyone said this was a terrible idea and that they would eventually cause a lot of collateral damage," Underwood said. "But it's also extremely unfortunate, because it shows how much the spammers are winning this battle."

The individuals responsible for organizing the attack on Blue Security appear to have been the principals at one of the largest pharmacy partnerkas at the time. Many of the plans laid out on Spamdot.biz for attacking Blue Security were shaped and encouraged by a heavyweight Spamdot .biz user who had adopted the nickname "Mr. Green." According to Spamhaus, Mr. Green was the alias used by a Russian named Vlad Khokholkov, a Moscow native who allegedly partnered with notorious spammer Leo Kuvayev.

The attack on Blue Security was a shot across the bow of anti-spammers everywhere. At the time, close to 90 percent of all email was junk advertisements, and Blue Security had tapped into a visceral sense of frustration among email users who were fed up with the daily deluge. But the top Spamdot members were running pharmacy partnerkas that were pulling in millions of dollars each month, and they viewed Blue Security as the vanguard of a new breed of anti-spam activity that posed a potent threat to the continued success of their money-making machines. They weren't willing to be sidelined, whatever the cost.

Spamhaus believes Kuvayev and Khokholkov ran the pharmacy affiliate programs Mailien and Rx-Partners. This is backed up by the leaked instant message chats from SpamIt administrator Dmitry Stupin. In a 2008 conversation between Stupin and "Joop"—the nickname used by a Russian who was one of GlavMed's top earners—the two are discussing a rival affiliate program called "Affiliate Connection."

"If it's no secret, do you know Leonid Kuvayev and Vlad Khokholkov (Mr. Green)?" When Stupin hesitated in answering, Joop apologized and changed the subject. "I am taking my question back. Something is wrong with my head. I forgot that their partnerka [was] Rx-Partners/Stimulcash."

Kuvayev, a Russian national, was convicted of violating U.S. anti-spam laws in Massachusetts in 2003 and ordered to pay $37 million for blasting botnet spam that touted counterfeit copies of Microsoft Windows and other name-brand software. He reportedly fled the country after that, avoiding jail time. But at some point after his conviction, Kuvayev returned to Russia.

Ultimately, however, Microsoft got the last laugh. The software giant paid consultants at Russian computer forensics company

Group-IB to monitor Kuvayev's activities and to share the information with Russian law-enforcement agencies.

In 2011, Kuvayev was arrested on child molestation charges. He is now in a Russian prison. Police raided Kuvayev's home after receiving a tip that he was having sex with underage girls. In his residence, they found hours of videotaped footage showing him abusing girls—some as young as fourteen years old—lured from a nearby Moscow orphanage. In 2012, Kuvayev was tried and convicted of child molestation, and he is currently serving a twenty-year prison sentence (recently reduced to ten years according to *MKRU*, a Russian weekly periodical).

Reached via email, Khokholkov denied being involved in the attack on Blue Security. Exactly who was responsible for orchestrating the attack remains unclear, but the leaked SpamIt chats and forum discussions clearly show that Vlad and Leo worked as partners, and that Kuvayev's spam gang was heavily involved.

Not long after the attack on Blue Security, Mr. Green asked Spamdot forum administrators to delete all of his postings and account information. But some of his forum messages survived as quoted text in forum conversations between other Spamdot members. They indicate that Mr. Green was working closely on the attack with a self-professed Satanist who used the nickname "Zliden," and the email address "domains@locu.st." According to Spamhaus, this was the last known email address of Leo Kuvayev.

Kuvayev is widely considered one of the most blatant and unrepentant spammers that ever worked the business. But like other masters of bulk email, he took care to separate his various online identities from his offline existence, switching email addresses and nicknames and deleting old posts every so often to elude digital-crimes investigators and anti-spam activists.

Even so, Kuvayev's experience (and that of his contemporaries like Cosma and Nechvolod) shows that while the Internet may occasionally lose track of online identities, anti-spam and Internet security activists have far longer memories and are willing to go to great lengths to bring spammers to justice.

Spamhaus DDoS

The denizens of Spamdot.biz also planned and executed several powerful attacks against Spamhaus, as well as against the widely used spam blacklists maintained by URIBL and SURBL. In a message to fellow members in October 2008, Spamdot administrator "Ika" posted a note on the forum to update the group's progress in collecting funds from spammers to launch a lengthy distributed denial-of-service (DDoS) attack against the websites of all three blacklist providers.

The message read, in part:

Dear Sirs,

We have collected more than $3,000 in the fund, of which portions will be allocated to the first four days of DDoS against URIBL and Spamhaus. We also bought $1,000 worth of bot installs at the rate of $25 for 1,000 bots.

Current DDoS targets: 1) Infrastructure lists.uribl.com/ 2) Home businesses of [Spamhaus founder Steve] Linford—www.uxn.com

and www.ultradesign.com/net where the Spamhaus backup
database is kept. 3) Both faces of Spamhaus.org.

A representative from the online pharmacy partnerka Affiliate
Connection said that his spammers could pool together several
million hacked PCs for use in a massive attack on Spamhaus.
But he noted that the opportunity costs from an assault like that
would be high, because anti-abuse companies would quickly
identify and blacklist all further communications (including
future money-making spam) from the spam zombies. What's
more, the Affiliate Connection leader said, URIBL and SURBL
had recently purchased denial-of-service protection services
from a leading anti-DDoS provider.

The SpamIt administrators responded that these factors were
hardly enough to deter their plans.

"Well, then, if they are sitting on strong anti-DDoS
channels, we will have to act strongly and decisively to fill their
pipes," Ika declared. "They will have to account for huge traffic
volumes and it will become a real problem for them. It will be
expensive, but I think that some of the affiliates can allocate a
few hundred bucks a day on it."

Weeks later, the Spamdot.biz thread on plans for attacking Spamhaus had generated pages of talk but little action.
Disgusted with his colleagues, GeRa—the SpamIt and
Rx-Promotion affiliate who operated the Grum spam botnet—
challenged other spammers to step up and make sacrifices for
the good of the industry.

I appeal to the largest spammers, you guys doing $50,000 to $200,000 in commissions per month, will you not be able to find $3,000 to solve this problem?

Docent, the curator of the Mega-D spam botnet, responded that he and his team were ready to lend funding to support a sustained attack on Spamhaus. But soon the discussion stalled on the question of who was going to take responsibility for directing and organizing the attack.

To complicate matters, not everyone on the spam forum was in favor of attacking Spamhaus and the other blacklist providers. Severa, the botmaster who built and operated the Waledac and Storm spam botnets, was more philosophical, observing that "Spamhaus is only a part of [a] huge evolution process," and that spam filters actually helped to separate the novice spammers from the pros and discourage inexperienced, would-be spammers from taking up the craft.

"Guys, we CAN'T live without anti-spam filters anymore," Severa reasoned in a reply on the Spamdot discussion. By advocating for the continued, widespread use of spam filters, Severa's comments must have sounded almost heretical to many of his colleagues. But this spam kingpin in all likelihood correctly identified inexperienced spammers as a plague on the industry and a drain on his profits. If spam filters mainly succeeded at keeping the ankle-biters at bay, then so be it.

"Really, it stops newbies and lamers. Imagine, if all filters were turned off now. Would you earn money? NO! It would just kill email as communication service, nothing more. So, Spamhaus is not good or bad; Spamhaus is just Spamhaus."

Spamdot member "Swank" said he agreed with Severa's general statement, but that Spamhaus nevertheless needed to be humbled.

"Severa, you make a great point and you are exactly right," Swank wrote. "Having anti-spam filters and more is good for technology and the Internet because both sides—spammers and anti-spam folks—are always adapting and changing things around to get past each other's latest. The end result is technology is constantly improving, which like you said also keeps the professionals going and the newbies out of the business. That being said, stupid companies like Spamhaus are not fair to the mailers who are compliant. Spamhaus is abusing their powers to take out ANYONE who is an email marketer, regardless of whether or not the person is compliant or not. Spamhaus hates all email marketers. That crap is absolute bullshit and is not fair to anyone. Spamhaus needs to realize they are not untouchable and they will soon realize this."

In October 2008, GeRa announced to Spamdot members that he was releasing an automated attack tool that his programmers had built to help the community participate in a massive attack on Spamhaus. The tool, which he called Anti-Haus v. 1.0, was distributed to major botnet owners who in turn installed the program on tens of thousands of hacked PCs that they controlled and that were already relaying spam.

A representative from Spamhaus who gave his name only as "Barry" said the organization doesn't recall this particular October 2008 attack, noting that Spamhaus has lost track of how many massive attacks it has been hit with over the years.

In March 2013, Spamhaus came under an attack that it would not soon forget. In fact, some experts called it the largest concerted cyberattack that the Internet had ever witnessed. A group of bullet-proof hosting providers united under the "Stophaus" banner decided to attack the anti-spam provider. Stophaus formed an online forum to coordinate the assault after Spamhaus listed one bulletproof hosting provider in particular on its block list: a network known alternatively as CB3ROB, a.k.a. "Cyberbunker" because it operated from a heavily fortified NATO bunker in the Netherlands.

Attackers allied with Stophaus launched a nine-day digital siege that hurled as many as 300 billion bits of data per second at the organization's website. As the *New York Times* described it, the data "fire hose" directed at Spamhaus didn't just swamp the anti-spam provider; the deluge spilled over onto neighboring networks, causing what the organization's content distribution network CloudFlare estimated to be hundreds of millions of people to experience delays and error messages across the web.

When the attackers allied with Stophaus decided that they were not going to be able to bring down CloudFlare, which Spamhaus had hired to protect it from DDoS assaults, they began pelting the "peering points" at which Internet networks exchange traffic, including Internet exchanges in London, Amsterdam, Frankfurt, and Hong Kong.

The *New York Times* reported that authorities in Spain later arrested Sven Olaf Kamphuis, a thirty-five-year-old Dutch man thought to be responsible for coordinating the unprecedented attack on Spamhaus. According to Spamhaus and media reports, Kamphuis made claims about being his own independent country in the Republic of Cyberbunker. The *Guardian* reported that Kamphuis was extradited to the Netherlands, but there is no indication that he is being prosecuted for crimes there. Kamphuis denies being involved in the attack and said he was merely acting as a press contact for CB3ROB/Cyberbunker. Meanwhile, in November 2014, a seventeen-year-old male pleaded guilty in the United Kingdom to participating in the unprecedented attack on SpamHaus.

The Stophaus assault was the loudest and latest reminder that such weapons of mass disruption are readily and freely available today to any person or organization that chooses to wield them. The attack that hit Spamhaus—known as a DNS reflection and amplification attack—leveraged unmanaged domain name system (DNS) servers on the web to create huge traffic floods intended to intimidate and silence targets.

To understand the significance of this, here's a bit of background. DNS servers act as the white pages of the Internet, transforming or "resolving" human-friendly domain names like example.com into numeric network addresses used by computers. Typically, DNS servers only provide services to machines within a trusted domain, in this case example.com. But DNS reflection attacks rely on consumer and business Internet routers that are configured to accept queries from anywhere on the web. Attackers can send spoofed DNS queries to these so-called "open recursive" DNS servers, forging the request so that it appears to come from the target's network. That way, when the DNS servers respond, they reply to the spoofed (target) address.

The amplification part of the attack takes advantage of the ability to craft DNS queries so that the responses are much bigger than the requests. They do this by leveraging an extension to the DNS standard that enables large DNS messages. For example, an attacker could compose a DNS request of less than 100 bytes, prompting a response that is sixty to seventy times as large. This amplification effect is especially pronounced if the perpetrators query dozens of DNS servers with these spoofed requests simultaneously.

The good news is that Internet and security experts have long understood how to block these extraordinarily powerful attacks. "Indeed, a number of computer security specialists pointed out that the attacks would have been impossible if the world's major Internet firms simply checked that outgoing data packets truly were being sent by their customers, rather than botnets," wrote John Markoff and Nicole Perlroth of the *New York Times*.

The bad news is that little has changed since these ultra-powerful attacks first surfaced more than a decade ago, said Rodney Joffe, senior vice president and senior technologist at Neustar, a security company that also helps clients weather huge online attacks. Joffe estimates that there are approximately twenty-five million misconfigured or antiquated home and business routers that can be abused in these digital sieges. Most of these are home routers supplied by ISPs or misconfigured business routers, but a great many of the devices are at ISPs in developing countries or at Internet providers that see no economic upside to spending money for the greater good of the Internet.

"In almost all cases, it's an option that's configurable by the ISP, but you have to get the ISP to do it," Joffe said. "Many of these ISPs are on very thin margins and have no interest in going through the process of protecting their end users—or the rest of the Internet's users, for that matter."

And therein lies the problem. Not long ago, if a spammer or hacker wanted to launch a massive Internet attack, he had to assemble a huge botnet that included legions of hacked PCs. These days, such an attacker need not build such a huge bot army. Armed with just a few hundred bot-infected PCs, Joffe said, attackers today can take down nearly any target on the Internet, thanks to the millions of misconfigured Internet routers that are ready to be conscripted into the attack at a moment's notice.

"If the bad guys launch an attack, they might start off by abusing 20,000 of these misconfigured servers, and if the target is still up and online, they'll increase it to 50,000," Joffe said. "In most cases, they only need to go to 100,000 to take the bigger sites offline, but there are twenty-five million of these available."

Chapter 11

TAKEDOWN

Nine months after my icebreaker cruise on the Russian trip to meet Vrublevsky, I found myself again gazing out at the starry night sky, standing on the deck of another large ship in a foreign country. This time, it was on the upper deck of an aging cruise liner that was docked at the harbor in downtown Rotterdam.

On the other side of the frosted porthole windows, a big band was jamming at a reception for attendees of the GovCert cyber-security conference, where I had delivered a presentation earlier that day on the turf war between Gusev and Vrublevsky. The evening was bracingly frigid and blustery, and I was waiting there to be introduced to investigators from the Russian Federal Security Service (FSB). Several FSB agents who attended the conference told our Dutch hosts that they wanted to meet me, but only in a private setting.

My hands had grown so cold that I could no longer hold on to my beer glass, which was glazing with ice. I set the glass down on the ledge, and at the same time heard the thick steel door swing open behind me, squeaking loudly on its hinges. Stepping out into the night air, a woman from the conference approached, formally presented the three men following behind her, and then hurried back inside to the warmth of the reception.

A middle-aged stocky fellow introduced as the senior FSB officer spoke in Russian, while a younger gentleman translated into English between drags on a Marlboro. They asked, did I know anything about a company in Moscow called "Onelia"? I said no, asked them to spell it for me, and inquired as to why they were interested in this firm. The top FSB official said they believed the company was heavily involved in processing payments for a variety of organized cybercriminal enterprises.

Later that evening, back at my hotel room, I searched online for details about the company but came up dry. I considered asking some of my best sources in Russia what they knew about Onelia. But a voice inside my head warned that the FSB agents may have been hoping I'd do just that. They would be able to divine who my sources were when those individuals began making inquiries about a mysterious (and probably fictitious) firm called Onelia.

My paranoia got the best of me, and I shelved the information. That is, until several months later, when I discovered that Onelia (turns out it is more commonly spelled Oneliya) was the name of the limited liability company behind Gateline.net, the credit card processor that processed tens of thousands of customer transactions for SpamIt and Rx-Promotion.

Gateline.net states that the company's services are used by firms across a variety of industries, including those in tourism, airline tickets, mobile phones, and virtual currencies. But according to payment and affiliate records leaked from both SpamIt and Rx-Promotion, Gateline also used to process most of the rogue pharmacy site purchases promoted by spammers working for the two programs.

The connection between Gateline and the spam programs is supported by chat logs seized in 2011 by Russian investigators who were looking into SpamIt. Those logs show hundreds of conversations between SpamIt co-owner Dmitry "SaintD" Stupin and a Gateline administrator, Nikolai Victorovich Illin, who used the nickname "Shaman" (shaman@gateline.net) and was referred to as "Nikolai," or the diminutive form, "Kolya." The logs show more than 205 conversations between Shaman and Stupin from 2007 to 2010.

The leaked Stupin chats suggest that Shaman held enormous sway over the day-to-day operations of SpamIt. The pharmacy spam sponsor had great difficulty offering buyers the ability to pay by MasterCard, mainly because MasterCard seems to have been far more vigilant than Visa about policing the use of its services by rogue online pharmacies. The payment records of SpamIt indicate that Shaman received a sizable cut (about 8 percent) from all sales processed by the SpamIt pharmacies, and that he sometimes earned tens of thousands of dollars per week for his services.

In the following chat between Shaman and Stupin, recorded November 23, 2009, Shaman chastises Stupin for not being more aware of transactions that they believed were from undercover buys made by MasterCard fraud investigators. At the beginning of the chat, Shaman posts a link to a story about the criminal case opened by Russian investigators into SpamIt and Stupin's copartner, Igor Gusev.

SHAMAN: www.runewsweek.ru/country/31283/

STUPIN: Yep, yep.

SHAMAN: I'd suggest you not to advertise (PR) banks too much.

STUPIN: We need it the least.

SHAMAN: Otherwise, the entire business will go down. There has been something like that already.

STUPIN: Igor is trying to remove those posts.

SHAMAN: Okay. What's the deal with information wars? We have to stop this thing somehow. You'll destroy the whole business.

STUPIN: We will??? There has been not a single post from us. Igor is removing them all the time. We are not doing anything else.

SHAMAN: Stop responding to him in forum posts and RedEye will calm down.

STUPIN: I will ask Igor whether he has been responding. If he has—I will ask him to stop doing it.

SHAMAN: [Pointing out an email address that apparently belonged to a MasterCard fraud investigator] Kill this asshole—he is MasterCard's officer [employee]. He made a purchase. www.iacva.org /PDF/William%20Hanlin.pdf

SHAMAN: Be more attentive with the batch. Kill these as well: Charles Wilson, Stephen Carpenter, Fredric Manger, Sandro Racheli…

SHAMAN: What's going on with you?

STUPIN: Our programmers are checking what's happened. This should not be happening.

When I met with the FSB officers, the noose was already beginning to tighten around Vrublevsky, and Gusev had long ago closed SpamIt and effectively scuttled GlavMed. Now, it appeared that the FSB was taking aim at the financial infrastructure that served both competing pharmacy partnerkas, as well as other rogue online pharmacy programs.

Vrublevsky and Gusev's Pharma Wars were extremely costly for the spam industry, and their internecine war cost everyone in their business plenty. The two are now widely reviled on cybercrime forums for costing spammers tens of millions of dollars in profits, and for focusing attention from law-enforcement officials and security experts on individual spammers.

"These two fuckers killed the spam business," Vishnevsky said in a May 2012 interview. "It was never super profitable for most guys; maybe five to ten guys earned really good money with spam. But after Pavel and Gusev started their war, everyone started thinking that every spammer is a millionaire and started hunting for spam and spammers."

Vishnevsky complained that as the revenues from his spam business dwindled, he was forced to take a second legitimate or "white" job to supplement his "black" deeds. He still sells his spam software to numerous other spammers, but he also now serves as a system administrator of a local company in Moscow, essentially being paid to defend against some of the threats he is helping to deploy with his spam business.

But his spam business is definitely way down since the golden years of pre- and post-McColo. It's not that spamming somehow became a more dangerous activity in Russia. Rather, Vishnevsky is having trouble attracting and retaining talented program-mers to help maintain his spam business. Legitimate high-tech and well-paying programming jobs are increasingly available to talented coders in Moscow, and many of his longtime employees have been hired away to legitimate jobs in Moscow's young but promising tech sector.

"Many representatives of the underground can't find good coders now, because their salaries in Moscow are much more than you can earn with spam," Vishnevsky said. "This business went to shit when Pasha [Vrublevsky] got busted. If Pasha and

Gusev [had] not start[ed] that stupid war, everyone would be much happier."

Vishnevsky's criticism may be harsh, but it is hardly an exaggeration. The spam industry has indeed taken a huge hit in the past few years. Prior to SpamIt's closure in October 2010, the volume of spam sent worldwide each day hovered at around 5.5 billion messages. Since SpamIt's closure, however, the volume of global spam sent daily has been in marked decline. According to Symantec, by March 2011, spam levels had fallen to just over one billion junk messages per day, and the total has hovered at or very close to that diminished level ever since.

Spam remains a major problem, but it has moved much farther underground, and the major players seem to be quite a bit more circumspect in their activities. Of course, the turf war between Gusev and Vrublevsky was only one (albeit considerable) contributor to the decline of the spam economy. If the spam industry has become less attractive for would-be cybercriminals, that may have something to do with a series of targeted takedowns against major spam botnets over the past several years.

Here are a few other notable takedowns that targeted botnet operators and their crime machines:

- In May 2009, the Federal Trade Commission convinced a court to force Internet providers to stop routing traffic for 3FN, a hosting provider in Northern California that had been identified by investigators and the FTC as a major source of harmful content online. Vrublevsky's forum Crutop.nu was hosted there and forced to find a new home after 3FN's closure.

- In November 2009, FireEye, a Milpitas, Calif.-based security firm, led a coordinated effort to take down the Mega-D botnet. A year later, Mega-D's alleged proprietor—twenty-four-year-old Oleg "Docent" Nikolaenko—was arrested in Las Vegas. He pleaded guilty to spreading malicious software to protected computers in 2013 and was sentenced to time served, plus three years' probation. (Nikolaenko had already served twenty-seven months in custody related to his trial prior to his conviction.)

- In January 2010, employees at the Internet infrastructure firm Neustar seized control over the Lethic spam botnet, a spam-spewing crime machine made up of more than 200,000 infected PCs.

- In February 2010, Microsoft unveiled what would be the first in a series of court-assisted takedowns of major spam botnets. The first target was Severa's Waledac spam botnet, which at the time was blasting billions of spam emails daily through a network of more than 60,000 hacked computers. In that effort, Microsoft convinced a U.S. federal court to grant the software giant legal ownership of 277 Internet domains that the Waledac botmaster was using to control his spam empire.

- In October 2010, Armenian authorities arrested twenty-seven-year-old Russian Georgiy Avanesov in tandem with a coordinated takedown of the Bredolab botnet, a spam engine that had hijacked millions of PCs since its debut in 2009. At the height of Bredolab's operation, experts say the botnet was blasting more than three billion messages each day. Investigators alleged that Avanesov made more than $130,000 per month renting his botnet out to other spammers. According to a BBC report, Avanesov was later convicted of computer sabotage and sentenced to four years in an Armenian prison. SpamIt records indicate he had multiple affiliate profiles generating income for him from that pharmacy program.

- In March 2011, Microsoft went after Rustock, launching a legal sneak attack through the U.S court system to seize control over the domains being used to control Cosma's spam engine. At the time, Rustock was running on an estimated 815,000 computers and was blasting huge volumes of junk email daily. Microsoft had help in the case from Pfizer, the drugmaker whose products and trademarks were most heavily abused by the spammers.

- In July 2011, Microsoft announced it was offering a $250,000 reward for information leading to the arrest and conviction of the Rustock botmaster. Interestingly, while Spamdot.biz closed its doors after Gusev was named the World's Number One Spammer by Russian law-enforcement officials in October 2010, the spam forum didn't go away. It merely changed its name and location. Not long after Microsoft offered its reward, Cosma—the Rustock curator (having changed his nickname by then to "Tarelka," or "plate" in Russian)—could be seen on the new forum asking for advice on how to obtain a new passport under an assumed name.

- In July 2012, FireEye and Spamhaus went after the Grum botnet, which had emerged as one of the top three most active spam machines, sending eighteen billion messages per day. Their collaborative takedown briefly shrank global spam volumes, but the source code for Grum subsequently fell into the hands of several other miscreants, prompting its revival. Grum remains active today.

- In July 2013, Microsoft and the FBI announced a joint operation that took down more than 1,400 distinct botnets that were using Citadel malware to control infected PCs. Citadel was primarily used by crime groups engaged in emptying bank accounts through online heists.

- In December 2013, Microsoft worked with the FBI again and with authorities in Europe to disrupt the ZeroAccess botnet. ZeroAccess was often bundled with other threats (including spam bots and fake antivirus software), but the botnet mainly was designed to hijack search engine results on infected PCs and to redirect people to websites that fraudulently charged businesses for online advertising clicks.

- In June 2014, the FBI in conjunction with multiple international law enforcement partners and private security firms took down the "Gameover Zeus" botnet, a collection of more than one million hacked computers. The FBI also named a Russian man—thirty-one-year-old Evgeniy Mikhailovich Bogachev—as the mastermind behind the operation and the principal author of the botnet. According to the U.S. Justice Department, the Gameover botnet was used to steal more than $100 million from victimized businesses. The botnet was also a major platform for deploying costly online extortion attacks against individual computer users.

But it wasn't only the spam industry that was temporarily

trashed by the war between Gusev and Vrublevsky. ChronoPay was deeply involved in processing payments for partnerkas that pushed rogue antivirus products, and when Vrublevsky became the subject of a criminal investigation in 2011, his processing networks fell apart. Overnight, the rogue antivirus affiliate networks ground to a halt because they had lost their connection to the credit card networks. Vrublevsky was arrested at the end of May 2011 on unrelated charges, and by August 2011, computer security giant McAfee noticed a 60 percent decline in users reporting problems with fake antivirus programs.

Downing Domains and Scrubbing Search

Another front in the war on spam has targeted the pharmacy websites advertised via junk email. Typically, spammers have sought out domain name registrars who turn a blind eye to spammers registering hundreds or even thousands of domains per month for use in pharmacy spam campaigns. For many years, some of the largest players in the website name industry brushed aside requests by the anti-spam groups to de-register domains that were clearly registered to benefit from spam activity.

John Horton, a former deputy in the White House Office of Drug Control Policy and now president of LegitScript, an Internet pharmacy verification service, has tracked the rogue pharmacy domains for years. Horton said that for quite some time, most registrars argued that it wasn't their job to inspect how their customers were using their domains.

That situation began to change in late 2008, when

EstDomains—a Estonian domain registrar that had emerged as a clear favorite of spammers and Internet scammers alike—had its accreditation revoked by the Internet Corporation for Assigned Names and Numbers (ICANN), the nonprofit entity that oversees the domain name registration industry. ICANN took action after a *Washington Post* story by this author observed that EstDomain's CEO—Estonian businessman Vladimir Tsastsin—had been previously convicted of money laundering, forgery, and credit card fraud.

ICANN acted after my *Washington Post* story called attention to a little-known clause in the contracts that domain name registrars like EstDomains had signed with ICANN, which stated that registrars were not allowed to appoint principals who had criminal backgrounds. As mentioned in Chapter 8, Tsastsin was an early, major investor in ChronoPay, and in 2011 was arrested in Estonia along with six other men accused of running an enormous botnet that spanned more than four million machines worldwide.

Horton said the EstDomains incident spooked many in the domain registration business. One of EstDomains' closest partners was an Indian registrar called Directi, which was grappling with its own deluge of abuse complaints about spammers using its service.

"Three to four years ago, nobody was suspending domain names engaged in rogue Internet pharmacy activity unless you could also clearly show that those domains were benefiting from spam activity," Horton said. "Directi was one of the first registrars that said, if we know websites are selling prescription drugs without a prescription, and [those drugs are] being shipped into another country in violation of that country's laws, we will take action to suspend the domain. After that, we saw GoDaddy and eNom and a few others do the same thing. If you look at registrars by market share, roughly 60 to 70 percent of [the] registrar market now does act [to suspend domains] on the basis of those allegations."

If the Internet community wasn't aware of the financial risks of getting too deeply enmeshed in the web of fake pharma sites, they got that message loud and clear in August 2011, when the U.S. Justice Department announced that Google had agreed to pay a $500 million fine to settle a criminal investigation that it allowed supposed Canadian pharmacies—including many rogue Internet pharmacies—to advertise drugs for distribution in the United States. The $500 million figure was intended to represent the company's advertising revenue from the Canadian pharmacies and the revenue the pharmacies received from American customers buying controlled drugs.

Visa Crackdown

Probably the most lasting impact on the spam economy over the past two years has come from research published by a ragtag group of academic researchers who mapped out the money-laundering networks relied upon by nearly all pharmacy partnerkas. More importantly, the researchers were able to use their findings to browbeat top commercial brands into pressuring Visa to take action against the financial institutions that enable this activity.

By early 2010, the rogue pharmacy programs and fake anti-virus peddlers were being infiltrated by a stealth band of white-hat researchers, university professors, and grad students who hoped to show that following the money could make it much harder for these businesses to obtain credit card processing. Over several months, these researchers made hundreds of "test buys" at websites from forty different shady businesses hawking knockoff prescription drugs, counterfeit software, and fake antivirus products. The researchers—from George Mason University, the International Computer Science Institute, and the University of California, San Diego (UCSD)—posed as buyers for these products.

The academic team believed that if they could locate and bring public attention to the financial institutions that were profiting from this trade, the industry as a whole would suffer. The reason is that although selling knockoff prescription drugs over the Internet is not illegal per se, it is illegal for foreign entities to ship prescription drugs into the United States. Such activity violates Visa and MasterCard card processing rules and can bring hefty fines.

As noted in Chapter 5, UCSD professor Stefan Savage and his team had a mountain of work to do just in gathering ground-truth data about the pharmaceutical spam economy.

"When we started this, we wanted to figure out the whole value chain for the spam economy," Savage said. "One big part of it was the back-end processing and banks, which no one was looking at."

Savage said that initially the University of California, Berkeley was none too interested in their research. The sticky ethical and legal issues of essentially violating federal law to conduct otherwise harmless research made the project a tough sell. The school and the researchers struck a bargain. They would only purchase generic drugs that were available in the United States over the counter and without a prescription, such as the abortion drug RU-486.

It turned out that the toughest part of their research was finding a reliable way to pay for their test orders. If they ordered the drugs with the same credit card over and over, the pharmacy partnerkas would cancel the transactions and flag the card number as suspicious. They settled on prepaid gift cards, since these payment instruments allowed their purchases to be anonymous. But it wasn't enough to be able to purchase the drugs with the prepaid cards. The team needed to coax the card issuers into divulging the names of the banks and merchant account numbers used to process the transactions.

"We found [that using] gift cards was the easiest thing because we could put a fake name in them or whatever," Savage said. "But with a lot of these gift cards, if you wanted to find out transaction information, you needed to call some customer support center. And even some of these fairly big prepaid cards had only a few customer service people. And they would quickly get suspicious because if you did a lot of buys, you ended up talking to the same people all the time."

Savage and the other researchers soon discovered the perfect prepaid network, although he declined to name it so as not to ruin similar ongoing and future research efforts. He would only say that it is a prepaid card issued by a fairly large grocery-store chain in the United States.

"So we asked another group that was exploring this, and they told us about a gift card from a grocery-store chain. [UCSD graduate student] Chris Kanich shows up at one of these grocery stores with like $5,000 in cash and buys a boatload of these grocery-store prepaids. They didn't bat an eyelash," Savage said. "We've still got a stack of them somewhere. But that really was a hard thing to get past the university: that we were going to take all this money and turn it into these untraceable payment instruments, and of course trust us that we're not just going to go off on some Brazilian vacations or something."

With the university's blessing and a stack of prepaids the size of several decks of playing cards, the researchers set off buying knockoff drugs from sites that were being advertised via spam. The grocery store's prepaid network worked like a charm at all of the online pill shops, and everything seemed to be humming along nicely. That is, until Uncle Sam decided that the largely unregulated and burgeoning market for prepaid cards was rife for abuse by money launderers.

"Everything was going fine until Congress decided to help the world with this Credit CARD Act of 2009," Savage said, referring to a law that went into effect in 2010 and included multiple restrictions on how credit card companies can charge consumers. "The U.S. Treasury Department's Financial Crimes Enforcement Network (FinCEN) had always been very concerned about gift cards from the standpoint of volume to untraceable money, because they totally rocked and were great for money laundering. I swear, if you had a suitcase full of these, you could move many millions of dollars and it would be a helluva lot lighter than several million bucks."

Somehow, the prepaid industry had escaped the "know your customer" regulations that govern all U.S. financial institutions. These rules require banks to take specific steps to profile customer activity for signs of money laundering, suspicious transactions, and terrorist financing. After passage of the Credit CARD Act, however, prepaid networks fell under those same rules.

"These cards were all reloadable, and you could just set the name on the cards to whatever you wanted, because there were essentially no 'know your customer' rules for prepaid networks," Savage said. "All of a sudden these networks needed to have anti-money-laundering protections on international transactions. The short-term impact of that was everyone in this industry basically said, 'Okay, no more international transactions with prepaids,' which instantly made my $5,000 in prepaid cards a useless pile of crap."

Savage said he was discouraged and ready to give up at that point, but one of his graduate students—Chris Kanich—was undeterred. It was close to the end of November 2011.

"That son of a bitch totally ignored me and started cold-calling credit card issuers. He just called them and said, 'Hi, my name is Chris Kanich and we're doing this pharmacy spam research and we need a financial product that can do X, Y, and Z.' He called like fifty banks until he found this little bank in the Midwest. The person he talked to was receptive and said the CEO of the bank was really interested in cybersecurity. So they cut us a special deal, and after that, it became way easier."

The research team became intimately familiar with the various schemes that different rogue pharmacy networks used to weed out suspicious transactions. The rogue pharmacy networks were extremely wary of any fraud that might drive up their transaction rates or get them shut down, so they tended to rely on many layers of anti-fraud measures. For example, they used geo-location services to check if the buyer's Internet address showed that he was from a geographic location that was in the same town as the billing address on the credit card.

"Over time, we learned that each transaction was awarded

a fraud score based on a number of criteria, and any transactions that went above a certain fraud score were just never put through by the merchant processors," Savage said. "We learned that having an email address at a public webmail provider increased your fraud score. We learned over time that you needed to have a name that had a real physical address and a working phone number because they would often call you back to verify the order."

Early in their bogus buying spree, the researchers got found out. They were trying to conduct at least one undercover purchase every month from each of more than two dozen online pharmacy partnerka programs, so that they could keep track of the acquiring banks that were processing the transactions. Little did they know that most of the partnerkas were using the same financial institutions—a handful of banks in Azerbaijan, Latvia, Cyprus, and Turkey.

"We tried to keep a low profile and put in one order per program per month, but since we didn't know they were all getting processing from the same place, we were doing like thirty-five orders per month from the same people," Savage said. "At one point Chris Kanich [still a coresearcher but by then an assistant professor at University of Illinois at Chicago] gets this call from customer service people from one of the partnerkas, and he's having to think on his feet because they wanted to know why so many people at his address were ordering Zyrtec, which is an anti-allergy drug. And he basically made up some story, saying he lived in a college dormitory, and that he and all of his roommates had allergies because they were all allergic to cats and one of the guys had a cat. So, over time, we all learned how to do this fake ordering."

Spamlytics, Microsoft, and Napalm

Following the money trail revealed an astounding fact: 95 percent of the credit card transactions for the spam-advertised drugs and herbal remedies that the researchers purchased were handled by just three financial firms—one in Azerbaijan, one in Denmark, and another in Nevis, in the West Indies. Many Americans probably would be hard-pressed to find these places on a map, let alone recall conducting business with a company in those areas. And yet, a huge percentage of the credit card processing for the spam industry flowed through financial institutions in these regions. Anti-spam experts wanted to know why banks couldn't spot this odd concentration of dodgy banking activity and put a stop to it.

The researchers published their findings in a paper, "Click Trajectories: End-to-End Analysis of the Spam Value Chain," which described their "spamalytics" method for targeting the central weakness in any spam operation—its reliance on credit card processing for the goods advertised in junk messages.

Savage said that five days after the *New York Times* wrote about their paper, the researchers received a phone call from the White House. On the line was Victoria Espinel, the Obama administration's intellectual property enforcement coordinator.

"She was having this come-to-Jesus meeting with the domain name registrars, big-name brands, and Google, saying, 'Hey, we should all be doing something about this spam problem.' In our paper, we said there were basically two ways of doing this: you can go bilaterally against the [pharmacy] merchant banks, but that's slow. Or you could try to shut it off at the credit card issuing side, because these pharma networks were mostly all Western money. That was in retrospect a stupid idea, because when we talked to issuing banks here in the United States, they said, 'Hey, our customers aren't complaining, and we're not in the business of policing what our customers do that appears to be legal in the transaction records.'"

Espinel connected Savage and his team with the International Anti-Counterfeiting Coalition, a nonprofit group created to help corporate brands tackle commercial piracy and trademark abuse cases. The IACC was putting together an online portal where any brand holder could sign up and report abuse of their trademarks directly to MasterCard and Visa, which would investigate the claim and ultimately levy fines against any banks processing transactions tied to that claim.

The IACC relied on contracts that all banks sign as a prerequisite to doing business with the credit card associations, which stipulate that all product sales must be legal not only in the jurisdiction where the merchant bank resides, but also in the home country of the customer. And since shipping prescription drugs to consumers from outside of the United States violates U.S. law, any claim reported to Visa or MasterCard via the IACC by an affected brand holder effectively caused fines to rain down on banks that were processing payments for the pharmacy partnerkas.

"These stipulations were always in the contracts, but for some reason people weren't paying attention to this," Savage said. "It turns out that the people who really give a rat's ass about the spam problem are the brand holders, because they're the ones whose products, copyrights, and trademarks are being counterfeited and violated. And the beauty of this approach is it's not a legal issue with criminal law. This is entirely a contract issue. In fact, there is no law enforcement involved in this process at all. It's just about getting Visa and MasterCard to enforce their own contract rules."

Ironically, it was not the pharmaceutical companies that stepped forward to use the IACC's cudgel against the pharmacy spammers but Microsoft. The same networks blasting spam to pimp online pharmacies were also being used to promote sites peddling counterfeit copies of Microsoft's Windows operating system, and Microsoft saw a golden opportunity in the IACC to make it much more expensive for counterfeiters to process credit card payments for knockoff copies of Windows.

"Microsoft decided they were going to go in whole hog. They were really committed," Savage said. "The idea was, as the lead guy over there said, 'a special Thanksgiving present.' They were going to simultaneously go after every bank being used in this program, all of the registrars registering domains, and all of the hosting companies, and then in a short time take down everything. And then go to Google and Bing and get [the spammers] out of search results too. There was a moment when they just dropped the bomb on the entire industry. And there is this transition going on in the underground where everyone is saying, 'Hey, we're having a little bit of trouble.'"

Savage said one major software vendor in particular went after affiliate programs that were selling its products. Affiliate programs that trade in pirated "OEM" or "original equipment manufacturer" software are those that principally traffic in high-dollar titles, including Microsoft Windows and Adobe products. It seems likely that Adobe was the vendor in question here, given the reaction on the OEM affiliate forums.

"This vendor went after everything. They did it so quickly—and not only for their own products—that it all but shut down the entire OEM ecosystem," Savage said. "A couple of [OEM affiliate programs] survived by getting rid of that company's brand, but in the beginning, when people had no clue what was going on, it shut down the entire business for everyone."

Contracts between the banks and Visa and MasterCard stipulate that merchants are prohibited from selling goods and services that are illegal in the country where those goods or services are being purchased or used, or both. The credit card associations have a standard process for accepting complaints about such transactions, in which they warn the online merchant's bank (including a notice of potential fines for noncompliance). After a complaint about such activity, the merchant's bank conducts its investigation and may choose to contest the issue if they believe the complaint is in error. But if the bank decides not to challenge the complaint, then they will need to take action to prevent similar future transactions, or else face an escalating series of fines from the card associations.

The researchers noticed that in case after case, merchant accounts that had been used in fraudulent activity for an extended time before the researchers filed a complaint with the IACC generally stopped being used within one month after a complaint was lodged.

Savage said the data suggests that the private sector can have a major impact on cybercrime merely by going after the funding for these operations.

"It doesn't require a judge, a law-enforcement officer, or even much in the way of sophisticated security capabilities. If you can purchase a product, then there's a record of it and that record points back to the merchant account getting the money," Savage said. "Visa and MasterCard frown on sales of illegal purchases made on their networks and will act appropriately on complaints from brand holders based on undercover purchases."

At approximately the same time that the researchers were submitting their findings to the IACC, Visa was enacting a series of changes to their operating regulations that seem designed to specifically target online pharmacies and sellers of counterfeit goods. First, sales of goods categorized as pharmaceutical-related were for the first time explicitly classified as "high risk" (along with gambling and various kinds of direct marketing services), and acquirers issuing new contracts for high-risk ecommerce merchants required significantly more due diligence (including $100 million in equity capital and good standing in risk management programs).

Also, the new documents explicitly call out examples of illegal transactions including "unlawful sale of prescription drugs" and "sale of counterfeit or trademark-infringing products or services," among others. Finally, these changes include more aggressive fine schedules for noncompliance.

Some of the best evidence of the success of the test-buy strategy comes directly from the folks operating the affiliate programs that reward spammers and miscreants for promoting fake antivirus and pirated software and dodgy pill sites. In June 2012, a leader of one popular pharmacy affiliate program posted a lengthy message to gofuckbiz.com, a Russian language forum that caters to a variety of such affiliate programs. In that discussion thread, which is now more than 250 pages in length, the affiliate program manager explains to a number of mystified forum members why the pharmacy programs have had so much trouble maintaining reliable credit card processing.

In May 2011, Visa initiated a new program, the so-called "Global Brand Protection Program." How this would turn out for banks and merchants no one knew at the time, so at the time nothing much changed—everything kept working as before. After several months, Visa begins to act, and beginning in November 2011, fines of $25,000 USD on every domain containing brands Viagra, Cialis, and/or Levitra or other copyrighted medications began raining down on merchants.

The manager continued:

All affiliate programs have come under fire. Today, all sizable affiliate programs have paid more than hundreds of thousands in fines under this program. Banks also come under fire, and although in most cases they can cover their financial losses at the expense of merchants—provided their turnover is sufficient—Visa's audits, reputation risks, and other hassles complicate their work. That is why some banks have completely refused to do business, some have greatly reduced the volume of "pharma" payments, [and] some have "overinsured" themselves in one way or another, leading to practically zero approval rates. Some (banks) continue to work, but today their number is very limited.

Another affiliate of a rogue pharmacy program put the situation in far less delicate terms, observing:

Right now most affiliate programs have a mass of declines, cancels, and pendings, and it doesn't depend much on the program IMHO, there is a general sad picture, fucking Visa is burning us with napalm.

After getting scorched by Visa's fines, many pill-shop processors have begun intentionally "miscoding" their pharmacy transactions, said Savage. The credit card companies require all transactions to be tagged with a transaction code that identifies the type of good or service being purchased. There are thousands of such codes (pharma is 5192, for example), and the contracts that merchants must sign with the card associations give the latter the power to levy huge fines against merchants that miscode high-risk transactions as lower-risk activity.

"At this point, most of the remaining pharmacy partnerkas start[ed] getting desperate, doing crazy things like laundering their transactions through parking garages and random banks in the United States," Savage said. "The miscoding was great because [initially] for most of the counterfeit stuff, we as researchers couldn't complain about it to Visa because we had no standing with Visa. We couldn't just say, 'Hey, here's a Pfizer product that's getting ripped off. Visa, you should do something about that.' Only the brand holder can actually take action.

"But on this miscoding stuff, anyone can report anything. If we find that one of these pharma shops is using a U.S. bank and miscoding their transactions, we can often just call the bank and say, 'Hey, did you know this is going on?' And most times, they'll say, 'Thank you very much,' because they can get big fines for processing these miscoded transactions. And so if you tell them, they get to shut it down without Visa finding out and fining them."

Damon McCoy, assistant professor at George Mason University's computer science department, said many pharmacy, scareware, and OEM software affiliate programs have responded to the payment system crackdowns by putting burdensome security measures in place to screen out test buys. For example, some rogue pharmacy programs—such as RxPayouts—began requiring buyers to send scans or faxes of their driver's licenses and physical credit cards. Others have decided only to process payments for existing customers.

But both security measures can be self-defeating, for customers and affiliates alike. The researchers note that RxPayouts' photo ID requirement for new customers (enacted in January 2012) caused an uproar among affiliates. According to the researchers, one affiliate wrote in response, "This new rule is killing me, my conversion rate for new customers [has] dropped to [zero]. As soon as my new customers find out they have to fax their customer service a photo ID, they cancel their order."

McCoy said the new requirements also serve to insulate affiliate programs from another potential source of headache and trouble:

rogue affiliates who join the program merely to reap the commissions for orders placed with stolen credit cards.

"Originally, the affiliate programs were doing this to defend against the carders, and in the past if there was a chargeback for a purchase, the affiliate program ate that chargeback cost," McCoy said. "Now, if a chargeback comes through, they'll take that charge out of the affiliate's subsequent earnings."

The researchers observed that pharmacy affiliate programs also have responded recently by replacing brand-name drugs with their generic equivalents (for example, sildenafil citrate instead of Viagra, tadalafil instead of Cialis, and so on). The operators of these programs argue to their affiliates that such actions will eliminate the brand and trademark issues and thus undermine the ability of brand holders to shut down both individual sites and the associated merchant accounts.

Whether this last step will allow banks that cater to such businesses to continue to do so undisturbed by the credit card networks remains to be seen, according to the program affiliate manager quoted above, who posted the following on gofuckbiz.com.

"What this will lead to in the end, time will tell. Either everyone will stop using well-known brand names, which are so well known to buyers, and will start using the Indian generic names or names of active ingredients, or everyone will continue to compete in this mad race of who will outsmart whom."

Chapter 12

ENDGAME

n June 2011, Vrublevsky made his second unscheduled trip to the Maldives that year. This time, he fled Moscow because he got word that prosecutors there were preparing to levy criminal charges against him in connection with a July 2010 cyberattack on Aeroflot's ticketing systems.

Investigators had already arrested Igor and Dmitry Artimovich, brothers who allegedly co-built and operated the Festi botnet. Both brothers deny operating a botnet or sending spam, and claim that the Russian police planted evidence on their computers. Russian prosecutors had obtained a signed confession from Igor stating that Vrublevsky had hired him to attack Assist, Aeroflot's payment processor. At the time of the attack, ChronoPay was among several companies bidding for a lucrative contract to process payments for Aeroflot, and prosecutors alleged that the attack was designed to ensure that Assist would not maintain the contract. Ironically, a month after the attack, Aeroflot awarded the contract to neither company, but instead to Alfa Bank, the largest private bank in Russia.

Russian authorities reminded Pavel that he could also be picked up by American or other national authorities while in the Maldives, and so he voluntarily returned to Moscow.

Upon his arrival, Vrublevsky was arrested and sent to Lefortovo, a high-security, fortress-like prison built in Moscow in 1881. The prison earned its infamy during the Cold War, when it was used by the Russian KGB to isolate and interrogate political prisoners. In 1994, control over Lefortovo was transferred to the Russian police, and later it was handed to the FSB, the successor agency to the KGB.

In prison, Vrublevsky admitted to ordering the attack on Assist, but later recanted that statement. Nevertheless, his lawyer— ChronoPay employee Stanislav Maltsev, the same former Russian policeman who was once in charge of investigating allegations of illegal business activities by Vrublevsky—argued that his client should be able to remain free pending his trial. The court denied that request and ordered Vrublevsky to be held in Lefortovo for six months, the maximum pretrial time allowed by law for the offenses alleged against him.

"The main risk of letting him out is not that he will run, but that he will do some negative thing to witnesses and try to persuade them not to give or testify to any information about him," Gusev said in a phone interview.

This is a bold statement for a man whose leaked chat logs show that he and Stupin paid $1.5 million to bring a criminal prosecution against Vrublevsky and $50,000 to start the case against Igor and Dmitry Artimovich, the brothers who—sharing the nickname "Engel"—allegedly used their Festi botnet to spam for

Rx-Promotion and to occasionally launch crippling attacks against online sites (including the Aeroflot DDoS that got Vrublevsky thrown in prison).

The following is from a leaked chat, allegedly between Gusev and Stupin, dated September 26, 2010. The two men had already decided to close SpamIt and were considering whether to do the same with GlavMed. Vrublevsky is referred to here as "Paul" (the Western equivalent of "Pavel").

> GUSEV: To my mind, you do not fully understand what's been going on for the last year. Paul has a plan to either throw me into jail or end me. His intentions are totally clear. There are only two choices: 1—Do nothing, and pay nothing to nobody, and at the end either go to jail or keep hiding until all the resources are exhausted; 2—Do the same thing as he is doing, with the same goal.

Gusev tells Stupin that "any war costs money, resources, and nerve cells. You cannot go to war little by little, you either fight to the end or do not start it at all. Engel is going to harm us all the time… If there is any potential opportunity to take him out of the game, we have to use such an opportunity. $50K is very little compared to the losses we've had because of his DDoS attacks and compar[ed] to future losses if he is going to DDoS us again."

Gusev tells Stupin that if he won't put up his share of the $50,000 bribe to bring a criminal investigation against the Artimovich brothers, Gusev will be forced to assume greater control over the pharmacy partnerka. Stupin ultimately acquiesces, but says he wants to go on record stating that he thinks it's a bad idea.

The chats also show that around this same time, Gusev visited the Russian FSB and was enticed into working with them and giving information on big players within the rogue pharmacy industry.

"They have tons of info, and a very good understanding of how everything works and where money comes in and comes out," Gusev told Stupin in January 2010. The FSB, he said, "definitely has information on the money movement of the wallets. In summary: If they want to put me in prison, they will. They also asked about you. For now they wanted me to work for them and give them info on others. They promised all kinds of benefits from working with them."

Interestingly, the leaked chat logs between Gusev and Stupin were obtained by FSB investigators who had detained Stupin and made a forensic copy of his hard drive. Somehow, Engel—perhaps via the bribes paid by Vrublevsky—obtained a copy of these logs and leaked them to several sources, including this author.

Conversations from those chat logs have been featured prominently throughout this book, but one of the most telling and honest conversations comes in a discussion thread on the Russian adult webmaster forum master-x.com. That conversation thread is full of comments from spammers who were sidelined from the business or lost money because of the Pharma Wars between Gusev and Vrublevsky. It currently spans more than one hundred pages.

The epic master-x.com discussion starts out with nearly everyone using nicknames and generally trying to hide their real-life identities, but about halfway through the thread Gusev starts to make references to himself that clearly identify him as the author. In this conversation, Gusev becomes uncharacteristically very emotional and launches into a series of increasingly hostile tirades directed at Artimovich.

Gusev says that Russian webmasters understood that the Pharma Wars between himself and Vrublevsky were just a contest to see who had more money and connections. Gusev also warns Artimovich that Vrublevsky is likely to turn his anger on him when he gets out of prison. (By admitting Vrublevsky hired him to DDoS Assist, Artimovich essentially sealed Pavel's fate.)

> Keep in mind that Pasha is a very vile man. And he has such a long memory! You see, the fact that I was doing better than him after leaving ChronoPay had caused him a severe butt hurt of 7 years!!! He could not sleep, was in a lot of pain over this! That's what envy is. It destroys one slowly but surely. Now imagine his psychological state after he finishes his prison term. Hungry, angry, abandoned by all butt-kissers, without any business, and worst of all—with a clear realization that he could not put me in jail after all. I think that Pasha's psyche will not be able to withstand such pressure. And since he will not be able to reach me, he will focus on you and your brother.

And then Gusev says he may actually exact *his* revenge on Artimovich before Vrublevsky does.

But this is all musing about a possible future. Speaking of the present, I think I will get to you beforehand anyway. I warned you before that if you try to get my family involved in this conflict, the consequences would be very harsh. I will personally find you, tear your head off, and swap it with your ass—most likely no one will see a difference.

◆   ◆   ◆

On Dec. 23, 2012, Russian prosecutors freed Vrublevsky from Lefortovo Prison, just three days before his birthday. Vrublevsky's release was hardly an act of mercy. Under Russian law, six months was the maximum time that prosecutors could hold him pending trial.

Within hours of returning to his Moscow home, Vrublevsky was tweeting and blogging about his triumphant release. He also wasted little time in calling this author, mainly to gripe about his treatment and living conditions in the famed prison. In a lengthy phone conversation, Vrublevsky lamented the presence of and constant utterances from numerous Muslim inmates who were held in captivity in his corner of Lefortovo.

"I didn't even have hot water or a fucking window, and the light was on twenty-four hours a day," Vrublevsky recalled. "This is the most strict prison in Russia, and half of the prison is there for some kind of Muslim terrorism. I was blocked from communication with my family for three months…no phone calls, visits, nothing. Just this 'Allah, Akbar!' crap five times a day!"

Vrublevsky's lawyer forbade him from discussing his case, but as always he had an amusing story to share about his situation. When prisoners of Lefortovo are to be released, they're ceremoniously informed by the more senior convicts of a solemn tradition whereby the freed captive is supposed to later burn the clothes he had on when he was released. Fearing it might be welcoming more bad luck not to observe this tradition, Vrublevsky invited some friends over to his house the day after his release to torch the clothes he was wearing when he was admitted and expunged from Lefortovo.

"Imagine this picture: It is gray, ugly weather, we are behind the house, standing there with my clothes that I came out of the prison with," Pavel recalled, barely able to stop laughing. "Standing there having a cigarette in front of the fire, having a funeral for the clothes. It's like a real Hollywood-type movie, minus the dramatic music at this moment. Serious things are being said, like, 'Dude, don't go back there, blah, blah.' All of a sudden, my wife runs out of the house screaming: 'Pavel, you're burning the wrong shoes!' Turns out, I burned my expensive Yamamoto shoes, not the ones I wore home from prison!"

During his imprisonment, Vrublevsky signed a full confession stating that he masterminded the attack on Assist, Aeroflot's credit card processor. Vrublevsky's confession stated that he had instructed a ChronoPay employee—Maksim Permyakov, an information security specialist for the company—to deposit $20,000 in WebMoney payments into a purse owned by Igor A. Artimovich, the alleged Festi spam botmaster and a former employee of Sun Microsystems in Russia. Indeed, a lengthy email thread in the cache of messages leaked from ChronoPay details this exchange precisely.

Arrested by investigators with the Russian Federal Security Service (FSB), Artimovich signed a similar confession stating that he'd been hired by ChronoPay to use Festi in an attack on Assist. The FSB also arrested Artimovich's brother, Dmitry, a freelance programmer.

All four men—Vrublevsky, Permyakov, and the Artimovich brothers—were charged with violating two articles of the Russian criminal code: Article 272, which covers "illegal access to computer information," and Article 273, which prohibits the use and distribution of malicious computer programs. Both articles provide for imprisonment for between three and seven years.

But in September 2012, the court hearing the case refused to consider charges brought under the latter statute, stating that the statute of limitations for charging the defendants with using and distributing malicious computer programs had expired.

All but one of the accused—Permyakov—would recant their jailhouse confessions prior to the start of their trial, claiming they were under intense psychological pressure from investigators at the time. Artimovich says police even beat him up.

Permyakov, however, ultimately admitted to his role in the scheme and agreed to assist prosecutors in their investigation. For many who followed the trial closely, this was not much of a surprise. Prior to joining ChronoPay, Permyakov himself was an official with the Russian FSB.

Permyakov may well have also been the source of the leaked ChronoPay emails and documents. In his many rants and musings about the source of the breach, Vrublevsky remained adamant in his belief that the ChronoPay compromat was not stolen by hackers but instead leaked by someone in the company's information technology department. Interestingly, while nearly all of the top ChronoPay employees saw years' worth of their company email communications leaked as a result of that breach, Permyakov's inbox was conspicuously absent from that archive.

In any case, it's perhaps fitting that the trial of Vrublevsky and his co-conspirators would unfold as a stellar example of the very corruption that the former ChronoPay CEO had schemed for so long to work to his commercial advantage.

Aeroflot claimed that its ability to accept plane reservations via its website and credit card processing facilities was sidelined for nearly a week by the DDoS attack from Festi, and that the attack cost the company at least 146 million Russian rubles (approximately $5 million). But as noted by Russian news media outlet *Novaya Gazeta*, which covered the Vrublevsky case perhaps more closely and skeptically than any other news organization, the judge in the case cited the monetary damages in her ruling even though an arbitration court refused to acknowledge the figures and denied Aeroflot's lawsuit to recover property damage claims in connection with the attack. Rather, the arbitration panel pointed out that most customers who could not purchase airline tickets online simply made their reservations through third-party booking services or else bought them by visiting Aeroflot ticket counters.

Toward the end of his trial—in June 2013, Vrublevsky was arrested and imprisoned yet again, allegedly for trying to intimidate a witness for the prosecution. The prosecutors charged that

Vrublevsky called one of the witnesses—a man named Nikita Evseev—and that he had offered money in exchange for his silence. Vrublevsky's lawyers denied that allegation, and charged that the signature of another witness—Anastasia Kurochkina— had been forged by the prosecution, and that she had never in fact viewed and confirmed the sanctity of evidence that the prosecution intended to present at trial.

Vrublevsky's lawyers argued that they'd discovered Kurochkina was in fact a friend or girlfriend of the law-enforcement officer who had investigated the DDoS attack for the prosecution.

Vrublevsky's attorneys were almost certainly correct in their assertion that the signature was forged, according to Aleksey Mikhaylov, an information security expert and Moscow native now living in New York City, who has followed the case religiously since its inception and has devoured news reports in the Russian press online and the occasional report in Western news publications. He explains the importance of the forged signature and the role of the witness in this case.

"Basically, the FSB investigators falsified some evidence, and unfortunately this is not uncommon in Russia," Mikhaylov said. "In the Russian criminal trials, there is a term called *panitoi*, and this is someone who is supposed to be an outside person— someone who has no interest in or connection to the case, like in America where random people are called to jury duty—who is taken into the room where the evidence is handled, and he or she is supposed to be witness that everything is okay for the prosecution's handling of evidence. In this case, the witness was supposed to verify that certain evidence gathered from Artimovich was not compromised. It's supposed to be a completely random person, but the fact that the witness in this case was a good friend, if not girlfriend, of an investigator in the case is very suspect."

Nevertheless, the court ignored the evidence presented by the defense and upheld the decision to imprison Vrublevsky for witness tampering.

For his part, Igor Artimovich gave an interview with the *New York Times* prior to his imprisonment stating that he was not responsible for Festi, and that his involvement with ChronoPay stemmed from a project within the company that had sought to develop a ChronoPay-branded antivirus product.

This may seem like a ridiculous and outlandish claim for a company that had been so instrumental in fostering the development and prosperity of the rogue antivirus industry—a business that sought to extort money from victims by planting malicious software on users' systems and then pitching the sale of a worthless security product supposedly designed to remove the infection that it caused.

But there appears to be a kernel of truth to Artimovich's claims. When I visited Vrublesky in Moscow in February 2011, he told me of plans to launch a ChronoPay-branded anti-malware solution code-named ChronoPay Antivirus. I recall that we both shared an awkward laugh about this at the time, but among the many documents leaked from ChronoPay are technical papers referencing the development of different antivirus software modules. The documents suggest that the company had hired programmers to reverse engineer the free version of the commercial anti-malware product Malwarebytes.

By the end of July 2013, the court had reached a verdict. All four of the accused were found guilty. Vrublevsky and the Artimovich brothers each were sentenced to two-and-a-half years in a penal colony. Permyakov received a slightly lesser sentence of two years because he assisted prosecutors in their investigation.

Mikhaylov said that he strongly believes that nearly everything that happened with Vrublevsky in connection with his criminal case—the inception, investigation, prosecution, trial, and ultimate conviction—had very little to do with the execution of justice the way Westerners understand it, but it has everything to do with his old business partner Gusev, and more specifically to bribes that Gusev paid the Russian FSB.

He notes that the Russian criminal code and the legal framework are not particularly well-suited for prosecuting many high-tech crimes.

"Many years ago, when the issue of hacking and cybercrime first surfaced, the government introduced a law that says it's illegal to gain unauthorized access to a computer system. And in this case, the prosecution argued that by attacking Assist [Aeroflot's credit card processor], the hackers basically gained unauthorized access to Aeroflot because they were able to switch off its credit card processing and website," Mikhaylov said.

"You cannot look at this and say it is logical or makes sense from a legal perspective. The prosecution had to work with what they had to work with. That's why they charged him with this thing even though in any normal court would have rejected it out of hand for any number of reasons. The prosecution did produce some of the evidence linking him to the Artimovich brothers. But it does seem that a lot of this evidence was either falsified, or due process wasn't followed in the case."

Mikhaylov noted that Aeroflot is 51 percent owned by the Russian government, and that the attack on this state asset was a source of shame and aggravation for many political powers-that-be in the country.

"The practice of businesses using corrupt law enforcement in Russia to fight each other and steal market share is very common," he said. "But when one party is willing to pay big amounts of money or there are political folks involved, all due process goes out the window immediately. In those circumstances, political connections and financial matters dictate the outcome of the case."

Mikhaylov said he believes Vrublevsky drastically underestimated the seriousness and potency of the case that his enemies had laid against him.

"When he initially got out of prison pending his trial, he tried to win the case on the merits, which was a big mistake and very naïve of him," Mikhaylov said. "Maybe he felt there was some financial support behind the scenes, because of his previous bribes to corrupt law enforcement. Unfortunately for him, Gusev eventually found a much stronger weapon to use in this conflict and gained the upper hand. [Providing] $1.5 million in a single payment is a serious effort on his part, even by Russian corruption standards. I seriously doubt Vrublevsky spent that much, even taking into account his past efforts on resolving the Fethard conundrum and hiring Maltsev as his security chief afterwards. Gusev won the war, or at least the battle, by upping the ante considerably. I'm sure that now Vrublevsky would gladly pay twice as much to get out, but it's a lot more difficult to negotiate from his current position."

Mikhaylov predicted that Vrublevsky would not end up serving that much time in the penal colony, or if he does serve his full term, the high-profile nature of his imprisonment may serve to insulate him while he's there.

"Pasha is rich guy, or at least he used to be rich guy. He had a house in the most affluent neighborhood outside of Moscow. He still owns a major share in ChronoPay. If I was him, I would sell everything to get out. In Russia it's relatively doable, unless you have FSB working against you. They are ruling the country. If someone in FSB took $1.5 million from Gusev, there is probably no way they will accept money from Pasha. But there is another thing that works for Vrublevsky. His case got a lot of attention, which means maybe he will be watched over by the prison's administration. There are hundreds of articles on him and this case. My guess is the prison and the Russian government doesn't want a public figure like him to get raped and cut in prison. That's bad publicity."

Mikhaylov is quick to note that he's no apologist for Vrublevsky, who he views as the inevitable target of karmic justice.

"At the very least, it produced something positive. Pavel was held accountable for a very tiny fraction of his crimes," Mikhaylov said. "His trial was obviously a fraud, and due process was not followed. But Pasha will get out of prison very angry, probably in a year or so. He will be looking for blood, and who knows? Maybe a few years down the road, Gusev will share the same fate."

Many of Mikhaylov's predictions have come true on several levels. It's not clear whether Vrublevsky paid for the privilege, but in June 2014—less than a year into his two-and-a-half-year prison sentence—he was released without any public explanation (as far as I could determine through extensive research) and allowed to return home to his family in Moscow.

Local Russian newspapers suggested that he'd been sprung from jail because his government needed him. In response to U.S. sanctions against Russia for funding and organizing pro-Russian separatists who were causing unrest and armed conflict in Ukraine, Visa and MasterCard in March 2014 stopped servicing payments for clients of at least two top Russian banks. Russian President Vladimir Putin responded by signing into law a bill that required the creation of a homegrown, cashless national payments system to route around the credit card companies. The law also imposed stiff new requirements on international payments providers operating in Russia.

In a telephone interview shortly after his release, Vrublevsky told me that his lawyers had strictly forbidden him from discussing his case. He said he had no idea why he was released early, but that he didn't think it had anything to do with the national payments system.

"It was probably because I've been a good fireman," Vrublevsky said, explaining that for the last five months that he was in prison he had volunteered to work as a fireman for the remote village that surrounded the penal colony—a former coal mining area in the Ryazan Oblast region of Russia approximately 200 kilometers southeast of Moscow.

"I've seen things and places that people shouldn't see, but I've seen some funny stuff as well," Vrublevsky said in response to questions about his prison sentence. "I get out and people are asking me about the national payments system, and I'm sitting there saying, 'Man, are you joking? I can pretty much tell you about how to feed cows with fireman water, but I don't know anything about the latest changes in the federal law'!"

Vrublevsky remains the principal shareholder in ChronoPay, a company he is looking to sell as soon as he can. When I asked whether he was concerned that his recent scandal and incarceration might hinder that effort, Vrublevsky intimated that whatever didn't kill him and his company would only make them both stronger.

"Do you think that BMW is a good car? This is a company that was making engines for German airplanes in World War II. So there's your answer. When someone is making a good product—and ChronoPay is a good product—all these other things are secondary."

Gusev remains in exile from Russia, where he is currently wanted on criminal charges of running an illegal business in GlavMed and SpamIt. Vrublevsky said he believes Gusev is hiding with his family somewhere in Spain or in Turkey, but that could not be independently confirmed. In any case, wherever Gusev is today, it's unlikely he'll be traveling anytime soon. In a 2011 interview, he said he was worried that the international organization of police agencies—Interpol—might post a notice for his arrest, should he decide to cross European borders.

"I'm expecting that very soon I could be in the Interpol database," Gusev said. "I'm already in the database of Russian police, so I'm not able to come to Russia, unfortunately. I'm sure Pavel is doing all he can to have my name put on the list of Interpol, and it could be very dangerous for me to go by plane or some kind of border transport."

Kimberly Zenz, a cybercrime expert with the Reston, Virginia-based firm Verisign iDefense, has tracked the feud for years. She said she believes Vrublevsky was the aggressor, and that he was brought down by an enormous ego and an overabundance of misplaced confidence.

"He loves the attention, and cybercriminals should not love attention," Zenz said. "But this way, he gets to very publicly be the big boss and get respect for his role in the underground community."

But according to Zenz, other factors worked to undermine Vrublevsky's spam and rogue antivirus empire.

"He really was on the wrong side of history," Zenz said. "At one point, people complained that Russia never cared about cybercrime. And I think Pavel misunderstood how far he could go and what he could attack. The part of his personality that made him grow ChronoPay the way he did was the same part that made him overstep his bounds and attack Assist, and think that he could take on Gusev and that there would be no problem with either."

Stefan Savage, the UCSD professor, said Vrublevsky seemed obsessed with always coming up with some newer and greater black-hat scheme.

"You have to see it in that light to understand how he could have this legitimate company and then still want to pump it full of pharma and fake antivirus and all this other stuff," Savage said. "He clearly felt driven to be the big man. And certainly, if you look at the interactions between him and other people at ChronoPay—and the fact that he would constantly show up at Visa security and fraud conferences in Europe—it's clear he sees himself as this larger-than-life figure. He didn't need to do all this to have a good standard of living. He could have been totally legit, although he might have done what he did to support a certain lifestyle. But I also suspect part of it as well was he had a certain social circle of people in this cybercrime space that he was trying to impress."

But while the Pharma Wars may be temporarily over, the global threat from spam is stronger than ever. The demise of many large spam affiliate programs like SpamIt and Rx-Promotion coincided with a marked and more malevolent shift in the way cybercrime is monetized. For starters, the work done by Savage, Microsoft, and the brand holders who worked with the International Anti-Counterfeiting Coalition (IACC) to make it far more expensive for partnerka programs to obtain credit card processing effectively killed off much of the rogue antivirus or scareware industry that ChronoPay had so carefully nurtured. But in its place, a far more insidious threat has taken hold: ransomware.

Much like scareware, ransomware is most often distributed via hacked or malicious sites that exploit browser vulnerabilities. Typically, these scams impersonate the Department of Homeland Security or the FBI (or the equivalent federal investigative authority in the victim's country) and try to frighten people into paying fines to avoid prosecution for supposedly downloading child pornography and pirated content.

Ransomware locks the victim's PC until he either pays the ransom or finds a way to remove the malware. Increasingly, ransomware attacks encrypt all of the files on the victim's PC, holding them for ransom until victims pay up. Victims are instructed to pay the ransom by purchasing a prepaid debit card or cash voucher, sold at convenience stores or retail outlets the world over. Victims are then told to send the attackers the voucher code or card number that allows the bad guys to redeem the information for cash.

"I don't think it's an accident that we've seen ransomware rise as it's become harder for these partnerka programs to find a continuous supply of banks to help them process cards for scareware payments," Savage said. "You have a bunch of people who are used to making good money for whom fake antivirus software and scareware have become problematic and for whom pharma is not really an option. There's a void in the ecosystem where people can make money. It's not at all an accident that these ransomware schemes essentially are bypassing traditional payment schemes."

The past few years have also witnessed a noticeable change in the ways that botmasters are using the resources at their disposal. By the first quarter of 2014, the proportion of email that is spam had dropped to 66.3 percent, 6.42 percentage points lower than the previous quarter, according to Kaspersky Lab, a Russian antivirus and security firm. But to supplement a decline in revenue from commercial email missives, many miscreants increasingly are hiring out their botnets to send malicious software that poses a far more serious threat to consumers, especially those of us who never open spam or junk emails, let alone buy anything from them.

One excellent example of this is the Rustock botnet, which started off in 2007 promoting pump-and-dump stock scams. For years, it was among the world's top promoters of pharmacy sites, but over the past few years, the miscreants at the helm of Rustock have dedicated more of their spamming resources to blasting malware wrapped in a thousand disguises, from phony missives from FedEx and UPS, to bogus audit alerts from the U.S. Internal

Revenue Service. In most cases, this password-stealing malicious software is aimed at small- to mid-sized businesses in the United States and Europe, with the goal of infecting the computer of the person in charge of the organization's finances. Armed with that person's username and password to the organization's bank account, the fraudsters will push through fraudulent bank transfers from that victim's account to accounts that they control.

Indeed, according to University of Alabama at Birmingham's Gary Warner, malware sent via Cutwail spam is among the leading causes of corporate account takeovers. This increasingly common cybercrime scourge affects thousands of small businesses each year, often resulting in hundreds of thousands of dollars in losses for individual victim organizations.

Another notable shift is that cybercrime entrepreneurs who run their own botnets increasingly are seeking to extract more value from each infected system, carefully harvesting every nugget of personal data (for example, passwords, software license keys, and social media accounts) that they can from the compromised systems of unsuspecting users, all of which can be resold in the cyber underground, Savage said. What's more, there are now more cybercrime bazaars than ever to help botmasters offload this data. In other words, it's very possible that a cybercriminal right now is selling your personal information to someone else and making a pretty penny off it.

"Much like the Inuit Eskimos made sure to use every piece of the whale, we're seeing an evolution now where botmasters are carefully mining infected systems and monetizing the data they can find," Savage said. "The mantra these days seems to be, 'Why leave any unused resources on the table?'"

While some are using ransomware and data harvesting, Savage said, many other former affiliates and managers of failed scareware, pharma, and pirated software partnerkas are casting about for the next big thing.

"It's a period of innovation, and people clearly are looking around for another sweet spot that's as good as pharma, which made more money more reliably than anything else out there," he said. "A few affiliate programs are trying to peddle pirated ebooks and movies; others are getting into [advertising] payday loans. There are now tons of programs that will write term papers for students. That seems to be a big thing now."

The other factor weighing on the spam industry, Savage says, is that many affiliates have found more success advertising websites using so-called "black SEO" techniques to manipulate search engine rankings for their sites. He notes that the biggest earner by far across thousands of GlavMed pharmacy affiliates was a black SEO expert who used the nickname "Webplanet." This enterprising young hacker appears to have earned all of his money by gaming the search engines.

"There are a lot of games being played now doing [advertising fraud] or black SEO," Savage said. "For now, a lot of these guys are becoming more diversified and are in kind of a regrouping period. And the subset of people doing well with pharma spam are either retrenching or saying, 'Yeah, we'll have to accept lower profits or find another niche.'"

Savage says he expects that online pharma as an industry will be dead two to three years from now.

"There will be some small affiliate programs, but I doubt there will be any big affiliate programs like Rx-Promotion or GlavMed," Savage said. "It just draws too much attention and pressure from the card systems like Visa and MasterCard."

Savage's comments eerily echo the words I heard from Igor Gusev in our last interview in mid-2011.

"It's very strange that some people need to have done so much expensive research to understand that [the] weakest part of this business is card processing," Gusev said. "They need to put pressure on the card processors which are monsters [that] only regulate [under] very negative public pressure. I think it would be a very powerful strike, and online pharma would be dead within two years if they could somehow switch off the merchants who [are] connected to online pharma."

Gusev, too, was wondering what the next big partnerka will be after pharmacy programs die off.

"I think that the next big thing will be connected to video, audio, and maybe social networking," he said. "It will be some kind of service like what Google and Apple are trying to do now with sharing and having all your MP3s and videos uploaded to a web service so you can access it from anywhere. The only question is what kind of model they will use to do billing for that, and how people will pay for it."

Gusev said he was considering going into the consulting business, advising online affiliate programs on how to navigate the choppy waters inhabited by the shady credit card processors and dodgy banks that support those industries.

"Honestly, I am looking into this business," Gusev said. "From one point of view, it's pretty risky because I want to stay as far as possible away from doing stuff which could lead to another criminal case. But from another point of view, I can earn some money just to make some consultations with merchants such as this, if the merchants agreed to pay some percentage for my expertise, because the banks are the vital thing to all of this stuff."

Most readers of this book probably have never ordered anything advertised in unsolicited junk email or ingested prescription drugs of uncertain origin that were ordered online. But there are myriad ways that even the wariest Internet users still end up supporting spammers, scam artists, and organized cyberthieves. And almost all of those ways invariably stem from one cause: apathy.

Whether we go online using a device powered by Microsoft Windows, Mac OS X, Linux, or Android, each of us has a role to play in combatting or contributing to online fraud. As such, we are all either part of the problem or the solution. There is no in-between anymore. Today's online threats take full advantage of people who fall behind on security updates, or those who wantonly open unbidden email attachments and click on random links in email or on Facebook and Twitter that seem legitimate. For more information on what all of us can do to fight spam and malware— and better protect ourselves online—check out the Epilogue that directly follows this chapter.

A SPAM-FREE WORLD: HOW YOU CAN PROTECT YOURSELF FROM CYBERCRIME

Many of us have had the experience of receiving a spammy email from a friend or loved one, only to have a frantic follow-up note arrive a few minutes later from that person stating that his or her email account was hacked and warning us not to open or respond to any of the messages sent by the intruder. To be sure, this is an alarming situation for many users. But the scarier truth is that if your inbox (or your phone, tablet, Twitter or Instagram account, anything really) gets hijacked by modern cyberthieves, spewing spam is about the most innocuous thing that can happen to it.

The true value of your email account to crooks is not merely in its ability to pump spam or even forward malicious software and viruses to your entire contact list. Depending on what you do with your account and how long you've had it, your inbox could be worth far more than you imagine.

For example, sign up with any service online, and it will almost certainly require you to supply an email address. In nearly all cases, the person who is in control of that address can reset the password of any associated services or accounts—merely by requesting a password reset email. Got your retirement fund, bank account, or insurance plan tied to that inbox? An attacker in control of your email account—either via phishing you or installing malware on your system—can simply visit the websites that manage those accounts, request a password reset, click a link in an email, and change your passwords (and they will start with your email password)!

Even if the person who hijacks your inbox doesn't have the time or inclination to seize control over all of your associated accounts, he likely knows that those accounts have a resale value in the cybercrime underground. How much are these associated accounts worth? There isn't exactly a central exchange for hacked accounts in the underground, but recent price lists posted by several ne'er-do-wells who traffic in nonfinancial compromised accounts offer some insights.

Several bad guys in the underground will sell purloined usernames and passwords for working accounts at overstock.com, dell.com, and walmart.com, all for two dollars each, for example. Other sellers peddle accounts at fedex.com and ups.com for five dollars a pop, and Apple iTunes accounts starting at eight dollars. Accounts that come with credentials to the email addresses tied to each site can fetch a dollar or two more.

Some crime shops go even lower with their prices for hacked accounts, charging as little as three dollars for active accounts at dell.com, overstock.com, walmart.com, tesco.com, bestbuy .com, and target.com, to name just a few. This may sound like peanuts and hardly worth the bother, but remember that the bad guys engaged in this activity very often run large botnets, meaning they can gather this information from hundreds or thousands of hacked computers simultaneously.

Even if your email isn't tied to online merchants, it is probably connected to other accounts you care about. Hacked email accounts are not only used to blast junk messages. They are harvested for the email addresses of your contacts, who can then be inundated with malware, spam, and phishing attacks. Those same contacts may even receive a message claiming you are stranded and penniless in some foreign country, and asking them to wire money somewhere. Trust me, countless people actually follow through on these fake pleas for help and wire money straight into the pockets of these cyberthieves.

If you've purchased software, it's likely that the license keys to those software titles are stored somewhere in your email messages. Do you use online or "cloud" file storage services like Dropbox, Google Drive, or Microsoft SkyDrive to back up or store your pictures, files, and music? The key to unlocking access to those files also lies in your inbox.

And worst of all, if your webmail account gets hacked and was used as the backup account to receive password reset emails for one of your other accounts, guess what? Attackers can now seize both of your accounts.

Hopefully, it's clear by now that keeping thieves out of your inbox is worth making the effort to take a few precautions. Fortunately, some simple tips and actions can help you maintain control over your email account—as well as lock down the system you use to access that account.

Until recently, some of the web's largest providers of online services offered little security beyond requiring you to enter a username and password. Increasingly, however, the larger providers have moved to enabling multifactor authentication to help users

282 | BRIAN KREBS

avoid account compromises. Gmail.com, Hotmail/Live.com, and Yahoo.com all now offer multistep authentication that users can and should use to further secure their accounts. These typically involve the sending of a numeric code via text message or smartphone app that needs to be entered along with your username and password. The code is sent and requested any time a suspicious login is detected—such as a login attempt from a computer or Internet address not normally associated with your account.

Dropbox, Facebook, and Twitter offer additional account security options beyond merely encouraging users to pick strong passwords. To check if your email or social network or other communications provider allows you to supplement your account security with two-factor authentication, check out the website twofactorauth.org. If your provider is listed with a check mark, click the icon under the "Docs" column next to that provider for a link to instructions on how to configure and enable this feature.

Password Madness

Enabling two-factor authentication is a good way to increase your account's security, but if you're relying on crummy passwords to begin with, you're still dangerously exposed. Plus, not every important service or site offers two-factor protections yet. Hardly anybody likes passwords—they can be such a pain to remember sometimes—but unfortunately we are stuck with them until we come up with stronger, more hacker-proof methods of securing our information.[17]

---

17. It's important to note that improved security and identification methods are in the works for certain digital technology and devices. Many banks in Europe, for example, put chips in their credit cards, which make the cards more difficult and costly to use for fraud. This is slowly being

Here are a few tips for creating strong passwords. Take a moment to review these tips and tools, and consider strengthening some of your passwords if they fall short.

If you're like me—and really detest passwords but recognize that life is too short to try to remember hundreds of them—it may be a good idea to consider a password manager. These are computer programs or online services that can help users not only pick and use much stronger passwords, but better safeguard them as well. They do so by using strong encryption to store your passwords.

If you want help picking strong passwords but don't trust that you can remember such cryptic and lengthy ones as "#$DG3dcLqziI%&*wp," then good news: password manager programs are built to do that for you. Nearly all of them hook into your browser and handle the retrieval and insertion of your passwords when you visit a site at which you've previously asked the program to remember your password. All you have to do is create and remember a single, strong "master password" that you'll be asked for when you visit one of these sites.

Some of the more popular password management tools include KeyPass, Password Safe, and RoboForm. LastPass is another excellent option that works entirely online. (It does not require special software to be installed on your computer, so you can access your passwords no matter which machine you're on—including your smartphone.)

If you prefer to pick and manage your own passwords—or if you just need a really good one to use as your master password in a password manager program—here a few tips for avoiding crummy passwords:

---

introduced in the United States as well. Another recent security measure worth noting is the addition of fingerprint ID technology on some phones and laptops as an option to lock or unlock them. And doubtless more is on the way.

- Create unique passwords that use a combination of words, numbers, symbols, and both upper- and lower-case letters.

- Do not use your network username as your password.

- Don't use easily guessed passwords, such as "password" or "user."

- Do not choose passwords based upon details that may not be as confidential as you'd expect, such as your birthday, your Social Security or phone number, or names of family members or pets or anything else you post about on social media. (The bad guys use Facebook, Twitter, and Instagram too!)

- Do not use words that can be found in the dictionary. Password-cracking tools freely available online often come with dictionary lists that will try thousands of common names and passwords. If you must use dictionary words, try adding a numeral to them, as well as punctuation at the beginning or end of the word (or both!).

- Avoid using simple adjacent keyboard combinations. For example, "qwerty" and "asdzxc" and "123456" are horrible passwords that are trivial to crack.

- Some of the easiest-to-remember passwords aren't words at all but collections of words that form a phrase or sentence, perhaps the opening sentence to your favorite novel or the opening line to a good joke. Complexity is nice, but length is key. Picking an alphanumeric password that was eight to ten characters in length used to be a pretty good practice. These days, it's increasingly affordable for hackers and spammers to build extremely powerful and fast password-cracking tools that can try tens of millions of possible password combinations per second. Just remember that each character you add to a password or passphrase makes it an order of magnitude harder to attack via brute-force methods like this.

- Avoid using the same password at multiple websites. It's generally safe to reuse the same password at sites that do not store sensitive information about you (like a news website or discussion forum), provided you don't use this same password at sites that *are* sensitive.

- Never use the password you've picked for your email account at any online site. If you do, and an ecommerce site you are registered at gets hacked, there's a good chance someone will be reading your email soon.

- Whatever you do, don't store your list of passwords on your computer in plain text. That's like handing your identity over to cybercriminals if your computer gets hacked. My views on the advisability of keeping a written list of your passwords have evolved over time. I tend to agree with security expert Bruce Schneier when he advises users not to worry about writing down passwords and having someone stumble across them in real life. Just make sure you don't store the information in plain sight. The most secure method for remembering your passwords is to create a list of every website for which you have a password and next to each one write your login name and a clue that has meaning only for you. If you forget your password, most websites will email it to you (assuming you can remember which email address you signed up with).

Keep Up to Date

All of the account security tools in the world won't prevent your inbox or Facebook account from being hijacked if your computer gets compromised by password-stealing malware. While having antivirus software and a firewall on your system can help ward off threats, these are far from panaceas, and today's cyberthreats are being built to evade detection by these, especially in that critical first twelve- to twenty-four-hour period after which the malware is blasted out via spam and social networking site links.

It's important to understand that a key tenet of securing any system is the concept of "defense in depth," or having multiple layers of security and not depending too much on any one approach or technology to block all attacks. And guess which layer is the most important one of all? You!

Memorize and practice Krebs's "Three Rules for Online Safety," and you will drastically reduce the chances of handing over your computer or mobile device to the bad guys. In short:

- Rule 1: *"If you didn't go looking for it, don't install it."* A great many online threats rely on tricking the user into taking some action—whether it be clicking an email link or attachment, or installing a custom browser plug-in or application. Typically, these attacks take the form of scareware or fake antivirus pop-ups that try to frighten people into installing a security scanner. Other popular scams direct you to a video but then insist that you need to install a special "codec," video player, or app to view the content. Only install software, software updates, or browser add-ons if you went looking for them in the first place. And before you install anything, it's a good idea to grab the software *directly from the source*. Sites like MajorGeeks .com and Download.com claim to screen programs that they offer for download. But just as you wouldn't buy a product online without doing some basic research about its quality and performance—and ensuring it's the actual product you want—take a few minutes to search for and read comments and reviews left by other users of that software to be certain you're not signing up for more than you bargained. Also, avoid directly responding to email alerts that (appear to) come from Facebook, LinkedIn, Twitter, your bank, or some other site that holds your personal information. Instead, visit these sites using a web browser bookmark and manage your online social networks that way. Fat-fingering a single character in a web address can lead to hostile sites set up to take advantage of typos.

- Rule 2: *"If you installed it, update it!"* Yes, keeping the operating system current with the latest patches (from Microsoft, Apple, or Google, for example) is important, but maintaining a secure computer also requires care and feeding for the applications that run on top of the operating system. Bad guys are constantly attacking flaws in widely installed software products, such as Java, Adobe PDF Reader, Flash, and QuickTime. The vendors that make these products ship updates to fix security bugs several times a year, so it's important to update to the latest versions of these products as soon as possible. Some of these products may alert users to new updates, but these notices often come days or weeks after patches are released. A wonderful resource for anyone feeling update fatigue is Secunia's Personal Software Inspector, a free tool that periodically scans for and alerts users to outdated security software. The latest version also can be set to update such products automatically. FileHippo also has a nice, free update checker.

- Rule 3: *"If you no longer need it, remove it!"* Clutter is the nemesis of a speedy computer. Unfortunately, many computer makers ship machines with gobs of bloatware that most customers never use even once. On top of the direct-from-manufacturer junk software, the average user tends to install dozens of programs and add-ons over the course of months and years. In the aggregate, these items can take their toll on the performance of your computer. Many programs add themselves to the list of items that start up whenever the computer is rebooted, which can make restarting the computer a bit like watching paint dry. It takes forever. And remember, the more programs you have installed, the more time you have to spend keeping them up to date with the latest security patches.

I hope you find these tips useful and timely. For more information about how to stay safe online—including news about the latest threats, criminal schemes, and software bugs being leveraged by the spammers and scam artists online, check out my website, KrebsOnSecurity.com. While you're there, drop me a note and let me know what you thought of this book, using the contact form at www.KrebsOnSecurity.com/about.

A CONVERSATION WITH BRIAN KREBS

Can you tell us a bit more of the backstory behind this book?

The great author Toni Morrison once said, "If there's a book that you want to read, but it hasn't been written yet, then you must write it." That fairly describes the genesis of this book, although in my case I would probably adapt that adage a bit to read, "If there's a book that has to be written and you're the only one who can write it, then you have to write that book!" By virtue of the fact that two warring cybercrime kingpins decided to hack each other and leak the other's core secrets to me and to law enforcement, I had a unique opportunity to invite the average person into a strange and somewhat terrifying world that even seasoned experts on cybercrime had never seen before.

Since your background is primarily in journalism, what drew you to the cybersecurity beat?

While never a programmer per se, I spent a great deal of my childhood noodling with computers and text-based bulletin boards online, communities that predated the modern Web. I became intensely interested in cybersecurity in 2001, after my home network was completely overrun by Chinese hackers. I grew somewhat obsessed with learning about the subject after that and it's an obsession that hasn't quite released its grip on me yet.

What are the primary motivations of the cybercriminals profiled in *Spam Nation*?

Their primary motivations are the same weaknesses responsible for most strife in life, including greed, lust for power, revenge, and perhaps most of all—pride. I was blown away that so many of the people so deeply involved in spreading spam and malicious software were willing to talk to me at all, let alone describe their businesses in great detail. But as we see in the book, many of these individuals were quite proud of their work and "accomplishments."

Law enforcement officials are fond of repeating several truisms when it comes to cybercrime, the most often-uttered being that today's cybercriminals are no longer interested in fame, but instead choose riches over renown. But from my perspective, while it's true that money is the central preoccupation of most modern cybercrooks, the majority still have tremendous egos and have trouble keeping those egos in check.

What is the biggest lesson you learned from this experience?

That writing a book is the single most challenging and rewarding experience of my professional career. The great master artist Leonardo da Vinci is said to have quipped that "art is never finished, only abandoned," and that has been the most challenging

aspect of writing a book as well: having the courage and conviction to stop tinkering with it and to declare that the book is
ready for publication (even if secretly, deep down inside, that
voice is still saying, "Yeah, but I bet we could still move this and
add that, and...").

**What would you like readers to gain from reading *Spam Nation*?
What advice or lessons should they take away in particular?**

I'd like readers to gain a better appreciation for how much they
depend on their computers and other networked devices for their
everyday productivity and well-being, and gain a better understanding of how to prevent thieves from hijacking their data, identities, and devices.

I'd like for readers to understand that spam is still the single
most popular and effective method of perpetrating and spreading
cybercrime. People tend to view spam as a solved problem because
of spam filters and junk folders. Yet we are reminded all the time
about how the biggest breaches—from Target to JP Morgan—
usually begin with someone opening an unsolicited email.

It's also important that users recognize the true value of their
own computers or inboxes. The crooks know very well how
much these assets are worth, and this awareness disparity puts
the average consumer at a severe disadvantage versus today's
online adversaries.

**You and your family have been threatened, bribed, and even
attacked in a variety of ways by the spammers and cybercriminals you expose for your work to bring their crimes to light.**

Have their actions ever made you consider giving up your work? Or do they make you more determined to find justice?

I've never considered walking away from this beat. If anything, the personal attacks that I and my family have grappled with over the past few years have only strengthened my resolve to keep shining a light on this space and validated my continued focus on this topic.

What would you do the same in your work on cybercrime and cybersecurity? What would you do differently?

I would have applied myself more diligently in school toward math and science. I never had much of a proclivity toward either field, but it would be helpful to have more skills in programming and scripting than I do at age forty-two. Thankfully, when I need these skills, I can usually rely on a network of sources that are all too eager to help, but I truly wish those skills came more naturally. I also would have learned Russian at an earlier age; that has opened up many more opportunities and avenues in my reporting that simply would not have been possible otherwise.

Did you always want to be an investigative reporter, or did you start off in a different career?

Ever since I was on the staff of my high school newspaper, yes. But I don't have formal training in journalism. Most of my experience there came from learning on the job. Prior to my employment at the *Washington Post*, I was in a dead-end job that I absolutely loathed. My best friend at the time helped me land a job at the *Post* answering phones in the circulation department, where the typical call came from a customer who didn't get their morning paper. From there, I "graduated" to a job in the newsroom, where I split my time between sorting mail and taking dictation from reporters in the field. Thankfully, there was enough downtime between dictation calls that I would frequently pitch story ideas to different editors at various sections of the paper. I ended up writing dozens of stories for half the sections of the paper before I landed an official reporting job—and that was for a newswire owned by the *Washington Post* in 1999.

What is the most challenging part of your work? Of writing this book? How about the most rewarding parts?

I'm a big believer in the idea that hard work is its own reward. While hard work and discipline alone never guarantee success, they are the best, most reliable paths to success that I know. Some of my best stories and biggest scoops come from weeks or months of reporting—often on stories that I nearly abandoned at one point from sheer frustration or exhaustion. But I'd say that's the most rewarding part of my work: seeing stories as they progress through that pipeline from a kernel of a hunch, idea, or scoop, and experiencing the payoff weeks or months later as that hunch, idea, or scoop grows into a story that ends up making international news.

I'm very fortunate because the very nature of my work allows me to see and experience cutting-edge developments on a fairly regular basis. Also, as an independent reporter, I mainly answer only to myself and have total freedom to focus on reporting news that nobody else is covering (as opposed to constantly chasing stories that other news outlets are following). So, the reporting aspect of my work tends to be a great deal more exciting and interesting than the actual writing part, which is by far the most challenging for me.

When I first began as a reporter at the *Post*, one of my early editors—an old-school newsman who was quite gruff and to-the-point—barked that he admired my reporting skills but that my writing was crap (he used a much more colorful word). He tried to soften the blow by stating that it was the rare journalist who was at the start of their career both a great reporter and a great writer; most, he said, were good at one of those skills at the outset, and only mastered the other through practice and careful observation over time.

Even so, I have learned to enjoy the process and much harder work of writing and describing my reporting, and have truly come to appreciate the iterative nature of the craft with a greater sense of patience and discipline. For me, the most rewarding aspect of writing is the deliberate, sometimes fitful process of starting with a blank page and assembling all of the story components one by one. Ultimately, it's about finding the best way to stitch all of those pieces together in a story that holds the reader's interest and hopefully prompts them to engage in a conversation about it. And that's exactly what I intended to do with this book.

ACKNOWLEDGMENTS

Writers tend to be a solitary lot, but they seldom produce enjoyable works with the length and complexity of a book without a great deal of assistance and patience from friends and colleagues.

Spam Nation would not have been possible without the help of several native Russian speakers who spent countless hours with me teasing out the conversations and links between various real-life characters profiled in this book. In particular, I would like to thank Alek Geldenberg, Aleksey Mikhaylov, and Maxim Suhanov for their tireless work in translating documents, emails, and chat logs, and in generally helping me connect the dots.

For their knowledge of the hacker underground and the denizens therein, my sincere gratitude goes out to Lawrence Baldwin, Adam Drake, Alex Holden, Lance James, Jon O, and Kimberly Zenz.

For helping me to extract patterns and meaning from epic truckloads of data, I am especially grateful to Damon McCoy, Stefan Savage, Brett Stone-Gross, Gary Warner (and their armies of grad students).

Joe Menn and Misha Glenny were there with encouragement and sage advice exactly when I needed it. Had it not been for the hours-long chat with Roland Dobbins in Snowmageddon 2009, I might not have had the courage to strike out on my own as an independent journalist. Thanks of an unspecified nature go also to J.B. Snyder, a great guy who always does just what he says he's going to do.

I owe more than I care to acknowledge for my continued physical and online safety to several folks. Chris Barton has kept me and my site online and out of trouble—even in the face of often withering attacks. Group-IB and Kaspersky Lab were instrumental in watching my back in Moscow. Various unnamed law enforcement officials have been helpful here in the States; thank you all.

Last but not least, I would like to thank the regular readers of my site—KrebsOnSecurity.com—for their encouragement, support, and inspiration these past five years. I could not have done this without you.

SOURCES

Chapter 1: Parasite

A November 2008 blog entry by ThreatExpert (now owned by Symantec) was helpful with the research on the car race that killed Kolya McColo, as well as a day-of-the-accident news report from the Russian publication *Rossiyskaya Gazeta* (ng.ru). I also relied on posts to the Crutop.nu forum, as well as leaked instant message chats between Stupin and Igor Gusev, talking about who was going to attend or was at McColo's funeral. As for information about Dmitry "Gugle" Nechvolod, I relied on instant message interviews with Igor Vishnevsky.

Chapter 2: Bulletproof

Much of the background information on RBN came from Russian and Belarusian news sources, including compromat.ru and Transitions Online, and Victor Chamkovsky's documentary, *Operation Consortium*, the text of which is still available

online via web.archive.org/web/20120112081516/http:/www
.detektiv.by/komputer. The connection between Alexander
Rubatsky and RBN also was supported by a letter to the Russian
government by Russian Duma lawmaker Ilya Ponomarev. The
section on Petrovsky's abduction was supported by news sources
and reports including the *Ecommerce Journal* (web.archive.org
/web/20120611001710/http://m.ecommerce-journal.com
/articles/hild_adult_in_internet_what_are_the_roots) and the
Belarusian electronic newspaper, *Diary*. The section about Russian
communication provider Eltel's role in RBN was supported by a
2009 story in *Russian Newsweek*. Eltel appears to have since been
purchased by Beeline, one of Russia's larger mobile firms.

Chapter 3: The Pharma Wars

Data to back up statements about Vrublevsky's apparent connection to Red & Partners was first published in a July 31, 2009,
Washington Post article called "Following the Money: Rogue-
Antivirus Software," (voices.washingtonpost.com/securityfix/2009
/07/following_the_money_trail_of_r.html). I revisited that story
in a May 2010 post on KrebsOnSecurity.com, titled "Following
the Money, Part II," (krebsonsecurity.com/2010/05/following-the
-money-part-ii/).

The public documents obtained from the Netherlands
Chamber of Commerce that concern Red & Partners, and
show how Igor Gusev (DPNet) and Pavel Vrublevsky (Red &
Partners) cofounded ChronoPay back in 2003 and became fifty-
fifty shareholders can be viewed online here: krebsonsecurity.com

/wp-content/uploads/2011/02/CP20051.pdf. (Note: This is a Dutch document that was publicly released.)

Some of the information that makes up this chapter is difficult to source precisely. For example, while it is assumed that Gusev or hackers closely allied with him obtained and released publicly several years' worth of emails, spreadsheets, and recorded phone calls from ChronoPay, I was not able to confirm this. As stated in this chapter, the information was shared anonymously by a source who used the alias "Boris." However, ChronoPay's CEO Vrublevsky did confirm that the documents in question were in fact stolen from ChronoPay. The data regarding GlavMed and SpamIt—including four years of ICQ chat records between GlavMed-SpamIt administrator Dmitry Stupin and his coworkers and employees (spammers) was paid for and released to this author and to U.S. authorities by Vrublevsky.

Chapter 4: Meet the Buyers

This chapter relied almost entirely on interviews with people who purchased drugs from GlavMed-SpamIt and Rx-Promotion. It also featured quotes and perspectives from online interviews with Igor Vishnevsky, the self-described spammer who acknowledged funding and reselling the Cutwail spam botnet. I also relied on information from government sources, including the FDA (www.fda.gov/ICECI/EnforcementActions/WarningLetters/ucm229010.htm). This chapter also references several news reports about the prices of prescription drugs in the United States. Those include a May 1, 2014, story at Bloomberg.com,

"Drug Prices Defy Gravity, Doubling for Dozens of Products."
The Tufts study was published November 18, 2014, and is
titled, "Cost to Develop and Win Marketing Approval for a
New Drug is $2.6 Billion." The FTC figures come from a report
the agency released on December 22, 2014, "FTC Staff Issues
FY2013 Report on Branded Drug Firms' Patent Settlements
with Generic Competitors."

Chapter 5: Russian Roulette

For the opening story about the death of Marcia Bergeron, I
relied on a 2007 piece in the *Vancouver Sun*. For additional background on the Bergeron story, I obtained a copy of Bergeron's
coroner report from authorities in British Columbia.

Several facts in this chapter refer to or cite stories in the
New York Times. The section that details how the anti-acne
drug Accutane came under new safety rules by the Food and
Drug Administration drew information from an August 2005
story by Gardiner Harris. An April 2013 story by the *New
York Times'* Harris and Katie Thomas helped with the research
on the role of Indian pharmacies producing the anti-leukemia
drug Gleevec at drastically lower prices than Western pharmaceutical companies.

A CNN story by David Goldman was the source for information about the $500 million settlement Google struck with the
U.S. Justice Department over illegally allowing online Canadian
pharmacies to advertise drugs to U.S. consumers. A discussion
of the $2.3 billion settlement Pfizer agreed to with the Justice

Department drew information from a *Wall Street Journal* article by Ron Winslow.

This chapter refers to an incident that had been reported recently in the news when I visited the University of Alabama at Birmingham—the case of the so-called "causeway cannibal" who reportedly chewed the face of a homeless man after allegedly ingesting bath salts. At the time, UAB's lab was testing the chemical composition of a substance that authorities suspected was bath salts. But as CNN and other news outlets later reported, follow-up toxicology tests on the suspect shot by police found not bath salts but marijuana.

This chapter also references a study by Merck. That study was never officially published; the references are in fact to online intelligence that Merck gathered between 2009 and 2010 and shared at the author's request.

The section that references a letter from the FDA to Vrublevsky's alleged partner in Rx-Promotion refers to a letter dated October 8, 2010, and addressed to one "Jorge Smark" at the email address hellmanh@gmail.com. See www.fda.gov /ICECI/EnforcementActions/WarningLetters/ucm229010.htm.

Chapter 6: Partner(ka)s in (Dis)Organized Crime

The inspiration for this chapter came principally from the seminal paper on partnerka programs "The Partnerka—What Is It, and Why Should You Care," by Dmitry Samosseiko of SophosLabs Canada. This chapter also relies heavily on data gathered by researchers at the University of California, San

Diego, the International Computer Science Institute, and George Mason University.

Chapter 7: Meet the Spammers

A section that details the rise of self-described spammer Igor Vishnevsky referenced an August 2006 article in *Wired*, "The Sleazy Life and Nasty Death of Russia's Spam King," by Brett Forrest, in which Vishnevsky himself also is interviewed. Some of the information about Vishnevsky's botnet—Cutwail, a.k.a. "0bulk Psyche Evolution"—comes from a March 2011 paper released at the fourth USENIX symposium by security researchers Brett Stone-Gross, Thorsten Holz, Gianluca Stringhini, and Giovanni Vigna, and titled "The Underground Economy of Spam: A Botmaster's Perspective of Coordinating Large-Scale Spam Campaigns."

Some of the information about infamous spammer Peter Severa's connection to convicted spammer Alan Ralsky comes from a forty-page indictment that the Justice Department lodged against Ralsky in its prosecution. Raw data about the spam-sending power of the major spam botnets drew principally from reports published by Dell SecureWorks and by M86 Security.

Chapter 8: Old Friends, Bitter Enemies

A discussion about raider attacks on Russian businesses references an April 20, 2009, paper by Brenden Carbonell, Dimitry Foux, Vera Krimnus, Ed Ma, and Lisa Safyan of the

2010 class of Wharton School's Lauder Institute, University of Pennsylvania, entitled "Hostile Takeovers: Russian Style" (see knowledge.wharton.upenn.edu/article/hostile-takeovers -russian-style/). The segment on Skolkovo, a technology park outside Moscow that Russian leaders envisioned as a Silicon Valley in the East, drew on a March 2012 story by Ingrid Lunden at TechCrunch. This chapter also benefited from an October 2010 story in the *New York Times*, "E-Mail Spam Falls after Russian Crackdown."

Chapter 9: Meeting in Moscow

A section explaining the likely reason that Russian police raided the Rx-Promotion party alludes to a series of police raids on Moscow gambling dens, which were documented colorfully in February 2011 articles in Russian news outlets Svobodanews, RIA Novosti, and *Rossiyskaya Gazeta* (rg.ru).

In the beginning of my interview with Vrublevsky, he makes an indirect reference to Said Amirov, the four-time mayor of the capitol city of Dagestan. For background on Amirov's arrest and ongoing trial for alleged weapons trafficking, I relied on stories in the *Moscow Times* and Business FM Radio.

Chapter 10: The Antis

Information about the percentage of email that was spam in the latter half of 2013 comes from statistics published by Kaspersky Lab, in a November 2013 posting on its securelist

.com blog. The story about the attack on Blue Security draws on my reporting of the incident at the *Washington Post*. A section on the March 2013 attacks on Spamhaus references *New York Times* stories in March and April about Sven Olaf Kamphuis.

Chapter 11: Takedown

A March 2013 story in the *Milwaukee Journal Sentinel* was the source of information about the guilty plea deal of convicted spammer Oleg Nikolaenko. Other references to botnet and spammer takedowns in this chapter draw on my own reporting published about these events at KrebsOnSecurity.com.

Chapter 12: Endgame

The beginning of this chapter includes information from a September 2013 *New York Times* article on Igor A. Artimovich, "Online Attack Leads to Peek into Spam Den." Russian news outlets Vedemosti, *Novaya Gazeta*, and RIA Novosti were indispensable for their accounts of Vrublevsky's convoluted trial.

According to multiple Russian news outlets, Maksim Permyakov was the only one of the four charged in connection with Vrublevsky's trial who admitted his role in the scheme, which was hiring the Artimovich brothers at Vrublevsky's request to launch a DDoS attack against Assist (a company that was competing directly with Vrublevsky's firm for a lucrative credit card processing contract with Russia's largest airline).

ABOUT THE AUTHOR

Brian Krebs is the editor of
KrebsOnSecurity.com, a daily
blog dedicated to in-depth
cybersecurity news and investigation. For the third year
running, KrebsOnSecurity.com
was voted the Blog That
Best Represents the Security
Industry by judges at the 2013
RSA Conference, the world's

© KRISTOF CLERIX

largest computer security gathering. KrebsOnSecurity also won
the Most Educational Security Blog award in 2013 and 2014,
and in 2013 Krebs was presented with the Security Bloggers
Hall of Fame award, alongside security expert Bruce Schneier.

From 1995 to 2009, Krebs was a reporter for the *Washington
Post*, where he covered Internet security, technology policy,
cybercrime, and privacy issues for the newspaper and the website.

His stories and investigations have also appeared in *Popular Mechanics*, Wired.com, the *Guardian*, the *Sydney Morning Herald*, and many other publications. Krebs is a 1994 graduate of George Mason University, where he earned a bachelor of arts in international relations.